D0075565

THE PLACE OF PREJUDICE

THE PLACE OF PREJUDICE

A Case for Reasoning within the World

Adam Adatto Sandel

Harvard University Press

Cambridge, Massachusetts
London, England
2014

Library of Congress Cataloging-in-Publication Data

Sandel, Adam Adatto.
The place of prejudice : a case for reasoning within the world / Adam Adatto Sandel.
pages cm
Includes bibliographical references and index.
ISBN 978-0-674-72684-0 (hardcover : alk. paper)
1. Ethics. 2. Reasoning. 3. Prejudices. I. Title.
BJ1031.S26 2014
170'.42—dc23   2013038551

To my parents

Contents

The Place of Prejudice

Introduction

Prejudice Reconsidered

Today prejudice is out of favor, and understandably so. It refers, more often than not, to a deplorable set of attitudes and practices based on animus and hatred for this or that group. Racial prejudice is a notorious example. It casts a dark shadow over any attempt to find a legitimate place for prejudice in moral and political judgment. Why would any decent person want to acknowledge a place for prejudice? What possibly can be said on its behalf? Insofar as prejudice refers to thought or action beclouded by hatred, the answer is nothing; such prejudice warrants condemnation, not defense. But prejudice also has a broader meaning.

Its meaning is well captured by Immanuel Kant's definition of "enlightenment" as "the emancipation from prejudices generally."[1] By "prejudice," he clearly means something more than unjustified hatred. Prejudice, for Kant, is any kind of *prejudgment,* any source of judgment whose validity we have not explicitly examined and justified. The kinds of prejudice that concern Kant include tradition, habit, custom, upbringing—even our natural

---

1. Immanuel Kant, *The Critique of Judgment,* trans. James Creed Meredith (Oxford: Oxford University Press, 1952), §40, 152.

desires. All tend to influence our judgment while evading our conscious reflection. The "maxim of unprejudiced thought," and the essence of enlightenment, says Kant, is to transcend such influences—to "think for one's self."[2]

We find a similar denunciation of prejudice in some of Kant's notable predecessors. Francis Bacon, for example, writes that the human intellect would be better off "cleansed of prejudice," purged of what he calls the "idols of the mind." By the "idols," he means the influences of tradition, habit, language, upbringing, and so on. We would judge more truthfully, Bacon writes, if our "understandings were unbiased, a blank slate."[3] René Descartes expresses a similar view when he resolves to rid himself of all "preconceptions" before reconstructing knowledge piece by piece.[4] Echoing the "blank slate" ideal, he maintains that our judgments would be firmer and less obscure if "we had had the full use of our reason from the moment of our birth, and if we had always been guided by it alone."[5]

The notion of prejudice that Kant, Bacon, and Descartes articulate goes far beyond unjustified animus. It refers to any source of judgment whose validity we have not verified for ourselves. The aspiration to banish prejudice in this broad sense is, I believe, a powerful intellectual ideal in our times. To be sure, we have reason to despise prejudice understood as hatred and discrimination. But the wholesale rejection of prejudice reflects the deeper, more pervasive assumption that rational judgment must be untainted by prejudgments of any kind, including the understandings and commitments that we acquire from tradition, habit, custom, and our upbringing.

This way of thinking about judgment, and the renunciation of prejudice it implies, is what I seek to challenge. My challenge rests on a distinction between two conceptions of judgment. The first might be called the *detached conception*. According to this conception, we judge best when we judge without relying on any authority or influence whose validity we have not explicitly confirmed for ourselves. Such judgment is "detached" in that it seeks to break free from all such influences.

---

2. Ibid.

3. Francis Bacon, *The New Organon,* ed. Lisa Jardine and Michael Silverthorne (Cambridge: Cambridge University Press, 2000), 18.

4. René Descartes, *Discourse on the Method,* in *Selected Philosophical Writings,* trans. John Cottingham, Robert Stoothoff, and Dugald Murdoch (Cambridge: Cambridge University Press, 1998), 26.

5. Ibid.

The second conception of judgment might be called the *situated conception*. According to this conception, the aspiration to a wholly detached way of judging is misguided; deliberation and judgment always work from within our life circumstance. According to the situated conception of judgment, our life circumstance is not an obstacle to reason but a perspective that informs and enables it.

My aim in this book is to elaborate and defend the situated conception of judgment. But I want also to show what is at stake in the contrast between the detached and the situated conceptions for the case against prejudice. If, as I hope to show, the situated conception is more plausible, then Kant's case against prejudice, and that of Bacon and Descartes, is called into question. If judgment is inescapably situated, then the very attempt to "cleanse" our minds of prejudice may be misguided. Perhaps the so-called idols of the mind should not be banished after all.

Now the notion of reasoning and judging from within our situation, or life circumstance, is admittedly obscure. One goal of this book is to make sense of it. To do so, I draw upon the work of two twentieth-century German philosophers, Martin Heidegger and Hans-Georg Gadamer. They argue that our understanding and judgment is always "situated" within a world, or horizon, shaped by the traditions, projects, and practices in which we are engaged. This means that whenever we exercise our judgment—in evaluating competing arguments in politics or law, in trying to understand a philosophical text, in deliberating about how to act in this or that circumstance—we never start from scratch. Our judgment is always informed by preconceptions and commitments that we have not justified in advance, that lie, for the most part, beneath the range of our conscious attention. But contrary to appearance, the prejudicial aspect of judgment is not some regrettable limitation. Certain prejudices, they argue, can actually enable good judgment rather than hinder it.

The assumption that good judgment must always be detached is influential today, not only in philosophy but also in politics and law. One striking example, from the American legal system, is the idea that a fair jury should be composed of members whose minds are ideally blank slates, untainted by any prior familiarity with the contending parties or the subject matter of the case. The justification frequently offered by judges and legal scholars is that this sort of jury selection eliminates bias and selects jurors who will approach the case with an open mind. But, as the inescapable influence of prejudice would suggest, this approach does not yield a truly prejudice-free jury. It might actually lead to a jury with the wrong prejudices—a jury that lacks the background understanding necessary to judge well or to even identify the relevant facts.

Consider, for example, the approach to jury selection in the 1990 obscenity trial of a Cincinnati art museum and its director, who were accused of exhibiting controversial photographs by Robert Mapplethorpe. The judge dismissed a potential juror simply on the grounds that she had seen the exhibit (not only the controversial photographs). She was also the only one who claimed to be a regular museum-goer. Among the jurors selected was someone who "never went to museums."[6] The judge assumed that people who had seen the exhibit, or even people who often visit museums, would be somehow prejudiced, perhaps in favor of artistic license, and would therefore be disposed to judge unfairly. In an attempt to avoid prejudice altogether, the judge apparently sought to fill the jury with people who had no prior familiarity with museums (or obscenity law).

But is such a jury really prejudice-free? A more plausible account is that a jury of people who almost never go to museums tends to be prejudiced in its own way: such a jury would seem to have little basis for determining what is appropriate in that context. How could people unfamiliar with the type of work normally displayed in museums accurately determine whether a certain photograph met "contemporary community standards of decency"—the standard they were asked to interpret? Jurors who lacked this background knowledge, or prejudice, would seem ill-equipped to judge the case fairly.

My use of "prejudice" will no doubt sound strange to those familiar with its pejorative sense. Isn't what I have here called "prejudice" simply a stand-in for "background knowledge"? In a sense, yes. My aim is precisely to connect these concepts. But what kind of background knowledge is at play? To say that I "know" what sort of work is typically displayed in museums is different from saying that I "know" the names of the photographs currently on exhibit. The second is mere information, whereas the first is a familiarity with content, with what counts as art versus trash. Beyond being value-laden, this sort of knowledge seems inescapably situated. It involves being

6. Jeffrey Abramson, *We, the Jury* (New York: Basic Books, 1994), 21–22.

raised in a certain community, going to museums, interpreting the art, developing a sense for what's "decent." In this sense, we might call such knowledge a "prejudice." Furthermore, insofar as such knowledge is situated, it would not be reducible to rules or principles accessible to anyone anywhere. This particularist quality of situated knowledge fits with the common association of "prejudice" with partiality.

A second example of the contemporary suspicion of prejudice lies behind the denigration of political rhetoric common today, well captured by the familiar expression "that's mere rhetoric"—eloquent nonsense crafted merely to persuade a particular audience. This denigration of rhetoric goes beyond a mistrust of politicians and their motives. It reflects a deeper view about the nature of political argument and how it should proceed. According to this view, political arguments depend for their justification on principles that can be specified "nonrhetorically," so to speak—without reference to the particular situations in which they arise. Rhetoric, which attempts to persuade through stories, images, and references geared to a particular audience, is, at best, an adornment to the "real argument." At worst, rhetoric is a form of pandering or deception. The suspicion of rhetoric, one might say, is based on the assumption that rhetoric appeals to people's prejudices and not their reason. Persuasive orators, the argument goes, lead their listeners to judge in a partial manner—influenced by their own perspectives, which others may not share. We assume that policies and principles should ultimately be justified in abstraction from the predispositions of a particular audience—justified by reasons ideally accessible to anyone anywhere.

But examples of great rhetoric force us to question this assumption. The speeches of political figures such as John F. Kennedy, Lyndon Johnson, and Martin Luther King arguably derive their moral force not simply from the principles they invoke, but from the way in which they appeal to the life circumstances of their listeners. In his campaign for civil rights, for example, Lyndon Johnson was famous for evoking feelings such as moral outrage, bound up with everyday roles and practices that resonated with his audience. He was even known to speak in a thicker southern accent in the South in order to forge a common footing with his listeners.[7] Although

---

7. Bryan Garsten, *Saving Persuasion: A Defense of Rhetoric and Judgment* (Cambridge, MA: Harvard University Press, 2007), 193.

Johnson spoke to people as situated, he used his rhetoric to challenge their views—to denounce segregation in light of other practices that mattered to them. Strange though it may sound, by appealing to people's prejudices, Johnson's rhetoric arguably gave moral force to principles of equality.[8]

The attempt at blank-slate jury selection and the suspicion of political rhetoric attest to the rejection of prejudice familiar today. But as I have suggested, this rejection is misguided. In order to establish the legitimate place of prejudice, I begin by exposing the ideal of detached judgment as *itself* a prejudice—an aspiration shaped by a questionable tradition of thought. Following Gadamer's lead, we find the source of this tradition in the early modern period and the Enlightenment. As Gadamer points out, "Not until the Enlightenment does *the concept of prejudice* acquire the negative connotation familiar today."[9] The word "prejudice," he explains, actually comes from "prejudgment," which used to have "either a positive or negative value." This meaning, he continues, seems to have been limited during the Enlightenment "to the sense of an unfounded judgment," a judgment shaped by human authority or tradition rather than one's own reason.[10]

In Chapter 1, I examine the case against prejudice as it emerged in early modern and Enlightenment thought.[11] In a way, this continues Gadamer's discussion of prejudice by offering a more sustained account of what he calls the "prejudice against prejudice."[12] My goal, however, is not to provide an exhaustive history of the concept of prejudice, nor to prove Gadamer's provocative suggestion that the "prejudice against prejudice" defines the essence of the Enlightenment.[13] My historical turn is intended, rather, to clarify the concept of prejudice and to lay out the detached ideal of judgment. To this end, I examine Bacon, Descartes, Adam Smith, and Kant—all of whom address "prejudice" or develop the detached ideal.

8. See Chapter 6 in this book.

9. Hans-Georg Gadamer, *Truth and Method*, trans. Joel Weinsheimer and Donald G. Marshall, rev. ed. (New York: Continuum, 1989), 273.

10. Ibid.

11. "Enlightenment" in this work refers to the self-description of the age in which the thinkers whom I examine wrote. I do not mean to assert that a single way of thinking defined what we today call the Enlightenment period.

12. Gadamer, *Truth and Method*, 273.

13. Ibid., 272–273.

As we will see, these thinkers sought to banish somewhat different conceptions of prejudice. Smith, for example, locates prejudice in our loyalty to family, friends, and country. Such prejudice, he claims, is parochial and irrational—the product of blind habit and custom.[14] But Smith does not consider all nonrational influence to be prejudice. He in fact defends love of humanity and "fellow feeling" in contrast to reason.[15] Smith reserves the term "prejudice" as a pejorative for our partialities. Kant, by contrast, considers *any* sentiment, however widely shared, to be a prejudice no different in principle from particular desires and loyalties. Prejudice, by his account, denotes anything "given" by any source other than detached reason.[16]

But despite their disagreements about the scope of prejudice, all of these thinkers agree that we judge best when we abstract from prejudice broadly conceived as our situation, or life circumstance the reason Smith exempts the basic moral sentiments from the category of "prejudice," even though the sentiments condition our judgment, is that he considers them to be fixed and universal in the human species. As such (so he claims) they provide a basis of judgment independent of habit, custom, and tradition.

In addition to highlighting the nuances of "prejudice," the thinkers whom I examine bring out two important senses in which escaping prejudice leads us to judge "well." The first sense of judging well, which Bacon, Descartes, and Smith emphasize, is judging *truthfully*. Our situation, they argue, especially our upbringing and the authority of tradition, tends to lead us astray. Escaping such prejudice is the first step toward discovering the *truth*, whether about the universe (Bacon and Descartes) or about the right way to act (Smith).

The second sense of judging well, which Kant highlights, is judging *freely*. Judgment influenced by prejudice, he argues, is not only erroneous but enslaved. Free judgment must be autonomous; it must come from the dictates of one's own reason, which Kant defines in contrast to habit, custom, culture, or even desire. Thus, the case against prejudice has two

14. Adam Smith, *The Theory of Moral Sentiments,* ed. Ryan Patrick Hanley (New York: Penguin, 2009), 229.

15. Ibid., 376.

16. Kant, *Critique of Judgment,* §40, 152.

strands—one to do with truth, the other with agency. My aim is to challenge both of these strands: to show that prejudice can be illuminating and also consistent with freedom.

Before exploring the place of prejudice by way of the situated conception of judgment, I conclude Chapter 1 by considering a more familiar case for prejudice—one that defends the unreflective embrace of tradition and sentiment over reason. The most prominent spokesman for this "sentimental" revival of prejudice is Edmund Burke. His notion of prejudice is important to consider in its own right and also as a contrast to the one I advance. Burke notoriously proclaims that "in this enlightened age, I am bold enough to confess, that we are generally men of untaught feelings; that instead of casting away all our old prejudices, we cherish them to a very considerable degree, and, to take more shame to ourselves, we cherish them because they are prejudices."[17]

By "prejudices," Burke not only means "untaught feelings," or sentiments in the abstract, but sentiments as shaped by particular habits, customs, and social roles. He often uses "prejudice" to denote the habits, customs, and social roles themselves. For example, he speaks of the church establishment as a "prejudice" insofar as it shapes the practice and judgment of Englishmen.[18]

On the face of it, Burke's defense of prejudice appears to be a radical challenge to his predecessors' way of thinking. But it actually shares one of their central assumptions. For he accepts a thoroughgoing distinction between prejudice and reason and merely flips the values—defending traditional sources of authority in terms such as "decent drapery," "untaught feeling," and "pleasing illusion." Rather than attempt to show that reason is somehow bound up with prejudice, Burke accepts that reason and prejudice are opposed and asserts the priority of prejudice.

But this defense of prejudice is unsatisfying. If prejudice is nothing more than sentiment and "pleasing illusion," then why should it override reason? Burke fails to offer a convincing answer. He actually offers two defenses of prejudice, neither of which justifies its superiority to reason. The first merely bemoans the decay of prejudice and sings a wistful praise of the past. The second simply argues for the social utility of tradition. Although Burke insists

17. Edmund Burke, *Reflections on the Revolution in France,* ed. Frank M. Turner (New Haven, CT: Yale University Press, 2003), 74.
18. Ibid., 77.

that traditional roles and institutions ground social solidarity, he does not show that they embody any inherent insight or reason. The utilitarian character of Burke's defense of prejudice emerges in his praise of the church establishment, which he considers a kind of "superstition" but defends nonetheless as the "basis of civil society, and the source of all good and all comfort."[19]

To understand prejudice as opposed to reason makes it difficult, perhaps impossible, to accept as a legitimate source of authority. But there is another way of understanding the relationship between prejudice and reason. In contrast to the sentimental conception of prejudice that we find in Burke, I defend what I call the *hermeneutic* conception. The latter is linked to what I have called the *situated* conception of understanding. According to this conception, prejudice is an inescapable feature of judgment; we always judge and understand from within our life circumstance. But as the term "hermeneutic" suggests, our life circumstance is an intelligible perspective open to *interpretation*. Moreover, certain features of our life circumstance, certain prejudices (habits, traditions, experiences), may actually enable us to judge well. In this sense, prejudice is an expression of reason, not a betrayal of it.

The hermeneutic conception of prejudice comes from Heidegger and Gadamer. Both understand prejudice in terms of our situation—what Gadamer calls our *horizon* and what Heidegger calls the *world*.[20] In Chapter 2, I derive the situated conception of understanding from Heidegger, first and foremost from his notion of "Being-in-the-World." My goal is to provide an interpretation of Being-in-the-World that challenges the ideal of detached judgment and that tries to make sense of what it means to reason from within our life circumstance. At the heart of "Being-in-the-World" is the idea that our most basic mode of understanding is not the detached scrutiny of our beliefs and their origin, but the practical understanding that arises

19. Ibid.

20. In *Being and Time*, Heidegger uses the term *world*, in his special comprehensive sense, without any quotation marks. When he speaks of *world* colloquially, in the various senses in which we typically use the term, he puts it in quotation marks—as "world" or 'world.' He uses the term 'world,' placed in single quotation marks, when speaking of "the totality of entities" around us, and "world," placed in double quotation marks, when speaking of a concrete world in the comprehensive sense, e.g., the "world" of the peasant woman (*Being and Time*, 93).

from making things, putting them to use, responding to situations, aiming at certain ends. This sort of understanding is not primarily an explicit awareness. It is not the sort of awareness we have when we examine things and note their properties (their size, shape, color, and so on). Our practical understanding is for the most part implicit. It operates beneath our conscious awareness. An example to which Heidegger frequently turns is the way in which a carpenter understands his hammer. As the carpenter works at his bench, he understands the hammer by using it. He understands it as a means to making a cabinet, the cabinet as part of a house, a house as part of living well. The workman knows all this as he hammers, even while his conscious attention lies elsewhere (perhaps in the upcoming lunch break, the weather, the news of the day).

Heidegger's notion of Being-in-the-World and its primarily practical character lead him to reject the familiar subject-object distinction.[21] When we are engaged in our activity, he points out, we are not subjects who contemplate objects. Rather, we are bound up with our purposes and ends, situated in the world we seek to understand.

To capture this notion, Heidegger introduces a key term of art. He replaces the subject-object distinction with the concept of "Dasein," literally "being-there."[22] Dasein expresses the idea that we are defined by what we do, by the activities we carry out, by the situations in which we find ourselves, and ultimately, by our comprehensive situation, or life circumstance—what Heidegger calls the *world*. The world is the totality of our involvements—the web of purposes, goals, and practices, that defines our life as a whole.

The paramount question for understanding the world is how to make sense of this totality. Two things are clear: First, our understanding of the totality is practical. We know it only by living within it, only by "Being-in" the world. Second, our understanding has a comprehensive character. To understand a part of the world, we must have some awareness of the whole. For the meaning of any particular activity or role makes sense only in relation to others, ultimately, in relation to the entire web. "Being-in-the-World" denotes our basic awareness of this articulated whole—an awareness that is

21. Martin Heidegger, *Being and Time*, trans. John Macquarrie and Edward Robinson (Malden, MA: Blackwell, [1927] 1962), 87.
22. Ibid., 27.

itself embodied in our way of life. Such awareness, Heidegger argues, is the condition for the possibility of all action and understanding, including all study and scientific research. Such reflection is one way of Being-in-the-World, not a privileged way of grasping reality.[23]

But how, exactly, the web of the world coheres is of crucial importance. Central to my interpretation of the world is that it coheres as a lived, or enacted, story. As such, the world has a point. It is not a set of arbitrary habits, customs, or social forces, but a unity of meaning. And yet, this unity is inexhaustible. The "moral of the story," so to speak, is open; no part is decided once and for all. The story is open because Dasein is "writing" it in every step of its life. How the world can be a partial whole, a unity of meaning still unfinished, is a core mystery in Heidegger's philosophy. My goal in Chapter 3 is to shed some light on it. At this point, my aim is simply to outline the narrative conception of the world in contrast to a familiar interpretation—what we might call the "sociological" view. According to this view, familiar among Anglo-American readers of Heidegger, the world is a contingent and ever-changing network of social practices; it has no ultimate point. In Piotr Hoffman's words, Being-in-the-World implies "the full contingency and groundlessness" of Dasein's existence.[24] To view the world in this way is a mistake. It overlooks Heidegger's crucial claim that the world embodies the "destiny of Being." Heidegger's own conception of the world in terms of "fate" (Schicksal) and "destiny" (Geschick) implies a narrative understanding of our situation. But beyond its fit with Heidegger, the narrative understanding makes best sense, I believe, of our actual experience. It captures the sense in which our life circumstance is intelligible and open to interpretation.

After developing the narrative reading of Being-in-the-World to clarify the situated conception of understanding and to challenge the ideal of detached

---

23. Ibid., 86–87.

24. Piotr Hoffman, "Death, Time, Historicity: Division II of Being and Time," in The Cambridge Companion to Heidegger, ed. Charles B. Guignon (Cambridge: Cambridge University Press, 2006), 239. For another prominent version of what amounts, I believe, to the "contingency" view, cf. also Hubert Dreyfus, Being-in-the-World: A Commentary on Heidegger's Being and Time, Division I (Cambridge, MA: MIT Press, 1991).

judgment, I consider, in Chapter 3, whether Being-in-the-World allows room for human agency. This question has special significance in light of the case against prejudice I seek to challenge. For one of the main arguments against prejudice (as I show in Chapter 1), is that prejudice is opposed to freedom. If understanding, deliberation, and judgment is unavoidably situated, then what becomes of freedom?

Although Heidegger does not attribute autonomy to a subject, I argue that his notion of Dasein nonetheless implies a conception of agency. The basis for this conception is his interpretation of Dasein as "thrown-projection," which highlights a passive and active dimension of Being-in-the-World. Thrown-projection captures the sense in which Dasein is at once the product and the author of its destiny. "Thrownness" means that any judgment, intention, or action, however revolutionary, makes sense only in relation to what is "given," namely, the world. Although we can question and revise any particular practice, aim, role, or judgment, we are incapable of overturning the whole order of things, of redefining ourselves from the ground up.

But the whole is not a fate to which we are enslaved. Rather, it is the source of a certain kind of agency. Heidegger develops this notion of agency in the concept of "projection." Even what appears to be mere habit, or thoughtless adherence to tradition, involves a sort of creative adaptation. However implicitly, we are always reshaping the world that conditions us. Projection thus involves a kind of freedom, which, I suggest, should be interpreted as a certain kind of autonomy. By comparing the sort of autonomy implied by thrown-projection to Kant's ideal of autonomy, I hope to show how Heidegger both undermines the Kantian tradition and continues it.

Central to the conception of agency that I derive from Heidegger is that Dasein is at once entirely passive and entirely active. We can make sense of this apparent contradiction by understanding the *unity* of thrownness and projection—the way in which each depends on the other. By highlighting this unity, I offer an interpretation of Dasein as neither self-creative nor subservient to an alien destiny. At the same time, I argue against a familiar understanding of Dasein as free to shape its identity but only within the "range of possibilities available in [its] culture."[25] To conceive of Dasein as partly

25. Richard Polt, *Heidegger: An Introduction* (London: Routledge, 1999), 63.

free and partly constrained mistakes thrownness, or what is "given," for a limit to agency rather than its source.

The unity of thrownness and projection points to Heidegger's special conception of time, which I interpret in the second half of Chapter 3. Understanding the connection between being and time is the key to grasping Heidegger's vision of human agency. By exploring Heidegger's conceptions of time, history, death, finitude, and eternity, I attempt to draw out the far-reaching implications of our situated understanding.

For those unfamiliar with Heidegger's thought, this preview of Being-in-the-World, Dasein, and thrown-projection will still, I imagine, seem somewhat obscure. To shed light on these key terms is my task in Chapters 2 and 3. At this point, I aim only to prepare this discussion by indicating how Being-in-the-World helps to clarify the situated conception of understanding.

To cast this conception in more familiar terms, we might describe our situation or life circumstance as a *perspective*. The situated conception of understanding expresses that all reasoning, deliberation, and judgment are from within a certain perspective. The concept of perspective affords us an intuitively plausible model for how our situation, or world, can inform our judgment rather than hinder it.

When we speak of "perspective" in the visual sense, we mean a particular range of view—the perspective from the valley, the mountaintop, or the edge of the sea. The curious thing about a perspective is its relation to the things it makes visible. A perspective itself is not identical to the totality of things it reveals. As the condition of sight, a perspective cannot be seen in the same way as any of the things it reveals can be seen. And yet, a perspective is inseparable from totality of what it reveals. Consider, for example, the perspective from a mountaintop. The perspective is inseparable from the fields that checker the landscape, the lake in the distance, and the hills beyond it. Without these things, the perspective would not be the distinctive viewpoint that it is. Nevertheless, the perspective, or the whole range of view, itself invisible, is what grants us the vision of these things and what gives them their distinctive look. If we change our perspective by descending the mountain, the same things appear in different proportions. If we turn away entirely, they all vanish.

This curious part-whole interdependence, and the elusive character of the whole, also characterizes what we call a "life perspective." By "life perspective," we typically mean a particular point of view shaped by many experiences but at the same time their condition. Consider, for example, the perspective of a child. The child's perspective is shaped, of course, by the characteristic activities of a child—preparing for "show and tell" at school, eagerly awaiting recess, playing "hide and go seek," waiting for the ice cream truck, watching cartoons, and so on. Without doing any of the childlike things, one would not have the distinctive perspective of a child. And yet, it is only from the perspective of a child, or a childlike sensibility, that any of these things "appear," or command the interest and excitement that they do. The perspective of a child is thus the condition of the many activities that shape it.

The same part-whole relationship defines our "life perspective" in the comprehensive sense in which we often speak of it: the point of view shaped by the experiences (i.e., activities, roles, practices) familiar to us. A life perspective is inseparable from these experiences, but it also grants them their distinctive meaning. In other words, any particular experience, or set of experiences, however "defining" of my identity, makes sense, or has the significance it does, only in light of my life as a whole. This is captured, I believe, in the familiar experience of having to tell a story in order to express the meaning of a significant event or person in our lives. When we attempt to elicit the meaning of particular things, we have to articulate, to some extent, the whole way of life in which they fit. We have to say something about our perspective.

To be sure, our perspective is for the most part inarticulate, and no account of it could be exhaustive. Just as a visual perspective conditions everything we see, a life perspective conditions everything we understand, including our particular attempts to elucidate the perspective itself. Moreover, a life perspective cannot be questioned or revised in the same way as any particular activity or practice can be. For our perspective directs in the first place what appears as question-worthy. What Heidegger means by the *world* is something like our life perspective in this comprehensive sense. This is the sense of "situation" I aim to develop. Perhaps it is easier to see how one's situation, conceived in terms of "perspective," admits of being more or less insightful.

In everyday speech, we distinguish "higher," "more expansive perspectives" from "lower," "more limited ones." Consider Plato's image from the *Phaedo* of someone's clouded view of the sun and the stars from the perspective beneath the sea compared to the clearer view of someone who could lift his head out of the water and gaze upon the world above.[26] Although it may be difficult, in certain instances, to distinguish among better and worse perspectives, in most cases, at least, we can distinguish quite easily. Although we may be unable to determine whether the view of Mount Everest is superior from above, as from an airplane, or from below, as from base camp, we could still say with certainty that both of these perspectives surpass that of a person climbing the mountain with his gaze directed toward his feet.

In the case of life perspectives, we also have a sense of higher and lower. Consider the perspective of a child compared to that of an adult. We recognize the superior perspective of an adult insofar as it reveals more clearly, or in truer proportion, the relative significance of certain interests, concerns, aims, responsibilities, and so on. The perspective of an adult thus informs deeper understandings and better judgments. We have this experience all the time in those instances of returning to a book or a movie that we read or watched when we were young and finding we are now able to interpret it in a new and more insightful way.

In general terms, we can say that the adult perspective reveals the child's perspective as partial and thus includes it in a more comprehensive awareness. This does not imply that the child's perspective is entirely immature or misguided. To the contrary, we recognize certain childlike sensibilities as correctives to the habits we fall into as adults. We appreciate, for example, the sense of wonder for the little things around us that we tend to pass by in the hustle and bustle of the work day. But these features of a child's perspective and their characteristic charm emerge only from the viewpoint of an adult, a viewpoint informed by alternative attitudes and stances toward the world. From this more expansive perspective, an adult can articulate the insight and shortcoming of a child's way of seeing things.

---

26. Plato, *Phaedo*, ed. Jeffrey Henderson (Cambridge, MA: Harvard University Press, 1914), 111a–c.

We can draw the same kind of distinctions among life perspectives in the comprehensive sense, that is, the variations of our fundamental awareness of the *world*, our situation writ large. Certain understandings of the world are more comprehensive than others. They enable deeper understandings and better judgments.

In a certain sense, judging from a perspective might seem to imply being limited, even hopelessly bound to a single viewpoint. The limited nature of situated understanding is well captured in the familiar expression "You would have had to be there to really understand." In this phrase we acknowledge the sense in which insightful commentary on certain topics (for example, what made the joke so funny) seems to presuppose a shared experience (having actually been "there," at the comedy show), an experience that cannot be fully reproduced in an account alone. But to think that such experiences form some fixed perspective that includes us (who attended the show) and excludes everyone else, would be a mistake. It would overlook how by giving an account of the situation, we invite others, who may not have been there with us, to consider our account by reference to their own, potentially analogous experiences. We thereby invite them within our perspective but also open it to expansion in light of what they say. Perhaps upon hearing another person's account of the situation, we revise how we had previously characterized our having been "there." The familiar experience of persuading someone else to see things your way—or of being persuaded—proves that our perspectives are open to expansion. As Heidegger shows, our fundamental experience of the world, our situation, or perspective writ large, is open to expansion in the same way. Because one's perspective is not a subjective viewpoint but embodied in one's life, others, at least in principle, can come to share it.

The standard of a "broader" or "more comprehensive" perspective is, of course, not some unconditional criterion of truth—for that would undermine the very notion of perspective. Rather, the standard is given *by the perspective itself,* by how it reveals the partiality of a previous perspective. In other words, the way in which we know that a perspective is "more comprehensive" is that it clarifies a previous one, exposing the previous as a shrouded view of what we now can see clearly. Only in light of the transition from a lower perspective to a higher one, by which the latter includes and supersedes the former, does the superiority of the higher emerge. Because the higher includes the lower and is thus inseparable from it (as the adult's perspective includes the child's) the problem of rival or incompatible perspectives does not arise. The problem would arise only if in asserting one perspective to be "higher" or "clearer" than another we assumed two entirely alien viewpoints and a standard by which we could compare each. But when we speak of "higher" and "lower" life perspectives, we mean that the higher is "higher" precisely because it contains the lower, revealing both its insight and shortcoming. The higher understands the lower better than the lower understands itself. In this sense, our understanding is always retrospective. We come to grasp the true merit of our perspective only by recapturing it within a broader one. As Georg W. F. Hegel famously maintained, "The owl of Minerva spreads its wings only with the falling of the dusk."[27]

Although the situated conception of judgment implies that some perspectives are higher than others, it does not imply Hegel's claim that there is a single highest perspective from which we attain absolute knowledge. As Heidegger shows, the "situated" character of understanding means not only that understanding is engaged, or practical, rather than detached, but that understanding is essentially *incomplete*. It is worth taking a moment to consider that practical understanding does not itself imply incompleteness. Although our understandings may be inseparable from the life in which we are engaged, from what Hegel calls "ethical substance," we might, at least conceivably, attain a perfectly clear understanding of that life. This understanding is precisely what Hegel claims to have achieved in his philosophy. He maintains that understanding is situated rather than detached. For the meaning of concepts only makes sense to someone engaged in the life from which the concepts emerge. But to such a person, at least at the end of history, the philosophical statement is the perfectly clear, perfectly complete, expression of that way of life. Hegel's "absolute knowledge" thus exemplifies only one dimension of what I mean by situated understanding. Absolute knowledge is situated insofar as it depends for its intelligibility on the actual life it knows. And yet, it is also complete, fully clear, and, in this sense, prejudice-free.

According to the conception of situated understanding I derive from Heidegger, even our broadest and clearest perspectives remain partial and

---

27. G. W. F. Hegel, *Philosophy of Right*, trans. T. M. Knox (Oxford: Oxford University Press, 1952), 13.

veiled. Put in positive terms, our perspectives are never fixed once and for all, but always open to further illumination. This openness has to do with the creative, or "projective," dimension of understanding—that any act of understanding comes to reshape the perspective from which it springs. The partiality of a perspective, together with its practical character, highlights the sense in which a perspective is a prejudice.

The connection of "perspective," or "situation," to "prejudice" finds explicit statement in Gadamer. By drawing upon Heidegger's notion of Being-in-the-World, Gadamer derives the idea that "all understanding inevitably involves some prejudice *(Vorurteil).*"[28] But prejudice, he argues, is not some regrettable limitation. For certain prejudices, or aspects of our life circumstance, can enable understanding. They can be, as he puts it, "productive of knowledge."[29] In Chapter 4, I show how this apparently puzzling claim is plausible.

Gadamer's reason for linking Being-in-the-World to "prejudice" is to rehabilitate the sources of judgment that became discredited during the Enlightenment. His primary aim is to show how our life circumstance, or "horizon," shaped by our traditions, practices, commitments, and concerns, is a perspective that informs our understanding in the human sciences. In particular, he seeks to undermine a certain ideal of detached historical research that arose in the wake of the Enlightenment. According to this ideal, which he calls "historicism," the proper method of research is to abstract from our own interests, concerns, and conceptions of truth so as to avoid imposing contemporary views upon a past age. Historicism teaches us to discover the "original" meaning of a historical work by escaping our own perspective and reconstructing the context in which the work emerged. Gadamer challenges historicism by arguing that contemporary prejudices are unavoidable, but also potentially illuminating. Although certain prejudices may obscure our understanding of a historical work (or epoch), others may clarify it.

28. Gadamer, *Truth and Method*, 272.
29. Ibid., 280.

My interpretation of Gadamer begins by laying out his general critique of historicism. My aim is to draw out the implications of the situated conception of understanding for how we relate to the past. Gadamer's crucial insight, in this regard, is that to be situated within a horizon means that one's own "present" is always in motion. It is not a fixed set of "opinions and valuations," but a comprehensive awareness that is open to question.[30] As such, it cannot be sharply distinguished from the past. Insofar as our own identity is open to question, so too is the extent to which we differ from past ages. And insofar as the past is intelligible, it is never truly behind us. In a sense, the past and present belong together. This belonging implies that the meaning of any aspect of our historical tradition can be recovered only in relation to the present. The notion that we should try to escape our contemporary perspective to attain prejudice-free historical knowledge is misguided.

After laying out this relation between past and present at a general level, I offer a concrete analysis of how contemporary prejudices can enable historical understanding. Gadamer's devotion to how prejudice informs the study of classical texts makes his work of special relevance for historians of ideas, political theorists, and those concerned with interpreting a tradition of thought. In order to highlight this relevance, I apply his theory of prejudice to interpreting Plato's *Republic*. I first consider how a certain contemporary prejudice can illuminate Plato's conception of poetry (*Republic*, Book 10). I conclude by showing how a certain misleading prejudice can be overcome through a careful reading of Plato's teaching on opinion versus knowledge (*Republic*, Book 5). My aim is to clarify how Gadamer's theory of prejudice works. Central to this challenge is working out the distinction between prejudices that illuminate and prejudices that distort. I also hope to show how interpretation involves a twofold gain in knowledge: a better understanding of the text and a better understanding of ourselves—of our own concerns and conceptions of truth.

Gadamer's suggestion that the past and present belong together motivates a turning point in my account of situated understanding. In Chapter 5, I move

---

30. Ibid., 305.

from twentieth-century Germany to ancient Greece, from Heidegger and Gadamer to Aristotle. Although Aristotle may seem far removed from Heidegger and Gadamer, he actually gives early and powerful expression to their way of thinking. In fact, both Heidegger and Gadamer were deeply influenced by Aristotle. In particular, they read his account of practical wisdom *(phronesis)* as a corrective to the detached ideal of knowledge. Following their lead, I attempt to recover from Aristotle an account of how judgment draws upon prejudice.

The apparent difficulty with thus appropriating Aristotle is that, strictly speaking, Aristotle does not work out a conception of "prejudice" or "situation." Both of these terms, after all, emerged in modern times. The very meaning of "situated understanding" depends on its contrast to the "detached" ideal, an ideal with which Aristotle was, in large part, unfamiliar. His work preceded, of course, that of Bacon, Descartes, Smith, and Kant. So in one sense, Aristotle cannot be said to articulate a "situated" conception of understanding—at least not in such terms. Nevertheless, Aristotle does, in his own way, offer such a conception. It is implicit in other concepts.

The most conspicuous is that of *phronesis,* or practical wisdom, which Aristotle develops in his *Ethics.*[31] *Phronesis* captures the way in which moral judgment involves a virtuous disposition of character *(hexis),* cultivated by one's upbringing *(paideia),* habit *(ethos),* and practice *(praxis).* The basis of moral judgment is thus irreducible to abstract principles. It is unattainable through book learning or instruction alone. In this sense, it is a kind of "situated judgment."

Aristotle clarifies the situated conception of understanding in two key ways. First, by contrasting *phronesis* to craft knowledge *(techne),* he highlights a crucial difference between practical reason and what we might today call "applied theory." Although both concern "practice" in that they aim at a kind of action rather than contemplation, *phronesis* is situated in a way that craft knowledge is not. Whereas craft knowledge involves only the theoretical grasp of the product's form *(eidos),* which is then, at a latter stage, applied to some given material, *phronesis* requires an engaged understanding of the situation of action. Such understanding involves a certain disposi-

---

31. Aristotle, *The Nicomachean Ethics,* ed. Jeffrey Henderson, trans. H. Rackham (Cambridge, MA: Harvard University Press, 1926), bk. 6.

tion of character *(hexis)*: the ability to balance competing goods and commitments, which is shaped by habit and upbringing. Second, Aristotle highlights an important distinction between situated understanding and blind habit. Aristotle shows that although moral judgment is conditioned by habit and upbringing, it nevertheless involves our own understanding and agency. We play a role in forging our characters through the activity of judging itself. By judging well and doing virtuous deeds consistently, we come to develop the characters that conditioned our judgment in the first place.[32] This is what Aristotle means when he says that we acquire virtue through habit *(ethos)*, through the repetition of virtuous actions. Habit, for Aristotle, is not the passive repetition of "the way" things are done. Each "repeated" action involves sizing up a situation that is similar to but never the same as what has come before.

Thus Chapter 5 sets out, first, to illuminate the situated conception of understanding by the torch of one of its forebearers and, second, to shed light on Aristotle. From the perspective of twentieth-century hermeneutic thought, we can make sense of some key parts of Aristotle's *Ethics* that might otherwise remain enigmas. These include Aristotle's conception of nature, the relation of nature to habit, and the sense in which natural justice changes yet remains the same. By making sense of these puzzles from the hermeneutic perspective, I hope to further show how a certain "contemporary" prejudice can actually reveal the truth of the past.

In Chapter 6, the final chapter, I draw out the implications of our situated understanding for political argument. In particular, that prejudice is a necessary feature of judgment forces us to reconsider the common assumption that political *rhetoric* is an illegitimate form of argument—one that appeals to people's particular passions, interests, and commitments rather than their reason. The suspicion of rhetoric is well summarized by Bryan Garsten, who notes its influence in contemporary political theory and practice:

> Political theorists tend to focus on reasonable dialogues of justification rather than passionate exchanges of rhetoric. While actual politicians

---

32. The acquisition of character is thus circular. We acquire good character through judging well, and we can only judge well if we already possess good character. Aristotle seeks to illuminate precisely this mystery.

have not abandoned persuasion (how could they?), they prefer not to acknowledge their art. They understand that when they hear an argument described as "rhetorical," it is being either decried as manipulative or dismissed as superficial. In both theory and practice today, the reigning view of rhetorical speech is that it is a disruptive force in politics and a threat to democratic deliberation.[33]

Perhaps not surprisingly, this conception of rhetoric went hand in hand with the suspicion of prejudice. We see this strikingly in Kant, who denounces rhetoric precisely on the grounds that it plays upon people's prejudices, thus bypassing their reason. He defines rhetoric as the art of "talking men round and prejudicing them in favor of anyone."[34] Consistent with his critique of prejudice, Kant argues that rhetoric inhibits autonomy. Rhetoric, he writes, "in matters of moment, [moves] men like machines to a judgment that must lose all its weight with them upon calm reflection."[35]

To be sure, what we today call "mere rhetoric" is often superficial pandering to people's unreasonable desires. The association of rhetoric with pandering goes back to Socrates, who famously compares rhetoric, as it was taught in his day, to the skill of cookery. Both, he suggests, seek merely to gratify desires without any concern with their goodness.[36] But rhetoric, conceived as the art of persuading people by appealing to their passions, predispositions, and loyalties, is not, as such, mere pandering opposed to reasoned argument. It is, rather, a way of reasoning from within people's perspectives and a way of engaging their situated judgment.

By defending this conception of rhetoric, I develop Garsten's work in *Saving Persuasion: A Defense of Rhetoric and Judgment.* Garsten argues that "a politics of persuasion—in which people try to change one another's minds by appealing not only to reason but also to passions and sometimes even to prejudices—is a mode of politics that is worth defending." Persuasion is worthwhile, he continues, "because it requires us to engage with others wherever they stand and to begin our arguments there, as opposed to assert-

33. Garsten, *Saving Persuasion*, 3.
34. Kant, *Critique of Judgment*, §53, 192.
35. Ibid., §53, 193.
36. Plato, *Gorgias*, ed. Jeffrey Henderson (Cambridge, MA: Harvard University Press, 1925), 465a.

ing that they would adopt our opinion if they were more reasonable."[37] I aim to develop this argument by reference to the conception of prejudice I defend. By considering prejudice as an aspect of reason, we see rhetoric in a new light. Instead of seeing it as a pernicious mode of argument that discourages people from judging detachedly, we come to recognize it as a compelling instance of the engaged understanding that defines our relation to the world.

To reveal rhetoric as exemplary of situated understanding and judgment, I examine some of the most compelling political speeches from American history. These speeches, I show, derive their moral and persuasive force not simply from the principles they may imply or invoke, but more fundamentally, from the way in which they appeal to and clarify the life perspective of the audience. Even those speeches that appear to rely solely on abstract principles of equality and justice also rely upon prejudices that make these principles intelligible.

By examining political rhetoric, we gain a deeper understanding of democratic politics and of what it means to reason from within a life perspective. In particular, we catch a glimpse of the agency connected to this notion of reasoning. The possibility of persuasion, made actual by the great rhetorical moments in our history, reveals that we are never bound to a fixed viewpoint. The practice of persuasion provides a compelling instance of how we are always defining the perspective that conditions us.

37. Garsten, *Saving Persuasion*, 3.

I

The Case against Prejudice

To understand today's suspicion of prejudice, we should consider its philosophical roots in early modern thought. By unearthing these origins and tracing their growth, we may better grasp the detached ideal of judgment. It seems that the case against prejudice did not arise in the realm of moral and political thought, but in seventeenth-century natural philosophy. The idea that we judge best when we abstract from "prejudice" can be traced to Sir Francis Bacon and René Descartes. Although neither philosopher extends his critique of prejudice to the realm of ethics, both powerfully shape the detached conception of judgment that informs Adam Smith's and Immanuel Kant's moral thought.

Prejudice as a Source of Error: Francis Bacon and René Descartes

Bacon and Descartes maintained that prejudice leads to scientific or philosophical error. They argued that in order to understand the universe, including not least ourselves, we must abstract from all prejudice and use our own reason. Each, of course, had a different notion of one's "own reason."

Bacon defended a method of empirical research and induction, whereas Descartes sought a method of finding "clear and distinct" first principles. But both emphasized "one's own" in contrast to one's life circumstance and, especially, to human authority, common opinion, and tradition. By means of such detached reasoning, they claimed, we can discover context-free truths accessible to anyone anywhere.

Bacon articulates his case against prejudice by invoking the "blank slate" ideal of knowledge, which has since become a familiar metaphor for detached judgment: men, he writes, would more easily discover nature's "deeper truths" if their "understandings were unbiased, a blank slate." But "as men's minds have been occupied in so many strange ways that they have no even, polished surface available to receive the true rays of things, it is essential for us to realise that we need to find a remedy for this too."[1] A real scientist, he continues, is someone who, "with faculties unimpaired and the mind cleansed of prejudice, applies himself afresh to experience and particulars."[2]

Bacon's "blank slate" ideal has come to inform today's suspicion of prejudice in realms far removed from natural science. One example, as we have already noted, is in the realm of jurisprudence. Bacon's idea that prejudice tarnishes the mind, leading it to misunderstand the facts, or "particulars," motivates today's search for jurors without any background familiarity with the case, whose minds are "blank slates." Judges and legal scholars often assume that a blank-slate juror is best prepared to receive and to assess the facts. A prejudiced juror, by contrast, is liable to misinterpret the facts— just as a prejudiced natural philosopher, according to Bacon, is liable to misinterpret the phenomena.

Bacon elaborates what he means by "prejudice" in his discussion of the "idols" of the human mind—the various influences that tarnish the intellect. Common to all of the idols is their tendency to influence our judgment in place of a "sure method" of inquiry. The idols, Bacon insists, must be overcome as the first step toward attaining knowledge.

1. Francis Bacon, *The New Organon*, ed. Lisa Jardine and Michael Silverthorne (Cambridge: Cambridge University Press, [1620] 2000), 18.
2. Ibid., 79.

It is notable that Bacon devotes as much space and emphasis in his *New Organon* (1620) to indicting prejudice as he does to developing the scientific method he sought to establish. Bacon envisaged the *New Organon* as the basis for his Great Instauration, an ambitious project of recording, reevaluating, and correcting all human knowledge of the natural world. But before laying out his principles of systematic observation, documentation, and induction, he devotes the entire first book of *The New Organon* to exposing the "idols."

The most general idols Bacon calls the "idols of the tribe." They denote our tendency to believe about the universe what we want to be true, to be influenced by our will and desires. The human understanding, Bacon writes, "is not composed of dry light, but is subject to influence from the will and the emotions, a fact that creates a fanciful knowledge; man prefers to believe what he wants to be true" and tends to reject "sensible ideas" because they "limit his hopes."[3] According to Bacon, hope and desire are merely subjective dispositions. They find no expression in nature as it really is. To grasp the "deeper truths of nature," he writes, we must rein in the tendency to believe that nature embodies a meaningful order or strives to realize certain purposes.[4] He dismisses such views as "superstition" and "fanciful knowledge"—the projection of human concerns onto the brute facts of the world.

A common example of our basic tendency to believe what we "want to be true," one that Bacon highlights, is our disposition to trust the senses, in particular, sight. Human thought, he laments, "virtually stops at sight; so that there is little or no notice taken of things that cannot be seen."[5] Thought "stops at sight" because visible things exert a certain pull on us. We see them as beautiful, ugly, threatening, inspiring. The interest we take in the visible world prompts us to believe that this world is real and not merely illusory. Our concern leads us to trust our vision even when our reason doubts it.

As evidence for such a tendency, we may consider the resistance to heliocentric theories of the solar system, despite compelling reasons in their favor. What finally convinced people that the earth orbits the sun was not the Copernican theory, but Galileo's confirmation of it through the telescope. (His telescope revealed the orbit of moons around Jupiter.) As Hannah Arendt

3. Ibid., 44.
4. Ibid.
5. Ibid., 45.

notes, the visual confirmation allowed people to behold what theorists had only speculated.[6] Bacon criticizes our tendency to accept the truth of what the senses reveal, stressing the need to abstract from appearance. For Bacon, appearance is the product of our own subjective faculty of perception, providing no hint at nature's "deeper truth." To reach such truth, we must correct our naive trust in the senses through detached scientific reasoning.

Bacon elaborates his doctrine of the idols by turning from the general kinds of human prejudice to their concrete sources. What gives shape to our allegedly misleading desires and emotions, according to Bacon, are the "idols of the cave." Each man, Bacon writes, "has a kind of individual cave or cavern which fragments and distorts the light of nature."[7] By "cave," Bacon means one's particular life circumstance, shaped especially by his "upbringing and the company he keeps" and by "his reading of books and the authority of those whom he respects and admires."[8] As the term "cave" suggests, Bacon conceives of one's life circumstance as an obstacle to understanding.

As strongly as Bacon denigrates the influences of habit and upbringing, he recognizes their force. He assumed that transcending the cave would be, for many, a difficult matter. In particular, it would require suspending all judgment on the teaching of one's most respected mentors—including philosophers as highly regarded as Aristotle and Plato. The truth of their teachings, if any, would have to be confirmed by a proper method of detached reflection.

One aspect of the cave that Bacon singles out as difficult but necessary to transcend is the pull of common opinion and conventional language. Words, he claims, insofar as the same ones are used differently among different people, "do violence to the understanding, and confuse everything; and betray men into countless empty disputes and fictions."[9] He suggests that if language is to aid thought rather than confuse it, the meaning of words must be reconstructed piece by piece such that everyone describes the same things by the same names.[10]

As part of this critique of language, Bacon condemns writing that is "rhetorical and prone to disputation." Rhetoric, he writes, is "inimical to the

6. Hannah Arendt, *The Human Condition* (Chicago: University of Chicago Press, 1958), 259.
7. Bacon, *New Organon*, 41.
8. Ibid.
9. Ibid., 42.
10. Ibid., 48–49.

search for truth."[11] According to Bacon, truth must be nonrhetorical; it must be derived from a "sure method" of reasoning and stated in abstract principles, principles whose validity does not depend on their concrete expression.[12] Bacon's scorn for rhetoric thus gives early expression to the idea, elaborated by Thomas Hobbes, that rhetoric, by means of metaphors and images, adds inconsistency to language and muddies clear, logical thinking. The suspicion of rhetoric along these lines, which developed in the seventeenth century and continues today, went hand in hand with the critique of prejudice.

In summary, Bacon's "blank-slate" ideal of knowledge, his rejection of the "idols," and, in particular, his account of our life circumstance as a sort of "cave," point to the renunciation of prejudice that has come to inform not only natural philosophy, but much of ethics, political thinking, and the human sciences in general. The wholesale rejection of prejudice is what I aim to challenge.

It might of course be said that our ability to free ourselves from certain traditional views has enabled the tremendous success of the natural sciences. If we had not stepped back from nature's apparent human meaning and trained our eye to see nature as a field of contingent events, we would have been ill-equipped to map the correlations that allow us to predict and control the things around us. This is true. What I seek to challenge is not the usefulness to modern natural science of stepping back from certain kinds of prejudice, but rather, the claim that such science reaches nature's "deeper truths." What I seek to challenge is Bacon's claim that to understand nature as a meaningful order is to fall prey to delusion. In Chapter 3, I draw upon Heidegger's conception of the world to show how nature must ultimately be understood as a sort of text. Bacon misunderstands his own view of nature as detached or prejudice-free. He overlooks the sense in which modern science presupposes a horizon of meaning that stretches beyond the scientifically knowable.

Although Bacon's critique of prejudice is one of the first and most vehement that we find in early modern thought, his critique has since been eclipsed by

11. Ibid., 58.
12. Ibid., 95.

that of René Descartes. Substantively, Descartes's critique of prejudice contains little that Bacon had not already covered. In fact, a striking feature of Descartes's discussion of prejudice is how consistently it lines up with Bacon's, despite the deep differences between their philosophies. Although Bacon and Descartes offer different accounts of the source of philosophical first principles, they agree that first principles must be prejudice-free, intelligible in abstraction from any particular life circumstance.

Although Descartes tends to use the terms "preconception" and "habitual opinion" more than "prejudice," he uses them to forcefully articulate what I have called the "prejudice-free," or detached conception of knowledge. "Preconception," for Descartes, is a broad concept including all of the understandings that we absorb from everyday life and our upbringing but have not validated by "the standards of reason." Descartes argues that we must suspend "preconception" in this sense and determine its truth (or lack thereof) through detached reflection.

The first rule of Descartes's *Discourse on the Method of Rightly Conducting One's Reason and Seeking the Truth in the Sciences* is "carefully to avoid precipitate conclusions and preconceptions."[13] He writes of preconceptions: "I thought that I could do no better than to undertake to get rid of them, all at one go, in order to replace them afterwards with better ones, or with the same one's once I had squared them with the standards of reason."[14] Similarly, at the beginning of his *Meditations,* he justifies his method of "extensive doubt," which he suspected would seem strange to his readers, on the grounds that it counteracts prejudice: "Although the usefulness of such extensive doubt is not apparent at first sight, its greatest benefit lies in freeing us from all our preconceived opinions."[15]

Like Bacon, Descartes was acutely conscious of the power of prejudice over our judgments. He considers prejudice to be reason's relentless rival for dominion over human understanding. Just as Bacon understands our escape from the cave as the most basic and challenging step toward enlightenment, Descartes considers the suspension of preconception to be the first and most

13. René Descartes, *Discourse on the Method,* in *Selected Philosophical Writings,* trans. John Cottingham, Robert Stoothoff, and Dugald Murdoch (Cambridge: Cambridge University Press, [1637] 1998), 29.

14. Ibid., 26.

15. René Descartes, *Meditation on First Philosophy* (1641), in *Selected Philosophical Writings,* 73.

challenging principle of philosophizing. He remarks, for example, that the proper use of his reason is an "arduous undertaking" because "my habitual opinions keep coming back, and, despite my wishes, they capture my belief, which is as it were bound over them as a result of long occupation and the law of custom."[16]

The way in which Descartes develops his notion of "preconception" reveals its deep affinity to Bacon's notion of "prejudice" and the "idols." Corresponding to the "idols of the tribe" is what Descartes calls the tendency to be misled by our will and the related "spontaneous impulse" to trust our senses.[17] The will, by which Descartes means our desiring and striving, tends to lead the intellect into error. In particular, he claims, we are misled by the body and its desires: we tend to mistakenly judge everything "in terms of its utility to the body," and to assess "the amount of reality in each object" by the extent to which the body is "affected by it."[18] For example, when you "judge that an apple, which may in fact be poisoned, is nutritious," you understand "that its smell, color and so on, are pleasant, but this does not mean that you understand that this particular apple will be beneficial to eat; you judge that it will be because you want to believe it." This holds true, he continues, for any object of reflection: "There may be many things about it that we desire but very few things of which we have knowledge."[19] Descartes concludes that philosophy, or the search for knowledge, requires abstracting from desire, and above all, the desires of the body.

The prejudice for which Descartes is most famous for denouncing is our "spontaneous impulse" to believe that what appears to our senses corresponds, in any way, to reality. Descartes famously raises the possibility that appearances are mere products of our subjective imagination, corresponding to nothing in the "external" or "objective" world.[20] But we naively as-

16. Ibid., 79.
17. Ibid., 89.
18. Ibid., 186.
19. René Descartes, *Objections and Replies to the Meditations*, in *Selected Philosophical Writings*, 133.
20. Descartes, *Meditations on First Philosophy*, 79.

sume, Descartes writes, that appearances are real. Just as Bacon impugns the tendency of thought to virtually stop at sight, Descartes laments that "we become tired if we have to attend to things which are not present to the senses." As a result, our judgments about such things are faulty, based on "preconceived opinion" rather than clear and distinct perception.[21] As the previous passage about our perception of the apple suggests, Descartes connects our tendency to trust the senses with the basic tendency of the will to mislead the intellect. The reason we get caught up in what appears to the senses is that we take a certain interest in it. The apple looks and smells good, so we neglect the invisible poison within. In general, we believe what we want to be true. Our "subjective" emotions and desires obscure the "objective" facts.

The general tendency to be misled by our will acquires its particular shape, according to Descartes, from our upbringing. He reflects, for example, on "how the same man with the same mind, if brought up from infancy among the French or the Germans, develops otherwise than he would if he had lived among the Chinese or cannibals."[22] He offers this reflection not to argue for the importance of a civilized education, but rather to show that one's upbringing as such is a limitation—a cave, as Bacon calls it—that one must try to escape through the use of his own reason. Just as Bacon claims our understanding would be superior if we began with blank-slate minds, Descartes maintains that our judgments would be firmer and less obscure if "we had had the full use of our reason from the moment of our birth, and if we had always been guided by it alone."[23]

As part of his critique of upbringing, Descartes also denigrates the influences of language. Words, he argues, are deceptive labels for concepts that often lead us into lazy thinking:

> Because of the use of language, we tie all our concepts to the words used to express them; and when we store the concepts in our memory we always simultaneously store the corresponding words. Later on we find the words easier to recall than the things; and because of this, it is very seldom that our concept of a thing is so distinct that we can separate it totally from our concept of the words involved. The thoughts

21. René Descartes, *Principles of Philosophy* (1644), in *Selected Philosophical Writings*, 187.
22. Descartes, *Discourse on the Method*, 28.
23. Ibid., 26.

of almost all people are more concerned with words than with things; and as a result people very often give their assent to words they do not understand.[24]

Descartes's separation of "word" and "thing" (or "word" and "concept") reflects his detached conception of understanding. The things themselves, according to Descartes, exist as separate from the particular terms in which we describe them. Words are mere labels that we invent and apply to things whose being we can ultimately grasp independently.

Perhaps the most striking feature of Descartes's critique of prejudice is his insistence on its universal scope. Whereas Bacon occasionally suggests that his prejudice-free method of study would benefit fields beyond natural philosophy, Descartes asserts that his rules for the direction of the mind, first and foremost the rejection of preconception, should "extend to the discovery of truths in any field whatever."[25] In rules "one" and "two" of the *Rules for the Direction of Our Native Intelligence,* he boldly claims that human wisdom "always remains one and the same, however different the subjects to which it is applied," for "all knowledge is certain and evident cognition."[26] He adds that "we should not regard some branches of our knowledge of things as more obscure than others, since they are all of the same nature and consist simply in the putting together of self-evident facts."[27]

The radical character of Descartes's claim can be seen in contrast to Aristotle's teaching that an educated person demands the kind of precision and clarity that each topic dictates. Certain topics, such as ethics and political science, argues Aristotle, do not admit of the same sort of clarity and precision as geometry. This difference in clarity, he continues, does not imply that the former are somehow less scientific but rather that they are of a practical nature. Ethical insight cannot be fully captured in abstract principles because it involves a certain engaged, or we might say "situated," under-

---

24. Descartes, *Principles of Philosophy,* 187.

25. Rene Descartes, *Rules for the Direction of Our Native Intelligence* (1628), in *Selected Philosophical Writings,* 5.

26. Ibid., 1.

27. Ibid., 17.

standing. In contrast to Aristotle, Descartes exempts no realm of understanding from his prejudice-free method of investigation.

Prejudice as a Source of Unfairness: Adam Smith

The case against prejudice that we find in Bacon and Descartes may be summarized as follows: rational judgment requires transcending prejudice, broadly understood as any influence that evades our self-conscious scrutiny. In particular, transcending prejudice means transcending our life circumstance—the perspective shaped by habit, custom, common opinion, our upbringing. According to Bacon and Descartes, our life circumstance is a merely contingent set of influences that tends to hinder our judgment. Although certain circumstances may, by chance, dispose us to judge well, we can discover what counts as good judgment only by means of detached reflection.

Adam Smith applies this way of thinking to moral judgment. Our life circumstance, he maintains, leads us to uncritically privilege our own interests over the interests of others. In particular, we tend to be prejudiced by our loyalties to family, friends, and country.[28] We accord such loyalties disproportionate moral weight, he argues, out of mere habit and custom. If we were to reason properly, we would recognize the contingent character of our loyalties; but habit and custom blinds us. As a result, we tend to judge unfairly, neglecting the interests of "all sensible and intelligent beings."[29] To attain a critical stance toward our motives and to judge the propriety of our conduct, writes Smith, we must examine our conduct as any "fair and impartial spectator would examine it."[30]

Pinning down what Smith means by the "impartial spectator" is not an easy matter. We can make sense of it, I believe, as a metaphor for the detached conception of judgment. We become "impartial spectators" when we step back from our life circumstance and assess our motives for ourselves, by means of our own reason, unburdened by the pull of particular

---

28. Adam Smith, *The Theory of Moral Sentiments*, ed. Ryan Patrick Hanley (New York: Penguin, [1759] 2009), 344.
29. Ibid., 277.
30. Ibid., 133.

loyalties. This is what Smith seems to mean when he speaks of removing ourselves from our own "natural station":

> We can never survey our own sentiments and motives, we can never form any judgment concerning them, unless we remove ourselves, as it were, from our own natural station, and endeavor to view them as at a certain distance from us. . . . But we can do this in no other way than by endeavoring to view them with the eyes of other people. . . . We endeavor to examine our own conduct as we would imagine any other fair and impartial spectator would examine it.[31]

Smith's notion of "viewing" our motives at a "distance" highlights the detachment he believes necessary for moral judgment. This sort of detachment, he concedes, does not imply that one should feel equally loyal to everyone: "The man who should feel no more for the death or distress of his own father, or son, than for those of any man's father or son, would appear neither a good son nor a good father."[32] Accordingly, Smith criticizes the Stoical philosophy, which prescribes us to "eradicate all our private, partial, and selfish affections."[33] Nevertheless, we should feel for "ourselves, our friends, our country" the "reduced passions of the impartial spectator."[34] When we weigh our loyalties in the moral balance, we weigh them not as our *own* loyalties to the actual people who are closest to us, but as generic loyalties to "one's closest" in the abstract. We imagine how an abstract anybody would feel for an abstract brother, friend, or fellow citizen. Our own particular loyalties have no special moral weight. They carry whatever relative weight our detached reason accords them.

Smith emphasizes the detached character of moral judgment in terms of leaping out of one's own situation and into the impartial spectator's. In doing so, one becomes two different people at once—the judge and the judged:

> When I endeavor to examine my own conduct . . . I divide myself, as it were, into two persons; and that I, the examiner and judge, represent a

31. Ibid., 133.
32. Ibid., 163.
33. Ibid., 344.
34. Ibid.

different character from that other I, the person whose conduct is examined into and judged of. The first is the spectator, whose sentiments with regard to my own conduct I endeavor to enter into, by placing myself in his situation, and by considering how it would appear to me, when seen from that particular point of view. The second is the agent, the person whom I properly call myself, and of whose conduct, under the character of a spectator, I was endeavoring to form some opinion. The first is the judge; the second person the judged of. But that the judge should, in every respect, be the same with the person judged of, is as impossible, as that the cause should, in every respect, be the same as the effect.[35]

Smith's reference to the person whom I must transcend, or the "judged," as "the person whom I properly call myself," reveals the sort of detachment he advocates. Moral deliberation requires putting one's own self aside and becoming an abstract anybody.

Smith's account of the impartial spectator follows the basic critique of prejudice that we find in Bacon and Descartes. Sound judgment requires abstracting from one's life circumstance. However, Smith's understanding of prejudice is complicated in one important respect: although he maintains that judging well involves abstracting from prejudice in the sense of one's particular situation, he does not argue that it requires abstracting from all influences given prior to reason. Smith offers a certain defense of the "given" by suggesting that the motivation to assume the role of the impartial spectator is, in the first place, given by human nature, by a universal sentiment of humanity.[36] Following David Hume, Smith claims that our first perceptions of right and wrong come not from reason, but from "immediate sense and feeling."[37] If moral judgment indeed has its source in feeling and is, therefore, not based ultimately on reason, one might say that moral judgment is based on a sort of prejudice. Although moral judgment

35. Ibid., 136.
36. Ibid., 344.
37. Ibid., 377.

involves transcending one's particular situation shaped by habit, custom, and upbringing, and in this sense, is detached, or prejudice-free, moral judgment remains bound to the human situation—to that which happens to be given in the human species.

Smith's moral philosophy thus rests on a distinction between two senses of "prejudice." In the most expansive sense, prejudice refers to any source of judgment given prior to reason. Among these sources would be any sentiment, however widely shared. In a somewhat more specific sense, prejudice refers to the influence of one's life circumstance—the influence of habit, custom, education, upbringing, common opinion, and so on. Smith denounces the second conception of prejudice, but offers a certain defense of the first.

To be sure, Smith never himself uses the term "prejudice" to describe what he takes to be the universal natural sentiments, the fixed aspect of human nature at the foundation of moral judgment. He uses "prejudice" only in the context of discussing the more specific sense of prejudice that he criticizes: habit, custom, and one's particular loyalties. Smith's critical use of "prejudice" attests to how "prejudice," by his time, had become a pejorative. But even though Smith does not understand himself as a defender of "prejudice," his claim that sentiment is ultimately prior to reason amounts to a certain defense of "the given," or of a source of judgment whose influence lies beyond our control. As we will see, Immanuel Kant denounces any such influence as a "prejudice." He claims that moral judgment involves transcending everything "external" to one's own reason—including any sentiment that happens to be universally shared. By understanding sentiment and even natural inclination as external to reason, Kant offers the purest case against prejudice.

Smith, of course, foreshadows Kant to the extent that he defends impartiality and argues that moral judgment must be detached from one's particular situation. But Smith's defense of impartiality is ultimately closer to Hume's claim that moral judgment requires one to "depart from his private and particular situation," and "chuse a point of view, common to him with others." By "common," Hume means that everyone happens to share this point of view.[38] Kant takes a further step: moral judgment must be based on

---

38. David Hume, *An Enquiry Concerning the Principles of Morals*, ed. J. B. Schneewind (Indianapolis, IN: Hackett, [1751] 1983), 75.

"pure practical reason," untainted by anything given. So although Smith has been interpreted as a forerunner to Kant, we should keep in view the difference in their critiques of prejudice. Kant rejects all prejudice, whereas Smith adopts Hume's claim that "reason is and ought only to be a slave to the passions."[39]

It should be noted that Smith comes very close to Kant in one passage where he seems to suggest that impartial judgment requires transcending not only one's particular situation, but also any prejudice whatsoever, even universal benevolence:

> It is not the soft power of humanity, it is not that feeble spark of benevolence which Nature has lighted up in the human heart, that is thus capable of counteracting the strongest impulses of self-love. It is a stronger power, a more forceable motive, which exerts itself upon such occasions. It is reason, principle, conscience, the inhabitant of the breast, the man within, the great judge and arbiter of our conduct. . . . It is not love of our neighbour, it is not the love of mankind, which upon many occasions prompts us to the practice of these divine virtues. It is a stronger love, a more powerful affection, which generally takes place on such occasions; the love of what is honourable and noble, of the grandeur, and dignity, and superiority of our own characters.[40]

Without knowing the source of this passage, one might easily mistake Kant for Smith as its author. The basis of moral motivation is not "love of our neighbour" or even "love of mankind," but the "dignity" of acting according to "reason, principle, and conscience," of expressing the better part of our nature. This passage is the only one in the *Theory of Moral Sentiments* in which Smith seems to suggest that moral judgment must be prejudice-free in the broadest sense of the term—based entirely on detached reason and not even on natural benevolence.

But Smith undermines this suggestion at the end of *The Theory of Moral Sentiments,* where he explicitly addresses the ultimate source of moral approbation:

39. David Hume, *A Treatise of Human Nature,* ed. L. A. Selby-Bigge, 2nd ed. (Oxford: Oxford University Press, [1740] 1978), 415.

40. Smith, *Theory of Moral Sentiments,* 159.

It is altogether absurd and unintelligible to suppose that the first perceptions of right and wrong can be derived from reason, even in those particular cases upon the experience of which general rules are formed. These first perceptions, as well as all other experiments upon which any general rules are founded, cannot be the object of reason, but of immediate sense and feeling. It is by finding in a vast variety of instances that one tenor of conduct pleases in a certain manner, and that another as constantly displeases the mind, that we form the general rules of morality. . . . But nothing can be agreeable for its own sake, which is not rendered such by immediate sense and feeling.[41]

In this passage, Smith firmly maintains that moral judgment is ultimately motivated by sentiment, not reason.

Smith's final position on prejudice seems to be this: moral judgment is prejudice-free insofar as it involves abstracting from one's own situation and assuming the position of the impartial spectator. But at the same time, the desire to see things from this abstract standpoint is motivated, in the first place, by a certain prejudice—a natural sentiment: "Nature has, accordingly, endowed [man], not only with a desire of being approved of, but with a desire of being what he ought to be approved of; or of being what he himself approves of in other men."[42] Smith concludes that morality demands detachment and that the desire to judge detachedly comes from a natural human attraction to fairness despite the opposite pull of particular interests. He ultimately defends an impartial morality based on an innate human prejudice for impartiality.

Smith's explicit case against prejudice, understood as life circumstance, and his implicit defense of prejudice, understood as natural sentiment, are both views that I seek to challenge. My goal is to show that one's life circumstance, including one's particular loyalties to family, friends, and country, is not a merely contingent obstacle to moral judgment, but an intelligible perspective that informs it. My goal is thus to question the very distinction between prejudice, on the one hand, and reason, on the other. Correspondingly, I reject Smith's implicit defense of prejudice understood

41. Ibid., 377.
42. Ibid., 140.

as natural sentiment distinct from reason. According to my argument, all human sentiments are shaped by the terms in which we describe them, terms which themselves arise from within our life perspective.

Smith's conception of life circumstance, which he discusses in terms of "habit and custom," provides a sharp contrast to the conception of perspective that I aim to defend. Smith considers habit and custom to be the basic source of prejudice, the source of the particular loyalties that lead us astray. Habit and custom, by his account, are mechanical dispositions into which we fall as an effect of our particular culture and upbringing. Smith highlights the rote aspect of habit as follows: "When two objects have frequently been seen together, the imagination acquires a habit of passing easily from the one to the other . . . [and] though, independent of custom, there should be no real beauty in their union, yet when custom has thus connected them together, we feel an impropriety in their separation."[43]

Smith considers habit and custom to be forces that pervert natural sympathy for mankind at large, leading to a parochial love of one's own. He calls "habit and custom" the "chief causes of the many irregularities and discordant opinions which prevail in different ages and nations concerning what is blamable or praise-worthy."[44] Habit and custom thus distort human nature, understood as the basic moral sentiments common to all men regardless of their particular situations—what Hume calls the "general unalterable standard, by which we may approve or disapprove of all of characters and manners."[45] Smith believes that the basic desire to be fair and impartial is "natural" in this sense, that this desire is a fixed aspect of human nature independent of habit and custom.

To understand Smith's account of the influence of habit and custom on moral reasoning, we should first consider his account of their influence on

43. Ibid., 227.
44. Ibid.
45. Hume, *Enquiry*, 49.

aesthetic judgment. Smith considers their influence to be strongest on judgments concerning beauty. Few are "willing to allow," he writes, "that custom and fashion have much influence on their judgments concerning what is beautiful, or otherwise, in the productions of any of those arts; but imagine, that all the rules, which they think ought to be observed in each of them, are founded upon reason and nature, not upon habit and prejudice."[46] Here Smith articulates precisely the distinction I aim to challenge—the distinction between "reason and nature," on the one hand, and "habit and prejudice" on the other.

With respect to aesthetics, at least, Smith tends to consider prejudice a more or less inevitable feature of judgment. For this reason, he is not severely critical of it. He accepts it with a certain resignation. For example, he concedes that "a man would be ridiculous who should appear in public with a suit of clothes quite different from those which are commonly worn, though the new dress should in itself be ever so graceful or convenient."[47] But Smith makes this concession in a critical tone. As the phrase graceful "in itself" suggests, Smith still defends the ideal of a prejudice-free aesthetic based on natural standards of beauty independent of anyone's particular situation. He laments that "few men have so much experience and acquaintance with different modes which have obtained in remote ages and nations, as to be thoroughly reconciled to them, or to judge with impartiality between them, and what takes place in their own age and country."[48] The most discerning aesthetic eye, he suggests, would view the "different modes" of beauty from the distance of a detached spectator, unprejudiced by the taste of his own age.

To bolster his defense of a prejudice-free ideal of aesthetic judgment, Smith suggests that utility and natural agreeableness recommend certain forms to us independent of custom:

> I cannot, however, be induced to believe that our sense even of external beauty is founded altogether on custom. The utility of any form, its fitness for the useful purposes for which it was intended, evidently recommends it, and renders it agreeable to us independent of custom. Certain

46. Smith, *Theory of Moral Sentiments*, 229.
47. Ibid.
48. Ibid.

colors are more agreeable than others, and give more delight to the eye the first time it ever beholds them. A smooth surface is more agreeable than a rough one. Variety is more pleasing than a tedious undiversified uniformity. Connected variety, in which each new appearance seems to be introduced by what went before it, and in which all the adjoining parts seem to have some natural relation to one another, is more agreeable than a disjointed and disorderly assemblage of unconnected objects.[49]

A cursory analysis of Smith's custom-free aesthetic reveals its weakness. Most significantly, his defense of utility as a criterion for aesthetic value uncritically equates the good with the beautiful. Just because something is useful, or fitting, does not make it attractive. We can imagine numerous examples of very useful forms that are hardly beautiful. In many cases, usefulness comes at the price of beauty. (Consider simple, more functional articles of clothing or utensils that lack beauty precisely because they are made to work well.) Smith's defense of the natural agreeableness of certain colors, surfaces, and arrangements is equally questionable. In response to his assertions, such as "a smooth surface is more agreeable that a rough one," one is inclined to ask: Are the "smooth" savannas of Africa more attractive than the "rough" mountains of the Himalayas? Is a scene depicted on a flat canvass more beautiful than a scene depicted in relief? Similar objections could be raised with respect to each of his other criteria. Smith's questionable claims attest to the difficulty of separating beauty and custom. His attempt to do so belies his desire for a standard of aesthetic judgment independent of any particular perspective.

As part of his staunch defense of impartial judgment, he excoriated the poets of his time who formed literary groups in an attempt to sway public opinion in favor of their respective styles—some advocating the model of classical literature, others defending a break from tradition. Smith refers disparagingly to such groups as "literary factions," each of which employs "all the mean arts of intrigue and solicitation to preoccupy the public in favor of the works of its own members."[50] Smith compares such attempts at

49. Ibid., 233.
50. Ibid., 149.

persuading the public to bribing a jury, declaring that the literary groups had "attempted both to obtain praise, and to avoid blame, by very unfair means."[51] Smith's analogy to bribery is far-fetched considering that the literary groups were offering arguments, not money for the support of their work. But the analogy makes sense in light of his ideal of prejudice-free judgment. By offering persuasive arguments for the merit of their work, the poets instilled a conspicuous prejudice in their audience. Those who came to be persuaded of a certain style's superiority would, of course, read the poetry in a new light—from a perspective shaped by the artist's testimony. According to Smith, this meant that the critics were no longer reading what was really on the page. Instead, they were interpreting the words through the distorting lens of the artist's rhetoric. As in Bacon's thought, Smith's case against prejudice goes hand in hand with a rejection of rhetoric. The fairest judge of literary excellence, according to Smith, is a blank-slate reader—one who is unprejudiced by the artist's persuasive arguments.

In the case of moral as compared to aesthetic judgment, Smith expresses more confidence in people's ability to overcome prejudice. He argues that in contrast to our sense of beauty, which may "easily be altered by habit and education," the "sentiments of moral approbation and disapprobation" are "founded on the strongest and most vigorous passions of human nature; and though they may be somewhat warpt, cannot be entirely perverted."[52] This echoes Hume's notion, in the *Enquiry Concerning the Principles of Morals*, that the basis of moral approbation lies in human nature, independent of custom:

> This principle, indeed of precept and education, must so far be owned to have a powerful influence, that it may frequently encrease or diminish, beyond their natural standard, the sentiments of approbation or dislike . . . But that *all* moral affection or dislike arises from this origin, will never surely be allowed by any judicious enquirer. Had nature

51. Ibid., 150.
52. Ibid., 234.

made no such distinction, founded on the original constitution of the human mind, the words *honourable* and *shameful, lovely* and *odious, noble* and *despicable,* had never had place in any language. . . . The social virtues must, therefore, be allowed to have a natural beauty and amiableness, which, at first, antecedent to all precept or education, recommends them to the esteem of uninstructed mankind, and engages their affections.[53]

Although Smith, like Hume, firmly defends a natural source of moral approbation, independent of education and upbringing, he readily admits that custom can, to some degree, shape moral sentiments for better or for worse. To the extent that Smith does defend habit and custom, he defends them as tools for getting us to consistently do the right thing. On the one hand, "when custom and fashion coincide with the natural principles of right and wrong, they heighten the delicacy of our sentiments, and increase our abhorrence for everything which approaches to evil." On the other hand, those "who have had the misfortune to be brought up amidst violence, licentiousness, falsehood, and injustice; lose, though not all sense of the impropriety of such conduct, yet all sense of its dreadful enormity."[54] For this reason, Smith stresses the ethical importance of education in good habits. Furthermore, he argues, good habits help make virtue our second nature, leading us to consistently do the right thing. But despite the benefits that habit and custom may bring, they at best reinforce virtue. In the first place, virtue is determined from the standpoint of the impartial spectator.

Reinforcing this point, Smith depreciates any manners or qualities of character to which we are favorably disposed by custom alone:

The different manners which custom teaches us to approve of in the different professions and states of life, do not concern things of the greatest importance. We expect truth and justice from an old man as well as a young, from a clergyman as well as from an officer; and it is in matters of small importance only that we look for the distinguishing marks of their respective characters. With regard to these too,

53. Hume, *Enquiry*, 40.
54. Smith, *Theory of Moral Sentiments*, 234.

there is often some unobserved circumstance, which, if it was attended to, would show us, that, independent of custom, there was a propriety in the character which custom had taught us to allot to each profession.[55]

In the last sentence, Smith suggests that even when we assume that custom is the source of our approval of certain manners, our approval actually derives from some "unobserved circumstance" independent of custom. Smith's eagerness to reject custom reiterates his claim that important moral judgments must be justified by detached reason.

The particular features of our life circumstance that Smith singles out for critique are the loyalties to our family, friends, and country, which he claims to be based on mere habit and not reason or nature. "What is called affection," Smith writes, "is in realty nothing but habitual sympathy" that arises from living in proximity with the same people.[56] Smith explains the affection for family members in this way. He reasons that since a person's family members "usually live in the same house with him," they are "naturally and usually the persons upon whose happiness or misery his conduct must have the greatest influence." Therefore, he is "more habituated to sympathize with them. He knows better how everything is likely to affect them, and his sympathy is with them more precise and determinate than it can be with the greater part of other people."[57]

Smith extends this argument to neighborhood and work relationships: "Among well-disposed people, the necessity or conveniency of mutual accommodation, very frequently produces a friendship not unlike that which takes place among those who are born into the same family."[58] In all of these cases, friendship arises from a "constrained sympathy," which has been "rendered habitual for the sake of conveniency and accommodation."[59] The only kind of friendship that Smith praises highly is friendship among "men of virtue," that is, among fellow impartial spectators who are willing to sacrifice the "inferior interests" of their "own particular order or society," and

55. Ibid., 244.
56. Ibid., 260.
57. Ibid., 258.
58. Ibid., 264.
59. Ibid., 265.

even of "the greater interest of state" to the "interest of that great society of all sensible and intelligent beings."[60]

Prejudice as a Source of Enslavement: Immanuel Kant

To this point, we have examined what I introduced as the "first strand" of the case against prejudice: the idea that prejudice leads us into *error*. According to this way of thinking, we must abstract from prejudice for the sake of learning the *truth*—whether the truth about the universe (Bacon and Descartes) or the truth about how best to act (Smith). Like his predecessors, Immanuel Kant maintains that prejudice tends to obscure our understanding of nature and morality. But he also develops another line of critique— what I have called the "second strand" of the case against prejudice. According to Kant, prejudice is opposed not only to truth but to *freedom*. By articulating both strands of the case against prejudice, and above all, by developing the opposition of prejudice and freedom, Kant brings the case against prejudice to its most powerful expression. Any compelling defense of prejudice must respond to Kant's critique of it.

Kant's deep concern with freedom is captured by his definition of "prejudice" as "the heteronomy of reason."[61] By "heteronomy," Kant means the opposite of autonomy, which he argues is the essence of freedom. To be free, Kant's maintains, is to be governed from within rather than from without, to be guided by one's own reason and not by nature, tradition, habit, or custom.[62] To be guided by the latter influences is to be "heteronomous" or "prejudiced." Kant thus understands "prejudice" quite expansively. It includes the influence of our life circumstance (as it does for Bacon, Descartes, and Smith), but it also includes any desire whatsoever. For if we consider the matter, argues Kant, we do not choose our desires. They act upon us as contingent facts of nature—in the same way as other influences typically considered "external." As part of his demanding conception of using "one's own reason," Kant rejects desire as a source of free judgment. In this sense, Kant's

---

60. Ibid., 277.

61. Immanuel Kant, *The Critique of Judgment*, trans. James Creed Meredith (Oxford: Oxford University Press, [1790] 1952), §40, 152.

62. Immanuel Kant, *Groundwork of the Metaphysics of Morals*, trans. and ed. Mary Gregor (Cambridge: Cambridge University Press, [1785] 1997), 52, 4:446.

critique of prejudice goes one step further than Smith's. As we have seen, Smith impugns life circumstance as "prejudice," but he defends what he considers to be the "natural" human sentiments. By contrast, Kant rejects even the latter as a kind of "prejudice" to be overcome for the sake of autonomy.

Like Bacon, Descartes, and Smith, Kant considers the overcoming of prejudice to be central to the progress of reason. In a telling passage, he defines "enlightenment" as the "emancipation from prejudices generally."[63] In positive terms, the "motto of enlightenment" is to "make use of one's own understanding without direction from another."[64]

In his essay "What Is Enlightenment" (1784), Kant reiterates that judgment influenced by prejudice is not merely error-prone but "passive," or enslaved. He compares the failure to think for one's self to being bossed around like a child: "It is so comfortable to be a minor!," he declares with scorn. "If I have a book that understands for me, a spiritual adviser who has a conscience for me, a doctor who decides upon a regimen for me, and so forth, I need not trouble myself at all."[65] Perhaps the book contains the truth, perhaps the priest knows what is moral, and perhaps the doctor knows what is healthy. The problem with following their prescriptions is not that I may err, but that I fail to "trouble myself," that I fail to exercise my own reason. Although, in the above passage, Kant singles out human authority as a source of prejudice, he makes clear that "prejudice" denotes any kind of "direction from another" (including direction from tradition, or even one's desires). His "maxim of *unprejudiced* thought" is the general injunction "to think for one's self."[66]

Notwithstanding Kant's somewhat counterintuitive inclusion of all desire in the category of "prejudice," his basic idea that prejudice, conceived as life circumstance, constrains one's freedom is quite familiar today. We often assume that free judgment requires abstracting from the influences of common opinion, convention, and our upbringing. We assume that to reason from such sources is to remain mired in what blind habit has taught us to

63. Kant, *Critique of Judgment*, §40, 152.
64. Immanuel Kant, "An Answer to the Question: What Is Enlightenment?," in *Practical Philosophy*, trans. and ed. Mary J. Gregor (Cambridge: Cambridge University Press, [1784] 1996), 17.
65. Ibid.
66. Kant, *Critique of Judgment*, §40, 152.

think. And even if judgment shaped by such sources proves to be reliable, we still view it as reflecting an undesirable lack of agency. Following Kant, we tend to think that free judgment means "thinking for one's self."

Kant's connection of prejudice to a lack of agency not only sheds light on our contemporary suspicions of prejudice but also on the suspicions of his philosophical predecessors. Although Bacon and Descartes focus primarily on how prejudice leads to error, their critiques of prejudice are also motivated by a deep concern with freedom. For example, although Bacon claims to be motivated by "the eternal love of truth," he goes out of his way to criticize the followers of Aristotle's philosophy not simply for being confused, but for having *"enslaved* themselves to it from prejudice and the authority of others" (emphasis added).[67]

The same concern with freedom lurks just beneath the surface of Descartes's case against prejudice. Although Descartes claims to reject preconception in order to form "true and sound judgments,"[68] he also affirms an interest in breaking free from authority. He considers his method of doubting and avoiding preconception a way of "emerging from the control of my teachers" and resolving "to undertake studies within myself . . . to use all the powers of my mind in choosing the paths I should follow."[69]

Most tellingly, Descartes associates his prejudice-free method of philosophizing with self-mastery, with being in command of one's own thoughts and desires. This alone, he claims, is sufficient to make philosophers "richer, more powerful, freer and happier than other men."[70] In these passages, Descartes ties the rejection of prejudice to being self-directed as much as to seeking the truth. Descartes also describes his method of doubt as a way in which "the mind uses its own freedom."[71] He conceives doubt as a source of liberty from the tutelage of his upbringing. We are at "our freest," Descartes adds, when "a clear perception impels us to pursue some object."[72] Although the claim that we are at the same time both "free" and "impelled" might appear contradictory, it makes sense in light of Descartes's view of

67. Francis Bacon, *New Organon*, 63.

68. Descartes, *Rules*, 1.

69. Descartes, *Discourse on the Method*, 24–25.

70. Ibid., 33.

71. Descartes, *Meditations on First Philosophy*, 73.

72. Descartes, *Objections and Replies*, 135.

the world. According to Descartes, the "clear perception" impels us from within—it is an achievement of our own self-reflection, and in this sense, an entirely different source of authority from the sources that lie outside us.

As these passages show, the ideal of freedom as autonomy motivates the case against prejudice even before Kant. What makes Kant such an important critic of prejudice is that he brings the views of his age to their clearest statement. He rejects prejudice as a source of error and unfairness, but most of all, as a source of slavery. Kant's thought thus unifies and completes the two strands of the case against prejudice that we have inherited.

Kant most famously writes against prejudice in his moral philosophy. He does so in the name of fairness and respecting the dignity of others, but more significantly, in the name of autonomy. The fairness rationale for rejecting prejudice finds expression in Kant's first formulation of the Categorical Imperative: "act only in accordance with that maxim through which you can will that it become a universal law."[73] If you can't consistently will your maxim and its universal application, implies Kant, you are favoring your own interests over the interests of others. The "universal law" test thus bears a certain likeness to Smith's "impartial spectator" exercise. Both are meant to express how moral judgment involves abstracting from one's particular situation and judging from a standpoint shared with everyone else.

But Kant's special concern for freedom leads him to a more thoroughgoing rejection of prejudice than Smith's. Whereas Smith accepts that praise and censure is based, ultimately, on a natural human inclination for fairness, Kant argues that moral judgment must be prejudice-free in a more demanding sense: It must be motivated by duty alone, by one's own reason defined in contrast to any sentiment of benevolence or inclination for fairness. This source of motivation is what Kant means by "pure practical reason." Practical reason is "pure" when it transcends the influence of all prejudice. The value at stake in exercising pure reason is not fairness, which could be achieved otherwise, but autonomy. Kant argues that one should take an interest in morality, even if it leads to unhappiness, because willing

73. Kant, *Groundwork*, 4:421, 31.

the Categorical Imperative is one way of transcending prejudice and realizing "the idea of freedom." Freedom, Kant maintains, is the source of human dignity; it distinguishes a human being "from all other things, even from himself insofar as he is affected by objects."[74] Kant's radical critique of prejudice thus reflects his demanding notion of autonomy.

Kant develops both the truth and freedom rationales for rejecting prejudice in his writing on aesthetics. It is in these rationales that we find some of his most illuminating accounts of the detached ideal of judgment. Kant praises our faculty of aesthetic judgment insofar as it involves abstracting from the "charm and emotion" of the work and trying to determine how anyone else would judge it.[75] His first reason for defending such abstraction is that it helps us avoid error, or "illusion":

> [Taste is] a critical faculty which in its reflective act takes account (a priori) of the mode of representation of everyone else, in order, as it were, to weigh its judgment with the collective reason of mankind, and thereby avoid the illusion arising from subjective and personal conditions which could readily be taken for objective, an illusion that would exert a prejudicial influence upon its judgment. This is accomplished by weighing the judgment, not so much with actual, as rather with the merely possible, judgments of others, and by putting ourselves in the position of everyone else, as the result of a mere abstraction from the limitations which contingently effect our own estimate.[76]

The idea that sound aesthetic judgment involves resisting "charm and emotion" recalls Bacon's and Descartes's parallel claims about judgments concerning nature. Understanding nature's "deeper truths," for Bacon, requires abstracting from the way that nature strikes us as useful, beautiful, threatening, or purposeful. To understand nature in such terms, he maintains, is to read human values into the objective world. In a similar vein, Kant

74. Ibid., 4:452, 57.
75. Kant, *Critique of Judgment*, §40, 152.
76. Ibid., §40, 151.

argues that we must abstract from the way in which a work of art, or any beautiful thing, charms us. What we find charming, he warns, might be a mere product of our subjective whim. It may have nothing to do with the value of the aesthetic "object" itself.

Kant's suggestion that we uproot ourselves from our own situations, or "positions," and try to place ourselves "in the position of everyone else," rests on his assumption that our particular situations are "subjective and personal conditions" that "contingently effect our own estimate." On the basis of this assumption, Kant equates a "man of enlarged mind" with someone who "detaches himself" from his personal situation and "reflects upon his own judgment from a universal standpoint (which he can only determine by shifting his ground to the standpoint of others)."[77] Kant denies the possibility that one's particular perspective might be more illuminating than the imagined standpoint of the abstract anybody. According to his view, particular implies parochial.

Kant's detached conception of aesthetic judgment is also motivated by his concern for freedom. He praises prejudice-free aesthetic judgment insofar as it cultivates our autonomy. Thus he measures the "aesthetic worth of the fine arts" by the extent to which they contribute to the free play of the "imagination" and "understanding." The worthiest forms of art, he claims, engage the mind and contribute to autonomy. The basest forms appeal to prejudice and foster heteronomy.[78]

Kant's most illuminating comparison, concerning the worth of art, is of poetry to rhetoric. He ranks poetry first "among all the arts," on the grounds that it "expands the mind by giving freedom to the imagination. . . . It invigorates the mind by letting it feel its faculty—free, spontaneous, and independent of determination by nature, . . ."[79] By contrast, he ranks rhetoric lowest among the arts. Rhetoric, he writes, "so far as this is taken to mean the art of persuasion . . . is a dialectic, which borrows from poetry only so much as is necessary to win over men's minds to the side of the speaker before they have weighed the matter, and to rob their verdict of its freedom. Hence it can be recommended neither for the bar nor the pulpit."[80]

77. Ibid., §40, 153.
78. Ibid., §53, 191–192.
79. Ibid.
80. Ibid., §53, 192.

Kant's suggestion that orators somehow bypass the reason and freedom of their listeners may seem unduly harsh. Surely persuasive speech elicits some sort of active participation, or "weighing," on the part of those persuaded. People do not just assent to a speaker's view for no reason, capitulating as if their arms had been twisted.[81] Kant's objection to rhetoric makes sense, however, in light of how rhetoric persuades people by appealing to their prejudices. Effective orators are typically masters at speaking to people from within their particular perspectives. The most persuasive politicians often encourage their listeners to judge, or to "weigh," the issues in light of the particular things they care about. On these grounds, Kant's calls rhetoric the art of "talking men round and prejudicing them in favor of anyone."[82] Such an appeal to prejudice, Kant argues, is at odds with cultivating autonomy. Rhetoric thus robs people of their freedom. Kant's deep suspicion of rhetoric is yet another example of the widespread condemnation of it that developed alongside the critique of prejudice.

Kant's renunciation of prejudice, thoroughgoing though it is, contains an important complication. On the one hand, Kant ties together the truth and freedom strands of the case against prejudice, defending a radically detached conception of judgment. On the other hand, however, in a subtle yet profound way, he provides the philosophical basis for a situated conception of understanding.

Kant prepares such a conception by undermining the version of the *subject-object distinction* assumed by his predecessors, including Bacon and Descartes. According to this version, we exist, first and foremost, as knowing subjects who take in bits of information from a supposedly external world, retain a memory of those bits, and then, at a latter stage, piece them together into beliefs. Our beliefs may, of course, be faulty. They may be our own subjective representations, bearing little or no resemblance to the actual objects "out there." To be sure that our subjective beliefs indeed correspond to the objects, we have to carefully scrutinize the belief-forming process.

81. Bryan Garsten, *Saving Persuasion: A Defense of Rhetoric and Judgment* (Cambridge, MA: Harvard University Press, 2007), 7.

82. Kant, *Critique of Judgment*, §53, 192.

We must proceed *methodically*—either by some system of observation and induction (Bacon) or of finding "clear and distinct" first principles (Descartes).

Kant undermines this way of thinking in his "transcendental deduction."[83] What his "deduction" establishes is that our awareness of an object, and even our awareness of the distinction between "in me" and "out there," presupposes a certain *unity* of experience, that the objects we perceive *already* stand in certain relations, that they cohere as parts of whole. The principle of unity is the *transcendental subject,* whose "categories" organize experience into once coherent consciousness. The "categories" reflect the presupposition that the "unity" of experience "in accordance with *a priori* rules," is the condition for the experience of "objects."[84] Although we never perceive this unity as an object, we must presuppose it as the condition of knowledge, or of any claim to knowledge.

The idea of "conditions of knowledge," at least in a faint sense, gestures toward the idea that knowledge involves a certain kind of prejudice. For Kant, what we know, including what we perceive "clearly and distinctly" (Descartes), rests upon a principle of unity that we do not *know* but must *presuppose.* On the basis of this way of thinking, Heidegger and Gadamer eventually rehabilitate prejudice *(Vorurteil).* As we will see in Chapters 2–4, they adopt Kant's basic notion of conditions of knowledge and develop a *situated conception* of those conditions.

But although in hindsight we must credit Kant with setting the stage for Heidegger and Gadamer's line of thought, Kant's own account of the conditions of knowledge lies far from a defense of prejudice. For the conditions, or the "prejudice," that Kant's transcendental deduction establishes is nothing other than the a priori categories of the knowing subject. To be sure, we, as knowers, can never "get behind" the categories that structure experience and have "pure," or unmediated, knowledge of things "in themselves," including our personal identity, or ego, in itself.[85] In this respect, Kant corrects Descartes by showing that the "I think" perceived in self-reflection presupposes a "unity of apperception," which itself (as the condition of con-

83. Immanuel Kant, *Critique of Pure Reason* , trans. and ed. Paul Guyer and Allen W. Wood (Cambridge: Cambridge University Press, [1781; 2nd. (B) ed.,1787] 1998), A95, 226.

84. Ibid., A108, 233.

85. Kant, *Groundwork,* 4:451, 56.

sciousness) cannot be brought before one's consciousness as an object.[86] One might therefore say that, according to Kant, knowledge is always "prejudiced" by the universal structures of subjectivity.

But this use of "prejudice" would be misleading. For unlike "prejudice" understood as one's world, or concrete life perspective, the "prejudice" that Kant may be said to articulate is unaffected by any actual experience or situation. Far from vindicating the idea that knowledge presupposes prejudice, Kant's transcendental deduction actually provides the metaphysical background for the possibility of the subject's radical autonomy—its ability to transcend all prejudice. The Kantian subject, which constitutes the world as it appears and can be known, is in principle, free of its own creation: free of the causal laws that govern nature and free of the conventions that order society.

But although Kant considers the condition for the possibility of knowledge to be the fixed, universal structure of subjectivity, Heidegger and Gadamer adopt his transcendental way of arguing and use it to undermine his own conclusion. Heidegger, as we will see, argues that the conditions of knowledge run deeper than the categories identified by Kant. For experience, according to Heidegger, is not primarily of an object as Kant assumes. Heidegger shows that the very possibility of what Kant calls the subject-object relation presupposes a way of life, or a world, in which the "subject" is situated. Heidegger's notion of situated understanding, as I will try to show, provides a framework for defending prejudice that overcomes the opposition of prejudice and reason. So in conclusion, although Kant is the thinker who brings the case against prejudice to its fullest expression, he is also, unwittingly, the philosopher who initiates its overcoming.

The Sentimental Revival of Prejudice: Edmund Burke

Any essay on prejudice and, in particular, any defense of habit, custom, and tradition as potentially legitimate sources of authority would be incomplete without a discussion of Edmund Burke—that rebelliously conservative thinker who offers the most famous and explicit defense of prejudice. In his

---

86. Kant, *Critique of Pure Reason*, A107–108, 232–233.

Reflections on the Revolution in France (1790), Burke shockingly declares: "In this enlightened age, I am bold enough to confess, that we are generally men of untaught feelings; that instead of casting away all our old prejudices, we cherish them to a very considerable degree, and, to take more shame to ourselves, we cherish them because they are prejudices."[87]

Burke's opening reference to "this enlightened age" highlights the sense in which he saw his defense of prejudice as a reaction against the spirit of his times. Like Kant, Burke identifies "enlightenment" with the overcoming of prejudice. But instead of lauding this development, he bemoans it. As his connection of prejudice to "untaught feelings" suggests, Burke's defense of prejudice builds upon Smith's and Hume's defense of sentiment over reason.[88] Echoing his Scottish predecessors, Burke declares that "our passions instruct our reason."[89] But by defending sentiment as a kind of "prejudice," Burke does not simply restate the views of Smith and Hume in more shocking terms. For the sentiments Burke defends are precisely those that Smith and Hume denounce as *mere* prejudice. In particular, Burke defends sentiments connected to traditional institutions and social roles—the feelings of reverence sustained by "the spirit of a gentleman, and the spirit of religion."[90] Smith, as we have seen, denounces such sentiments as parochial. He defends instead what he considers to be the general, "natural" sentiments—those supposedly untainted by habit and custom. Burke, by contrast, defends precisely those sentiments shaped by traditional sources of authority.

When Burke speaks in praise of "prejudice," he rarely means "untaught feelings" in the abstract, but feelings as shaped by particular habits, customs, and roles. In fact, he often uses "prejudice" to denote the habits, customs, and roles themselves. For example, he speaks of the "church prejudice," by which he means the established Church of England insofar as it

---

87. Edmund Burke, *Reflections on the Revolution in France*, ed. Frank M. Turner (New Haven, CT: Yale University Press, [1790] 2003), 74.

88. The phrase "untaught feelings" appears somewhat strange given that these "feelings," according to Burke, are specifically those cultivated by habit and custom. In this sense, they would seem "taught," not "untaught." But the phrase makes sense if we consider "untaught" to mean "from a source whose authority does not depend on rational justification." This is precisely how Burke understands tradition.

89. Burke, *Reflections*, 69.

90. Ibid., 67.

shapes the practice and judgment of Englishmen. He ranks the church establishment "first of our prejudices" and defends it at great length.[91]

Burke's defense of prejudice consists of two arguments for tradition, both of which conceive of tradition as based on sentiment rather than reason. Therefore, we may call Burke's the "sentimentalist" case for prejudice. Burke's first defense of tradition, or "prejudice," lauds the customs, manners, and moral sentiments of feudal society, praising them as "pleasing" and "noble." This way of life, he laments, is being destroyed by "the new conquering empire of light and reason."[92]

To the extent that Burke praises traditional roles and institutions as "pleasing" and "noble," he apparently ascribes to them a sort of intrinsic value. Upon closer examination, however, he does not mean to say that such prejudice expresses some special insight. He instead considers traditional institutions to be "pleasing illusions," practices whose value arises from "the human mind."[93] Meaning, or value, according to Burke's account, is not embodied in the social world but projected upon it by human subjects. In this crucial respect, his defense of prejudice adopts a basic premise of Bacon, Descartes, and Kant—namely the subject-object conception of the world. Each of these thinkers, in his own terms, assumes that world *in itself* is meaningless—an array of *objects* devoid of intrinsic value. By contrast, the world *for us* is meaningful. It is meaningful insofar as we stamp it with our subjective values. In the case of the social world, to say that its meaning is a product of subjective values is also to say that it comes from *convention,* not nature. To think that meaning is embodied in society—either by the will of God, by nature, or by any other source—is to be deceived by "pleasing illusion."

Although Burke, at one point, defends what he calls "the reason in prejudice," he means by "reason" its social utility, not its inherent worth or insight.[94] This utilitarian argument is his second defense of tradition, which, in the final analysis, seems to be his strongest. According to Burke's utilitarian defense of prejudice, tradition provides a strong, arguably necessary basis for social solidarity and willingness to obey the law. He warns that if all

91. Ibid., 78.
92. Ibid., 66.
93. Ibid.
94. Ibid., 74.

traditional prejudices are to be dissolved, nothing but brute force and the fear of punishment will preserve society. In this way, Burke connects prejudice to a sort of republican freedom—the liberty born of identifying with the traditions and customs of one's society. Citizens inspired by such prejudice, Burke argues, revere their rulers, willingly accept their commands, and do not perceive political life to be coercive. Needless to say, Kant, and others, considered this sort of freedom to be a sham. But Burke defends it as a firm source of decent political life. For this reason, he excoriates the French revolutionaries for seeking to abolish all prejudice in favor of the abstract "rights of man."[95] A wise statesman, Burke claims, prudently uses prejudice to advance the common good.

My aim is not to take a stand on whether Burke is right about the social necessity of prejudice. I aim, rather, to highlight the sense in which his utilitarian defense of prejudice preserves the opposition between prejudice and reason. Although prejudice, for Burke, may "have reason" in the sense of be useful, it has no intrinsic meaning. Prejudice is not a source of reasoned political judgment. What Burke calls the wise politician's "political reason" is, upon close analysis, decisively detached. Such reason, as Burke understands it, does not work within the perspective of tradition but from outside of it. By Burke's account, the wise politician steps back from the habits, customs, and roles of his society, surveys them from a bird's-eye view, and carefully selects which to manipulate toward the common good—a good he perceives with the detached eye of a craftsman toward his product.

Burke's sentimentalist defense of prejudice offers a clarifying contrast to the sense of prejudice I aim to develop. My goal is neither to sing a wistful praise of the past nor to defend the social utility of tradition. It is rather to connect prejudice and reason by developing the situated conception of understanding. According to this conception, our habits, customs, and traditions are more than sentimental dispositions or mechanical ways of behaving. They are more or less informed understandings that emerge from and articulate our life perspective—an intelligible outlook that, for better or worse, always influences our judgments and actions. To distinguish my argument from Burke's "sentimentalist" defense of prejudice, I call my argument the "hermeneutic" defense. The term "hermeneutic" comes from Hei-

95. Ibid., 49.

degger and Gadamer. It captures the sense in which one's life perspective is an intelligible viewpoint open to interpretation.

Burke is ultimately blind to the reason in prejudice. Although he vehemently defends prejudice, in sharp contrast to the thinkers we have thus far examined, his defense accepts their basic opposition of prejudice and reason. Burke thus adopts the distinction grounding the case against prejudice and merely flips the values—defending prejudice over reason. By examining Burke's thought, I hope to illuminate a prominent case for prejudice easily mistaken for my own.

Let us first examine what appears to be Burke's claim for the intrinsic value of prejudice, his claim for the beauty and nobility of tradition. It should be noted that Burke's *Reflections* were intended to inoculate his countrymen against the revolutionary spirit of France. He had a pragmatic interest in praising traditional British institutions. Nevertheless, it is difficult to read Burke's praise of such traditions without believing that he indeed saw something genuinely noble in them. Consider the following passage:

> To fortify the fallible and feeble contrivances of our reason, we have derived several other, and no small benefits from considering our liberties in light of an inheritance. . . . The idea of a liberal descent inspires us with a sense of habitual native dignity. . . . By this means our liberty becomes a noble freedom. It carries an imposing and majestic aspect. It has a pedigree and illustrious ancestors. It has its bearings and its ensigns armorial. It has its gallery of portraits; its monumental inscriptions; its records, evidences, and titles. We procure reverence to our civil institutions on the principle upon which nature teaches us to revere individual men; on account of their age, and on account of those from whom they are descended.[96]

In this passage, Burke praises England's "inheritance" for instilling a sense of dignity, nobility and majesty. But this sense does not respond to some

96. Ibid., 30.

inherent meaning that our inheritance embodies. We revere the "civil institutions," "ancestors," "portraits," "monuments," and everything else, Burke
suggests, not because they have some intrinsic value that makes a claim on
our reason, but because they are *old*. The mere fact that our institutions are
old triggers a certain "natural" reverence in us. Reverence comes not from
reason, which is "fallible and feeble," but from nature, which he calls the
avenue leading to the heart as distinct from the mind. Our prejudices, according to Burke, are sentimental affects, "well-placed sympathies of the human
breast."[97]

Burke's separation of prejudice and reason comes to powerful expression
in his defense of tradition as "pleasing illusion." As this expression suggests,
Burke considers tradition to be at odds with enlightenment and reason. But
instead of celebrating enlightenment, he bemoans the decay of tradition:

> All the pleasing illusions, which made power gentle and obedience lib-
> eral, which harmonized the different shades of life, and which, by a
> bland assimilation, incorporated into politics the sentiments which
> beautify and soften private society, are to be dissolved by this new con-
> quering empire of light and reason. All the decent drapery of life is to
> be rudely torn off. All the superadded ideas, furnished from the ward-
> robe of a moral imagination, which the heart owns, and the under-
> standing ratifies, as necessary to cover the defects of our naked, shiver-
> ing nature, and to raise it to dignity in our own estimation, are to be
> exploded as a ridiculous, absurd, and antiquated fashion.[98]

This passage highlights two key aspects of Burke's conception of prejudice
(understood as the authority of tradition). First, as "pleasing illusion," prejudice is not only opposed to reason but *threatened* by it. The "pleasing illusions," Burke laments, are "to be dissolved by this new conquering empire
of light and reason." The "decent drapery of life is to be rudely torn off."
Burke's fears express a notable reversal of Bacon's and Descartes's concern
that reason is threatened by prejudice. It seems that by Burke's time, Europe
had become sufficiently swayed by the case against prejudice that the scales

97. Ibid., 55.
98. Ibid., 66.

had tipped in favor of reason. Recognizing this, Burke tries to buck the trend. His passionate defense of prejudice tries to "one up" reason in the face of reason's impending dominion:

> The age of chivalry is gone. That of sophisters, economists, and calculators has succeeded; and the glory of Europe is extinguished for ever. Never, never more shall we behold that generous loyalty to rank and sex, that proud submission, that dignified obedience, that subordination of the heart, which kept alive, even in servitude itself, the spirit of an exalted freedom.[99]

Burke's second crucial claim concerns the source of tradition's value. Tradition is a "pleasing" illusion that *human beings* create. Burke's metaphor of throwing "drapery" over social life powerfully belies his notion that we adorn the brute facts, or conventions, with our own subjective values. He makes this explicit when he writes that the drapery is "furnished from the wardrobe of a moral imagination." The wardrobe, we might say, represents the inner sphere of subjectivity. We draw from the wardrobe and throw its contents upon society in order to "cover the defects of our naked, shivering nature." Burke thus implies that reverence for tradition is the product of a human need, a need to find value in a world that, in itself, is meaningless. Most telling is Burke's claim that our traditions raise our nature to dignity "in our *own* estimation" (emphasis added). In other words, the roles, customs, and institutions that constitute tradition are elaborate artifacts created by human beings to convince themselves of their own worth. Tradition derives its meaning from the values which human subjects ascribe to it. Accordingly, Burke at one point refers to tradition as "artificial."[100]

Burke further reveals his "artificial" view of tradition when he defends institutions, roles, and titles as most "valuable in the human breast," but at the same time considers them mere conventions and names. As such, Burke writes, traditional practices are incapable of being the "causes of evil." They are benign adornments to life, which reformers should not abolish. Paradoxically, Burke defends prejudice by playing it up as a harmless illusion.

99. Ibid., 65.
100. Ibid., 117.

The real enemies to social order, he writes, are "pride, ambition, avarice, revenge, lust . . . and all the train of disorderly desires." These are the real causes of the "storms of history."[101] Disorderly desires, he claims, will always spring up in the human breast, quite apart from titles, roles, and prerogatives, which are mere names:

> Religion, morals, laws, prerogatives, privileges, liberties, rights of men, are the *pretexts*. . . . As these are the pretexts, so the ordinary actors and instruments in great public evils are kings, priests, magistrates, senates, parliaments, national assemblies, judges, and captains. You would not cure the evil by resolving, that there should be no more monarchs, nor ministers of state, nor of the gospel; no interpreters of law; no general officers; no public councils. . . . You might change the names. The things in some shape must remain. A certain *quantum* of power must always exist in the community, in some hands, and under some appellation. Wise men will apply their remedy to vices, not to names.[102]

The final sentences powerfully express Burke's conventionalist understanding of tradition. The terms in which we describe roles, institutions, and laws are mere names that designate brute units of authority. A certain "quantum" of power is a fact of social life. This "quantum" remains the same regardless of the names that express and articulate it. Thus, the traditional titles of "king," "priest," "monarch," "magistrate," and so on, are harmless labels that divide power in a certain manner. The titles have no significance in themselves. But as they have inspired people for centuries and "beautified" social life, such titles ought to be preserved. Consistent with his praise of "pleasing illusion," Burke defends mere names rather than denigrating them. Both formulations bring out the contrast Burke maintains between prejudice and reason.

In one significant formulation, however, Burke seems to call the contrast between prejudice and reason into question. He refers to the "reason" and "latent wisdom" that prevails in prejudice.[103] But upon examination, what Burke means by "reason" and "wisdom" is *social utility,* not intrinsic

101. Ibid., 119.
102. Ibid.
103. Ibid., 74.

value. Burke's argument for the social utility of prejudice fits with his claim that prejudice is a "pleasing illusion." The first is an extension of the second. Insofar as "pleasing illusion" not only provides a semblance of meaning to individual lives but instills a sense of lawfulness, it helps forge social unity.

We might consider this "utilitarian" defense of tradition to be Burke's second case for prejudice. Our prejudices are not only beautiful and noble, but contain something like the collective political wisdom of the ages. Burke's argument is, in a sense, quite simple: the roles and institutions that have persisted throughout time, such as the "church prejudice," have proven themselves to work. In short, they have proven themselves to peaceably organize social life. We should, therefore, exercise the utmost moderation when considering whether to revise them. Above all, he warns, we should not act like the French revolutionaries and overthrow our traditions in light of some novel political theory. Burke famously argues that abstractions such as the "rights of man" are empty "political metaphysics" incapable of replacing the prejudices that foster loyalty among citizens.[104]

In a key passage on prejudice, Burke defends England's prudent political thinkers for wisely employing prejudice instead of denouncing it. The passage brings out what Burke means by the "reason," or "latent wisdom," in prejudice:

> Many of our men of speculation, instead of exploding general prejudices, employ their sagacity to discover the latent wisdom which prevails in them. If they find what they seek, and they seldom fail, they think it more wise to continue the prejudice, with the reason involved, than to cast away the coat of prejudice, and to leave nothing but the naked reason.[105]

In the first sentence, Burke suggests a certain unity of reason and prejudice. He sunders this unity, however, in his conception of prejudice as a "coat" that covers a "naked reason." He thus maintains that, in principle, prejudice and reason are separable. What Burke really means by the "latent wisdom" in prejudice is not some inherent insight that prejudice affords, but some

104. Ibid., 49.
105. Ibid., 74.

independent good that prejudice adorns and makes persuasive. We can imagine, for example, how the "church prejudice" might incline citizens toward patriotism—a social good whose validity Burke defends on nonreligious, utilitarian grounds. Even when the "coat" of piety is "cast off," the validity of the "naked reason" (patriotism, conceived as beneficial) remains. Burke's reference to prejudice as a "coat" recalls his comparison of prejudice to "decent drapery." Both highlight the sense in which prejudice, for Burke, is a superficial illusion, however pleasing and beneficial.

Burke reiterates the instrumental value of prejudice for judgment in the following passage:

> Prejudice, with its reason, has a motive to give action to that reason, and an affection which will give it permanence. Prejudice is of ready application in the emergency; it previously engages the mind in a steady course of wisdom and virtue, and does not leave the man hesitating in the moment of decision, sceptical, puzzled, and unresolved.[106]

When Burke writes that prejudice "gives action" to reason, he seems to mean that prejudice helps impel one toward a wise course of action. But he does not claim that prejudice itself informs the wise course.

He mentions two additional benefits of prejudice, both of which attest to its utility, but not its intrinsic value. First, prejudice "previously engages the mind in a steady course of wisdom and virtue."[107] Although one could interpret this claim to mean that prejudice is a necessary condition of wisdom and virtue, one could equally interpret it to mean that prejudice merely inculcates wisdom and virtue, whose contents we learn from some other source. The latter reading fits better with Burke's overall position and, in particular, with his claim that prejudice "renders a man's virtue his habit."[108] (This formulation suggests that we first learn virtue, and then, as a separate matter, make it our "habit." Prejudice, by his account, plays a role in the second stage, not the first.) This instrumental defense of prejudice recalls Smith's claim for the significance of habit and custom. Smith, as we have seem, denounces habit and custom as mere prejudice, but still defends them

106. Ibid.
107. Ibid.
108. Ibid., 74–75.

insofar as they inculcate virtue as derived from the detached standpoint of the impartial spectator. Burke seems to defend prejudice in similar terms.

Second, Burke argues that "prejudice does not leave the man hesitating in the moment of decision, sceptical, puzzled, and unresolved."[109] Prejudice fosters decisiveness. But decisiveness does not imply wisdom or good judgment. And a timely decision is beneficial only if it hits upon what is wise or good. Again, Burke suggests that prejudice is an auxiliary to sound reason, not a perspective that informs it.

Burke's utilitarian defense of prejudice in general comes to concrete expression in his discussion of the "church prejudice." The church establishment, Burke writes, is "not a prejudice destitute of reason, but involving in it profound and extensive wisdom."[110] This statement might seem to suggest that the church provides some true teaching, that a Christian way of life embodies some intrinsic good, or that it provides an illuminating perspective on the world. But Burke means none of these things. What he means by the "reason" of the church is simply that religion is the "basis of civil society, and the source of all good and all comfort."[111]

In a striking passage that would likely offend any true believer, Burke offers the following defense of the church: "There is no rust of superstition, with which the accumulated absurdity of the human mind might have crusted over in the course of ages, that ninety-nine in a hundred of the people of England would not prefer to impiety."[112] Thus Burke intimates that piety is an absurd superstition; but he nevertheless defends it as beneficial to society.

An examination of each of Burke's examples of the "reason" of the "church prejudice" confirms that by "reason" he means social utility. His defense of the church amounts to a set of familiar arguments in favor of a civil religion. None of his arguments suggests that the church's teaching is true or that the Christian way of life provides an illuminating perspective on the world. First, the church is necessary to inspire awe among free citizens.[113] Burke invokes Cicero's claim that the citizens should be convinced

109. Ibid., 74.
110. Ibid., 78.
111. Ibid., 77.
112. Ibid.
113. Ibid., 79.

"that the gods are lords and masters of everything; that what is done is done by their decision and authority; that they are, moreover, great benefactors of mankind and observe what kind of person everyone is. . . . Minds imbued with these facts will surely not deviate from true and wholesome ideas."[114] Second, by consecrating the commonwealth, the church instills in all rulers the idea that "they act in trust," and that their own individual will is not the standard of right and wrong.[115] Third, the church "nourishes the public hope." The poorest man "finds his own importance and dignity in it."[116] Fourth, it humbles the rich, "tying their pride and ambition to the yoke of moderation and virtue."[117] Fifth and finally, by consecrating the state, the church creates stability. Those who revere the state, Burke claims, will not "approach to look into its defects or corruptions but with due caution." The church thus wards off the "evils of inconstancy and versatility," which, he adds, are "ten thousand times worse than those of obstinacy and the worst prejudice."[118]

All of Burke's arguments for the church's "reason" turn on its social utility. As Burke does not conceive of the church as possessing any intrinsic meaning, or as providing a distinctively illuminating perspective on the world, he does not consider its preservation strictly necessary. In principle, he implies, all of the church establishment's benefits could be reaped from some other source. To be sure, Burke considers this unlikely. But he entertains the possibility of a substitute institution for the church that would have the same effect. His critique of the French revolutionaries is not simply that they abolished religion, but that they abolished "the natural human means of estimation" without supplying anything that "may be presented *in the place of it*" (emphasis added).[119]

Burke's defense of the "reason" of the church reveals the sense in which he understands the "reason" of prejudice in general. The "reason" of prejudice refers to its utility, not its inherent value or insight. In this sense, Burke accepts the distinction between reason and prejudice. Prejudice may "give

114. Ibid., 77.
115. Ibid., 79–80.
116. Ibid., 84.
117. Ibid., 86.
118. Ibid., 82.
119. Ibid., 78.

action" to reason but the two are, in principle, separate. Rather than effecting a paradigm shift, Burke offers a correction to the case against prejudice within its own framework. Specifically, Burke challenges Hume's assumption that superstition is "frivolous, useless, and burdensome" in contrast to true principles of justice, which are "absolutely requisite to the well-being of mankind."[120] Burke concedes that traditional institutions may "savor of superstition in their very principle," but he argues that this should not hinder the statesman "from deriving from superstition itself any resources which may thence be furnished for the public advantage."[121]

The statesman, Burke continues, uses prejudice as a workman his tools:

> A politician, to do great things, looks for a *power,* what our workmen call a *purchase;* and if he finds that power, in politics as in mechanics, he cannot be at a loss to apply it. In the monastic institutions, in my opinion, was found a great *power* for the mechanism of political benevolence.[122]

Just as the workman employs his power, or "purchase," to create the form he envisions, so the politician employs the prejudice of his society in order to strengthen "political benevolence."

In a striking passage, Burke compares the statesman's prudent manipulation of prejudice (specifically the "monastic institutions") to the scientist's conquest of nature. He expresses both his notion that tradition is a human creation and his view that tradition is especially beneficial—at least if "tamed" and rendered useful by a wise statesman. He condemns the unwise statesmen, namely the revolutionaries, for destroying tradition instead of skillfully manipulating it:

> To destroy any power, growing wild from the rank productive force of the human mind, is almost tantamount, in the moral world, to the destruction of the apparently active properties of bodies in the material. . . . These energies always existed in nature, and they were always discernible. They seemed, some of them unserviceable, some noxious, some

120. Hume, *Enquiry,* 31.
121. Burke, *Reflections,* 135.
122. Ibid., 133.

no better than a sport to children; until contemplative ability, combined with practic skill, tamed their wild nature, subdued them to use, and rendered them at once the most powerful and the most tractable agents, in subservience to the great views and designs of men. . . . Had you no way of using the men but by converting monks into pensioners? . . . Your politicians do not understand their trade; and therefore they sell their tools.[123]

Burke's claim that the monastic institutions grew "wild from the rank productive force of the human mind" speaks to his view that tradition and, in a larger sense, the social world are the creations of human subjects. Society embodies no meaning beyond the value that human beings ascribe to it. Burke denounces the revolutionaries not because they destroy intrinsically meaningful institutions, but because they "sell their tools." He implies that traditions, like natural forces, may, in fact, be "unserviceable" and "noxious." But through the statesman's "contemplative ability" and "practic skill"—what Burke elsewhere calls "political reason"—traditions may be made to serve the common good.

Burke contrasts "political reason," which prudently preserves prejudice, to "political metaphysics," which rejects prejudice in favor of the "rights of man." But in one crucial sense, the "political reason" Burke lauds overlaps with the "political metaphysics" he rejects. Both, according to Burke, operate outside of tradition. To be sure, the wise statesman's "political reason" must draw upon the lessons of history and tradition—the "great volume" that is "unrolled for our instruction," that reveals the tendencies of men and the sources of their loyalties.[124] But the statesman's turn to the "great volume of history" inscribed in tradition does not imply his being informed by the *perspective* of tradition. The statesman, according to Burke, does not live within the volume he studies—at least he does not accept it as a source of authority. The statesman flies above the traditions of his time, viewing them as mere superstitions to be tamed and employed toward the common good. He uses his detached reason to act upon tradition from the outside, to master the prejudices of the past by molding them to his design.

123. Ibid., 133–134.
124. Ibid., 119.

In summary, Burke wavers between singing the wistful praise of prejudice and advocating its social utility. Prejudice is either a "pleasing illusion" that covers "the defects of our naked, shivering nature," or it is an instrument of prudence "in subservience to the great views and designs of men." In neither case is prejudice a perspective that informs political deliberation and judgment.

2

The Case for Situated Understanding

Heidegger on Being-in-the-World

As we have seen in Chapter 1, today's suspicion of prejudice in politics, law, and everyday life is part of a larger way of thinking that emerged in seventeenth-century natural philosophy and came to full expression during the Enlightenment: To know reality, or to critically assess our motives, we must step back from our life circumstance. We must escape the perspective shaped by tradition, habit, custom, and our upbringing. We must, in other words, cleanse our mind of all prejudice and methodically use our own reason to confirm the validity of our beliefs and motives.

Heidegger undermines this way of thinking. Our most basic way of knowing the world, he argues, is not through the self-conscious scrutiny of our beliefs and their origin but through dealing with the world "concern-fully," through being at work, building things, putting them to use, living out certain roles.[1] This "knowing" is not the detached relation of a subject to an object. It is a practical kind of knowledge that is simultaneously an understanding of one's self. It involves knowing how to deal with things,

1. Martin Heidegger, *Being and Time*, trans. John Macquarrie and Edward Robinson (Malden: Blackwell, [1927] 1962), 83.

how to use them properly, how to fulfill one's daily activities. Heidegger points out that the items of equipment we deal with in everyday life—a hammer or a pair of shoes, for example—"are not objects for knowing the 'world' theoretically";[2] furthermore, insofar as we use them proficiently, they do not appear as objects "present" to our consciousness at all. A strange, yet familiar feature of our experience, to which Heidegger draws our attention, is that when we are engaged in work, the equipment we use *vanishes* from our perceptual and cognitive range altogether: "It must, as it were, withdraw in order to be ready-to-hand quite authentically."[3] In our engaged activity, we understand the world as continuous with ourselves, not as a collection of objects that we could reflect upon, doubt, or affirm. At the same time as our tools withdraw, so does our self-consciousness. The notion of "I" in contrast to what I do, dissolves into the work I carry out.

The disappearance of self-consciousness that characterizes our basic activity explains Heidegger's peculiar term for human being: "Dasein." Heidegger uses this term precisely to avoid the suggestion that human life is defined by subjectivity, inner consciousness, or cognition. Translated into English, "Dasein" *(Da-sein)* literally means "being-there," where "there," in Heidegger's sense, denotes a situation rather than a physical location. "Dasein" captures the way in which we are defined by the activities we carry out, by the situations in which we find ourselves, and ultimately, by our comprehensive situation, or life circumstance—what Heidegger calls the *world*.

But although "Dasein" indicates that personal identity is inseparable from one's situation, or world, Dasein does not imply that personal identity is the product of some cultural mold. Dasein can be considered, in each case, an individual who participates in shaping context and whose being is never identical to anyone else's. Thus, Dasein's world, the basis of its being, is not a set of social forces that acts upon it from the outside—as if an entity called "Dasein" with its own inner life, or psychological and biological tendencies, gets stamped by some social template or molded by a complex array of influences. Dasein *is* its world, and its world is always its own.

Stated in basic terms, and in a way that wards off familiar suggestions of "social context," Dasein's world is something like its *story*—a lived, or

2. Ibid., 95.
3. Ibid., 99.

enacted, story of which Dasein is simultaneously the sufferer and author.[4] This conception of the world makes best sense, I believe, of Heidegger's own account in which "meaning," "fate," and "destiny" are key terms. But first and foremost, this conception of the world captures the sense of "situation" I mean to defend. Unlike a social context, or a set of irrational influences, a story has a point; it is about something, which is to say it always has a certain "moral," however trite or profound. A story, moreover, always has a protagonist—someone who carries it out. Only through the action of Achilles, for example, is there an *Iliad*. But at the same time, it is only through the story that the protagonist becomes who he is. Although there would surely be no *Iliad* without Achilles, there would also be no Achilles without his story as a whole. As soon as Achilles has emerged, so too has the *Iliad*. Dasein's world is intelligible in a similar way.

But unlike a typical story, whose plot line eventually comes full circle, the world is open-ended. Dasein is a sufferer and author who never ceases to write, *who never has any option to cease*. The absence of this option is itself an essential dimension of the story. What this means and what it implies for human agency is a crucial question. At this point, we can say the following: The sense in which Dasein is both sufferer and author of its destiny—and perpetually so—implies a passive and active dimension to human agency. Heidegger has a special term for each of these dimensions. The passive he calls "thrownness," and the active "projection." Dasein's agency consists in "thrown-projection." By interpreting "thrown-projection" in the second half of this chapter, I aim to articulate a situated conception of freedom.

A second key feature of the world, as a kind of story, concerns the distinction among "characters." Dasein is in each case a sufferer and author of the world in its own way. Although Heidegger recognizes a tendency in Dasein toward conformity, he insists that no human being is identical to any other. And yet, *each of us is defined by the same world*. The sense in which human life is at once differentiated and identical is difficult to grasp. What

---

4. For the notion of human life as a story or narrative, cf. Hannah Arendt, *The Human Condition* (Chicago: University of Chicago Press, 1958), 184; cf. also Charles B. Guignon, "Authenticity, Moral Values, and Psychotherapy," in *The Cambridge Companion to Heidegger*, ed. Charles B. Guignon (Cambridge: Cambridge University Press, 2006), 277–278. As I explain later, considering the world as a sort of story fits with Heidegger's own interpretation of the world as a "fate" *(Schicksal)* or "destiny" *(Geschick)*.

makes it especially difficult is Heidegger's suggestion that Dasein is in each case wholly identical and wholly different! It is not as though you and I and the guy next door each differs in some respect but shares at least one common trait or set of traits. Dasein is, in each case, in the whole of its identity, both different from and identical to every other.

How might we make sense of this apparent contradiction? The concept of the world as a lived story points to a provisional answer. Dasein is, in each case, a unique sufferer and author of the same story. Take any story—whether expressed in a novel, a play, or a movie. Each character in that story is manifestly different. And yet, each is identical in that his or her identity is part of the same "moral," the same unity or meaning, the same whole. If one were to express the identity of any particular character—to say what makes that character unique—one would have to say something of how he or she fits into the story as a whole. And if one were to perform the same exercise for the other characters, one would end up with multiple versions of the same story. In a similar sense, Dasein is in each case simultaneously identical and different. Each instance of Dasein is its own reflection of the same world.

There is, however, a key difference: Unlike a typical story, which comes "full circle" by the end and thereby reveals a clear distinction among characters, the world is open-ended and holds the distinctions open too. The relation among "characters," the identity and difference of the many instances of Dasein, is never fixed. The extent to which one instance of Dasein "overlaps" with another is always a question. Although this question puts human community on precarious footing, it also holds open the possibility of common ground. Common ground is at once given and achieved. Although there is no guarantee of solidarity in advance, there is no inherent limit to it.

The conception of the world as a lived story diverges from a familiar interpretation according to which the world is a network of practices with no ultimate point. Piotr Hoffman expresses a version of this view when he speaks of "the full contingency and groundlessness" of Dasein's existence.[5] Richard Polt implies the same when he calls the world a "complex of options" (although he then interprets it as a "sphere of meaning," leaving ambiguous

---

5. Piotr Hoffman, "Death, Time, Historicity: Division II of *Being and Time*," in *The Cambridge Companion to Heidegger*, 239.

whether he understands the world as a story or a pointless network of practices).[6]

Perhaps the most prominent version of the "contingency" view comes from Hubert L. Dreyfus in his commentary on Being-in-the-World.[7] Dreyfus's commentary has been an aid to my own understanding of Heidegger, especially of the sense in which Dasein is not a self-conscious subject. Dreyfus does a remarkably clear job of distinguishing Heidegger's notion of practical, or engaged, understanding from the understanding of a subject related to an object.[8]

But his analysis overlooks the sense in which Dasein's practical reason in various domains points to a comprehensive notion of "reason" tied to the world as a destiny. The only sort of larger whole that Dreyfus describes is the "holistic background coping that makes possible appropriate dealings in particular circumstances."[9] His conception of this "holistic background" as devoid of any ultimate meaning leads him to statements such as "man is the result of a cultural interpretation," or Dasein is "passively formed."[10]

The very term "culture," which interpreters frequently invoke to make sense of Heidegger's notion of the world, is somewhat misleading. An example is Polt's claim that according to Heidegger, "personal choice is dependent on the range of possibilities available in one's culture."[11] The term "culture" is misleading because it implies a normalized, collective, or conventional way of doing things in contrast to a distinctive or individual way. To inject "culture" into Heidegger's thought is thus to suggest precisely the worldview he seeks to challenge—that of choosing selves constrained by a menu of impersonal social (or "cultural") options. According to Heidegger, Dasein is not a "self" who faces another entity called the "world" or "society" or "culture." Dasein, in a sense, *is* its world, and its world is a totality of

6. Richard Polt, *Heidegger: An Introduction* (London: Routledge, 1999), 72.

7. Hubert Dreyfus, *Being-in-the-World: A Commentary on Heidegger's* Being and Time, *Division I* (Cambridge, MA: MIT Press, 1991).

8. Although I offer an account of practical understanding, or what Heidegger calls "concernful circumspection," the account assumes a basic familiarity with how understanding can be embodied in action (rather than represented in a mind). For anyone interested in learning more about this topic, and for anyone interested in how Heidegger's thought relates to contemporary questions in analytic philosophy, I would recommend Dreyfus's book, especially chapters 1–6.

9. Dreyfus, *Being-in-the-World*, 104.

10. Ibid., 26.

11. Polt, *Heidegger*, 63.

purposes and ends, a totality that coheres as a lived story. Rarely does Heidegger himself speak of "culture," and he seems, in fact, to avoid it when elucidating the concept of the *world*. He speaks instead of particular purposes and practices "for-the-sake-of-which" Dasein exists and which ultimately point to a fate *(Schicksal)* or destiny *(Geschick)*. In this way, Heidegger forces us to consider that the world cannot be reduced to the familiar concepts of "culture" or "zeitgeist." Although the world certainly includes such influences, it is by no means defined by them.

The sense of contingency that Dreyfus highlights in his reference to "culture" is captured in the following passage:

> Not only is human being interpretation all the way down, so that our practices can never be grounded in human nature, God's will, or the structure of rationality, but this condition is of such radical rootlessness that everyone feels fundamentally unsettled *(unheimlich)*, that is, senses that human beings can never be at home in the world.[12]

In this passage, Dreyfus equates Heidegger's important notion of being "unsettled" *(unheimlich)* with "radical rootlessness," a term that Heidegger, to my knowledge, does not use. "Radical rootlessness" fails to account for the "thrown" dimension of human life, which involves bearing a destiny. To make sense in light of thrownness, "unsettled" or "not-at-home," must be understood, I believe, as a positive concept, capturing the "projective," or transcendent dimension of human life: that our nature is to be always exceeding ourselves, that there is more to us than we can possibly know.[13] The open-ended character of our lives, which Heidegger certainly does emphasize, implies neither contingency nor radical rootlessness. Perhaps Dreyfus's most telling formulation of the "contingency" view paints Heidegger as a sort of nihilistic libertine, one who believes that "nothing is grounded

---

12. Dreyfus, *Being-in-the-World*, 37.

13. In contrast to Dreyfus, Stephen Mulhall interprets Heidegger's *"unheimlich"* along the lines I have suggested. According to Mulhall, *unheimlich* captures the fact "that our existence is always capable of being more or other than its present realizations, and so that, for all our worldliness, we are never fully at home in any particular world." His phrase "never fully at home" is an instructive contrast to "radical rootlessness." Cf. Stephen Mulhall, *Inheritance and Originality: Wittgenstein, Heidegger, Kierkegaard* (New York: Oxford University Press, 2001), 259.

and that there are no guidelines for living."[14] In formulations such as these, Dreyfus likens Heidegger's understanding of social practices to the view that sees them as mere prejudices. Such interpretations, which stray far from Heidegger's own key terms, attest to the influence of the "prejudice against prejudice" on contemporary thought.

The conception of the world as a contingent set of practices overlooks the basic fact that we can give an account of our actions and of the world in which they make sense.[15] Dreyfus suggests that "once a practice has been explained by appealing to what one [typically] does, no more basic explanation is possible."[16] But he overlooks an alternative: rather than appealing to convention, or to "the way things are done in our culture," we can tell a story that makes sense of the practice within the narrative of our life as a whole, that explains why the practice is necessary, or essential to our identity and why other people, perhaps, should also adopt it. Although the story will surely never exhaust the meaning of the practice, or justify it once and for all, the very fact that we can tell one implies that our practices are not merely contingent. They cohere as parts of a world, which, however veiled and inexhaustible, gestures toward an intelligible whole.

Insofar as Dasein is always a story that I live out, and a story not identical to anyone else's, Dasein "is in each case mine," and for this reason, "one must always use the *personal* pronoun when one addresses it: 'I am', 'you are.'"[17] But we must not assume, Heidegger insists, that the personal pronoun denotes some inner self in contrast to the external world. It is the bias of modern thought, he argues, beginning most conspicuously with Descartes, to equate individuality, or self-possession, with having an inner life that is shielded, so to speak, from what goes on around me. The "I" is not

---

14. Dreyfus, *Being-in-the-World*, 38.

15. Moreover, if the world is, indeed, a contingent set of practices, as Dreyfus suggests, if there is really no necessity whatsoever that things be the way they are, then, in principle, at least, Dasein should be able to entirely transcend its world by spontaneously remodeling it. In other words, if the practices that define the world are ultimately meaningless cultural norms, then one could live according to his or her own taste, the norms be damned. Heidegger insists, however, that Dasein cannot get beyond the world into which it is thrown (*Being and Time*, 330). This impotence of Dasein in the face of its thrownness forces us to consider the world as a pre-given unity of meaning, a narrative, of a sort, which conditions any attempt to change it.

16. Dreyfus, *Being-in-the-World*, 155.

17. Heidegger, *Being and Time*, 67–68.

some "cabinet of consciousness," but myself expressed in the way I live.[18] Although explicit self-reflection is, of course, a possibility of Dasein, and although it may enrich one's life in certain ways, it is not constitutive of Dasein's identity or self-possession. Heidegger maintains that even in moments that do not involve self-conscious reflection, my life can, in principle, be an authentic expression of who I am.

Although being absorbed in life does not involve self-consciousness or cognition, such absorption is by no means mechanical behavior, mere instinct, or blind continuity with one's environment. We are inclined to understand it as such because we assume that detached theoretical reflection is the only type of "knowing," or reason, properly so called. We therefore understand practical activity as "atheoretical in the sense of 'sightlessness.' "[19] But our ability to handle things "has its own kind of 'knowledge.' "[20] It is a situated kind of understanding, the most basic mode of what Heidegger calls "Being-in-the-World." In analyzing Being-in-the-World, my aim is to make sense of the situated conception of understanding, thereby revealing the sense of "prejudice" involved in judgment.

In general terms, "Being-in-the-World" denotes Dasein's practical understanding of life as a whole. "Being-in" must be taken as "being in a situation," and the "world" as Dasein's situation writ large—the totality of practices in which Dasein is engaged and which cohere as one destiny. Heidegger's ambitious project is to give a concrete account of Being-in-the-World and to reveal it as the condition of any possible understanding or relation to the world whatsoever, whether theoretical or practical. In this sense, he aims to show that Being-in-the-World is the most basic, or fundamental, mode of human existence. Being-in-the-World is not one possibility among others, as if sometimes we are "in the world" and other times we exist in another way: Dasein is never "an entity which is, so to speak, free from Being-in, but which sometimes has the inclination to take up a 'relationship' towards the world. Taking up relationships toward the world is possible only *because* Dasein, as Being-in-the-World, is as it is."[21] This holds true, Heidegger shows, for any possible relationship, including the modes of scientific study that

18. Ibid., 87.
19. Ibid., 99.
20. Ibid., 95.
21. Ibid, 84.

appear to be detached reflection. Thus, what Bacon and Descartes consider the only legitimate path to knowledge, Heidegger reveals as a narrow species of understanding, a mode of knowing that is "founded" on our practical understanding of life as a whole.[22]

In the following interpretation of Heidegger, my primary goal is to clarify the situated conception of understanding by reference to Being-in-the-World. What I mean by "situation" and "life perspective" is well captured in Heidegger's account of the world. As part of interpreting Being-in-the-World, I address how it undermines the first strand of the case against prejudice: the idea that in order to judge truthfully, we must judge in a detached manner. By showing that our ability to step back and explicitly assess our beliefs and motives presupposes an engaged understanding of life, Heidegger exposes the supposedly prejudice-free standpoint as itself a prejudice—a particular stance made possible by our prejudice writ large.

After showing how Heidegger undermines the ideal of detached reflection, I turn to a deeper analysis of Being-in-the-World to derive a conception of situated agency that undermines the second strand of the case against prejudice—the idea that prejudice is opposed to freedom. My suggestion is that Being-in-the-World implies a conception of agency that actually preserves a certain notion of autonomy.

I hope to contribute an interpretation of Heidegger that clarifies the conception of prejudice I defend, that articulates a vision of situated agency, and that frees his thought from the distorting language of "culture," "contingency," and "rootlessness." My approach is to hew closely to Heidegger's own language and to avoid formulations of the world in the subject-object or individual-society frameworks. Because these frameworks have come to pervade not only our philosophical discourse but also our everyday reper-

22. Ibid., 86.

toire of expression (and for the most part without our notice), avoiding their influence is no small task.

Even among well-known and otherwise illuminating interpretations of Heidegger, we find the misleading use of "subject" and "object" to describe Dasein and the world. According to Hoffman, for example, "Dasein reveals itself as rooted in its historical community only by exploring the full depths of its own *subjectivity*" (emphasis added).[23] In the conclusion to his otherwise astute summary of Heidegger's standard of truth, Polt misleadingly invokes "objectivity" to describe a right interpretation. Heidegger, Polt writes, "believes in *objectivity*" (emphasis added). But "objectivity," Polt adds, "does not mean the complete absence of prejudices and points of view. Instead, true objectivity involves a willingness to revise one's point of view in light of what one discovers."[24] Although acknowledging that prejudice, for Heidegger, is consistent with truth, Polt falls back on the familiar equation of "right" or "true" with "objective." This obscures Heidegger's crucial insight that a "right" interpretation does not conform to an object of detached reflection.

The Subject-Object Conception of the World Contrasted to Heidegger's Interpretation of the World

The ideal of detached reflection that emerged in seventeenth-century natural philosophy was based on a certain conception of the world. According to this conception, the world is a collection of meaningless objects governed by contingent forces rather than ultimate purposes. It does not embody rationality or exist to express some notion of goodness or beauty. Meaning is not a feature of the world, as Plato and Aristotle believed, but originates in the minds of human subjects. To conceive of the world as inherently meaningful is to project onto things what human beings "most desire to find."[25]

This view holds true for the social world as well as for the natural. The practices that organize human life do not themselves embody reason or have an essential nature. They are merely conventional, owing their meaning

23. Hoffman, "Death, Time, Historicity: Division II of *Being and Time*," in *The Cambridge Companion to Heidegger*, 240.

24. Polt, *Heidegger*, 71.

25. Charles Taylor, *Hegel* (Cambridge: Cambridge University Press, 1975), 4.

to the human subjects who create them. To think otherwise is to be deceived, as Burke says, by "pleasing illusion."[26] According to this view, traditional roles and institutions are products of the human mind that have taken hold through habit and custom. Having taken hold, they become features of "culture," which, to a greater or lesser degree, puts its artificial stamp upon the individuals born into it.

Thus arises the ideal of detached reflection as the only means for knowing reality (what *is* in the natural realm) on the one hand, and for determining how to act (what *ought* to be in the social realm) on the other. Understanding "the true rays" of nature, as Bacon writes, requires abstracting from the way nature appears as beautiful, threatening, or purposeful.[27] We must rein in our hopes and desires and rationally examine the brute facts. Of course, different thinkers had different conceptions of what it meant to rationally examine the facts. For Bacon, it involved careful experimentation and induction. For Descartes, it involved finding clear and distinct first principles. But both Bacon's "empiricism" and Descartes' "rationalism," though different in many respects, rested on the subject-object distinction. They both strove to eliminate subjective prejudice in order to know the world "objectively."

Heidegger challenges the subject-object distinction because he thinks it misses the basic way we understand and relate to the world. Understanding the world is not just a matter of looking at things, surveying the facts "out there," and then processing them in our minds. It involves engaging with the world—knowing our way around, being competent to do things. For Heidegger, understanding has an inescapably practical dimension that recalls Aristotle's notion of *phronesis* (practical knowledge). The world, according to Heidegger, is not a meaningless array of objects that the human mind surveys and takes in. It is constituted instead by the web of projects and ends towards which we aim. Only on the basis of the world in this sense—the world in which we act and deal with things, and which has a point—can "nature," "society," or any theme for reflection, including ourselves, appear as such.

26. Edmund Burke, *Reflections on the Revolution in France*, ed. Frank M. Turner (New Haven, CT: Yale University Press, [1790] 2003), 66.
27. Francis Bacon, *The New Organon*, ed. Lisa Jardine and Michael Silverthorne (Cambridge: Cambridge University Press, [1620] 2000), 18.

According to Heidegger, we cannot come to know reality through self-conscious reflection or empirical observation alone. To understand the world, we must live within it. This leads to a special conception of philosophy. The goal of philosophy, according to Heidegger, is to give a comprehensive interpretation of the world, to illuminate the perspective that limits and makes possible all understanding. But we can reflect upon this perspective philosophically only insofar as we already exist within it, only insofar as we are engaged with the world and understand it as a world of *concern* to us. In this sense, philosophy does not teach us something new, as if it connected us to reality for the first time. Illuminating the world means clarifying what we, on a certain level, already know.

Heidegger developed his conception of the world and demonstrated its priority in light of a single question—the question of the meaning of *being*. What do we mean when we say that something *is*? Heidegger recognized that the question might appear dauntingly abstract, "a mere matter for soaring speculation about the most general of generalities."[28] But he insisted that it was both the most basic question and the most concrete. He gave it concrete direction, first and foremost, by placing it within the western philosophical tradition. The question of being, he pointed out, was not some novel speculation of his own but an ancient puzzle that had since been forgotten. In particular, it was a puzzle raised by Plato, which Heidegger acknowledges in the first line of *Being and Time*. The line comes from Plato's *Sophist:* "For manifestly you have long been aware of what you mean when you use the expression '*being.*' We, however, who used to think we understood it, have now become perplexed."[29] Heidegger sought to reawaken Plato's question.

Although Heidegger does not himself mention it, there is something strikingly Socratic about the question of being. Socrates's famous question—the one he always would ask his fellow Athenians—was "what *is*. . . ." For example, what is justice?, what is virtue?, what is the good? Socrates, in

28. Heidegger, *Being and Time*, 29.
29. Plato in Heidegger, *Being and Time*, 19.

other words, was concerned first and foremost with the *being* of what he investigated rather than its composition or generation. This distinguished him from the physiologists of his day, who attempted to explain the nature of things by reference to their parts and the causes of their coming into being. According to Socrates, the question of being was more fundamental. He would often point out that to determine the composition of something or the cause of its coming into being, one must presuppose an understanding of what that thing *is*. Without some understanding of the thing itself, the whole, completed thing, any investigation about it is blind.[30]

Heidegger adopts this Socratic line of thought, but his distinctive twist is to explicitly investigate the being of being rather than to start, as Socrates did, by asking about the being of justice, virtue, and so on. Nevertheless, Heidegger gives his investigation concrete direction in broadly Socratic fashion. For in approaching the question of being, Heidegger, like Socrates, turns not toward the visible things, but toward the practices, ends, and opinions that constitute human life.

By doing so, Heidegger suggests that the comprehensive study of being, what he calls "fundamental ontology," has, broadly speaking, a *political* character. His ontology is "political" not because it treats of regimes, legislatures, presidents, kings, and the like (which it doesn't) but because it deals, first and foremost, with human beings in community. His ontology is "political" in Aristotle's comprehensive sense—when he writes that man is by nature a political animal. Aristotle uses "political" to describe not only political regimes but also the general realm of human action and speech. In this latter sense, fundamental ontology is political. It is not primarily the study of objects, much less of the elements, atoms, and particles that comprise the physical universe. It is first and foremost a study of human practices. Only on the basis of such a study, suggests Heidegger, does the rest of the universe become intelligible.

Heidegger's concern with human practices makes his ontology of special relevance for political philosophers. This becomes clear as his provisional answer to the question of the meaning of being emerges. Being, Heidegger shows, is something like the *world*, that is, the world of *concern* to us.

---

30. Cf. Leo Strauss, *Natural Right and History* (Chicago: University of Chicago Press, 1953), 123.

Only on the basis of this world do beings appear as what they are. Investigating the meaning of being thus involves addressing the nature of human understanding and action. Accordingly, Heidegger begins *Being and Time* by examining everyday life.

To make sense of Heidegger's conception of Being-in-the-World, we must think our way beyond the familiar subject-object distinction. Heidegger proposes that we do so by distinguishing two ways in which beings appear to us in everyday life. The first is "presence-at-hand" *(Vorhandenheit)*, the basic character of things insofar as they appear to our conscious awareness and veil their link to our concern. When we balance a teacup in our hand to guess its weight, or when we gaze at the moon and imagine it as a mere shape moving across the grid of the sky, we relate to these things as present-at-hand. On the basis of things appearing as present-at-hand, it becomes possible to raise the question: do they really exist in the "external world," or do they merely reflect our own "subjective" representations of that world? As Descartes famously speculates, perhaps what we take to be reality is merely a figment of our imagination, a dream implanted in our own consciousness by a malevolent god.

Heidegger regards "presence-at-hand" as a superficial (or nonbasic) way in which beings appear. It is derivative of another mode of being, which he calls "readiness-to-hand" *(Zuhandenheit)*.[31] We encounter beings as ready-to-hand when we deal with them rather than look at them. When we deal with things (such as a hammer or a pair of shoes), when we engage with them, when we put them to use, we become absorbed in doing so. But when we are absorbed, the things we use no longer appear as present to our consciousness. They become, in Heidegger's phrase, "ready-to-hand." This term captures the sense in which the things we use vanish from our perceptual range as we work with them. Things ready-to-hand are "there," in that we have a practical awareness of them, but they do not appear as themes of reflection.[32]

31. Heidegger, *Being and Time*, 98.
32. Ibid., 99.

This notion of "ready-to-hand" differs from the standard way of describing the world in terms of subjects and objects. While absorbed in activity, we do not distinguish ourselves from the things we put to use. Only when our activity is disrupted, when the spell of absorption is broken, so to speak, and our attention is drawn to the things we are engaged with, only then do we come to regard these things as "present-at-hand." By distinguishing these two understandings of being, both grounded in familiar experiences, Heidegger challenges the ontological priority of presence-at-hand. The world, he argues, is not a collection of objects that we come to know through detached reflection. What we typically regard as objects are actually things present-at-hand, things whose readiness-to-hand has been veiled.

By inquiring into the nature of the ready-to-hand, Heidegger concretely develops his conception of the *world*—the basic structure of any situation that makes possible things ready-to-hand and present-at-hand. Only on the basis of Being-in-the-World, he shows, can we put things to use or reflect upon them as topics of study.

The Structure of Our Situated Understanding: The World as a Referential Totality of Equipment, Nature, and Dasein

By starting his inquiry from the experience of using equipment *(das Zeug),* Heidegger does not mean to suggest that human life is defined primarily by labor or productive activity. The use of equipment is simply one feature of our experience, which, if examined carefully, affords us a glimpse at Being-in-the-World. In his writings after *Being and Time,* Heidegger devotes less attention to equipment and develops his conception of the world through other means, for example, by examining the work of art.[33] But his derivation of the world from equipment is his most famous and perhaps his most concrete. By analyzing Heidegger's conception of the world, I aim to clarify the concept of "situation"—to show how it can be understood as a life perspective that enables our understanding.

Heidegger begins his account of the world by pointing out the following: "Taken strictly, there 'is' no such thing as *an* equipment. To the Being

33. Martin Heidegger, "The Origin of the Work of Art," in *Poetry, Language, Thought,* trans. Albert Hofstadter (New York: Harper & Row, [1935–1936] 1971).

of any equipment there always belongs a totality of equipment, in which it can be this equipment that it is. Equipment is essentially 'something in-order-to. . . .'" And "in the 'in-order-to'" lies "an *assignment* or *reference* of something to something. In other words, equipment "always is *in terms of* its belonging to other equipment: ink-stand, pen, ink, paper, blotting pad, table, lamp, furniture, windows, room."[34] Without this "totality of equipment," or some such totality, none of the particular things could exist as the things they are. The parts presuppose the context as a whole: it is in this arrangement that "any 'individual' item of equipment shows itself."[35]

The way in which equipment "shows itself" is in our dealings *(um-gang)* with it—when we actually go about using it. In such dealings, the equipment "is not grasped thematically as an occurring Thing, nor is the equipment-structure known as such even in the using."[36] If the equipment performs its function and is "ready-to-hand" authentically, it vanishes along with the references it implies. Paradoxically, the equipment is "there" most authentically when it is not there for us to look upon or consider. Things ready-to-hand are "not grasped theoretically at all."[37] Nevertheless, our dealing with the ready-to-hand "is not a blind one." It "has its own kind of sight," which is guided by the *work*—by "that which is to be produced at the time." The work "is accordingly ready-to-hand too," and "as the *"toward-which"* of such things as the hammer, the plane, and the needle, likewise has the kind of being that belongs to equipment." As such, "the work bears with it that referential totality within which equipment is encountered."[38]

But the work refers not only to a context of things made by human hands. It also refers to materials that human beings harvest, cultivate, and harness—what is typically called "nature"—the things of the earth and sky:

34. Heidegger, *Being and Time*, 97.
35. Ibid., 98.
36. Ibid.
37. Ibid., 99.
38. Ibid.

> In the environment [of the workshop] certain entities become accessible
> which are always ready-to-hand, but which, in themselves, do not need
> to be produced. Hammer, tongs, and needle, refer in themselves to
> steel, iron, metal, mineral, wood, in that they consist of these. In equip-
> ment that is used, 'Nature' is discovered along with it by that use—the
> 'Nature' we find in natural products.[39]

Heidegger reiterates that the "nature" to which the work refers is ready-
to-hand and thus discovered within the totality of equipment. Nature "is
not to be understood as that which is just present-at-hand, nor as the
power of Nature."[40] In other words, the things of the earth and sky are not
encountered as objects of theoretical study or as things that can be defined in terms of physical properties. Rather, they are implicitly understood along with the work: "A covered railway platform takes account
of bad weather; an installation for public lighting takes account of the
darkness, or rather of specific changes in the presence or absence of
daylight—the 'position of the sun.'"[41] When we are absorbed in building
the railroad platform or in using it, we understand "bad weather" without reflecting upon it explicitly. The very structure of the platform and
the way we position ourselves beneath the covering expresses such an
understanding.

Heidegger's casual treatment of the work's reference to nature disguises
a subtle and significant insight: from the perspective of being absorbed in
work, what we typically distinguish as "natural" things in contrast to "fab-
ricated" ones are discovered as ready-to-hand; both "kinds" have the same
value-laden mode of being. The rain, for example, is "bad weather," not
droplets of water produced by condensation. The sun is the "vaulting sphere
of light" whose rising and setting marks the time of day (morning, noon,
and evening); it is not a collection of mass around which the earth revolves.
As ready-to-hand within a totality of involvements, natural things are discovered as meaningful in their own ways. The distinction between what
human beings produce and what arises spontaneously, between "artifice"
on the one hand, and "nature" on the other, is foreign, Heidegger shows, to

39. Ibid., 100.
40. Ibid.
41. Ibid., 100–101.

our basic experience of the world. The very conception of something as "made" in contrast to "grown of itself" presupposes an abstraction from our engaged relation to things. While absorbed in work, we do not separate the "natural" from the "artificial." We distinguish things only by their *place* in the totality of references.

From Heidegger's initial description of nature in *Being and Time*, one can see how radically he begins to rethink our familiar categories. "Nature" no longer denotes the way things are independent of human action. What distinguishes a street light from the sun is not that one is made and the other found. The difference between the two lies is the different *purpose* each serves. To articulate this difference is to say something of how each has its own place in the context of Dasein. Heidegger thus forces us to reconceive "nature" in terms of the "basic character" of things, as when we speak of the "nature" of art or of politics. He replaces "nature," as a general term for things such as rives, lakes, mountains, and stars, with simply "the things of the earth and sky." The latter formulation implies no contrast between these things and the "artificial" or "manmade."

Heidegger's usage of "nature" recurs to the ancient Greek conception of *phusis*, which is synonymous with "being." The Greek conception aligned with a teleological view of the universe in which everything, including human action, is part of a harmonious whole. Although Heidegger rejects the notion of a single fixed order of things, of an all-encompassing whole that explains, once and for all, what and how the world is, he seeks to recover, in his own way, the Greek conception of a meaningful universe. His rethinking of nature aligns with this project of recovery.

Beyond referring to equipment and to nature (which, as we have seen, are ultimately inseparable), the work "also has an assignment to the person who is to use it or wear it. The work is cut to his figure; he 'is' there along with it as the work emerges."[42] The work thus refers to Dasein— not just to my own Dasein (i.e., the one doing the work) but to *others* who inhabit different roles. In other words, the work transcends the

42. Ibid., 100.

bounds of the workshop and reaches into a *public* world, a world shared with others:

> Along with the work, we encounter not only entities ready-to-hand but also entities with Dasein's kind of being—entities for which, in their concern, the product becomes ready-to-hand; and together with these we encounter the world in which wearers and users live, which is at the same time ours. Any work with which one concerns oneself is ready-to-hand not only in the domestic world of the workshop but also in the *public world.*[43]

The others "who are thus 'encountered' in a ready-to-hand, environmental context of equipment, are not somehow added on in thought to some Thing which is proximally just present-at-hand."[44] For example, we do not explicitly conceive of a shirt-thing which is intended for another entity, the wearer. Our consideration of the wearer is just as implicit, or "inconspicuous," as our consideration of the rain when we build the railway platform. That is to say, the "others" to whom we relate are not present-at-hand subjects "over against whom the "I" stands out." They are rather "those from whom, for the most part, one does *not* distinguish oneself—those among whom one is too."[45] Heidegger recognizes that "theoretically concocted 'explanations' of the Being-present-at-hand of Others urge themselves upon us all too easily; but over against such explanations we must hold fast to the phenomenal facts of the case which we have pointed out, namely that Others are encountered *environmentally* [i.e., within the context of equipment]."[46]

The way in which we "encounter" others, however, is manifestly different from the way we encounter things ready-to-hand. Heidegger expresses this difference by the term "solicitude." Our concern for others, our solicitude, is always guided by roles and terms of "being-with." In everyday existence, for example, being-with is often "being for, against, or without one

43. Ibid., 100.
44. Ibid., 153.
45. Ibid., 154.
46. Ibid., 155.

another, passing one another by, not 'mattering' to one another."[47] These are not explicit thoughts or beliefs, but attitudes expressed in one's action: "When material is put to use, we encounter its producer or 'supplier' as one who 'serves' well or badly. When, for example, we walk along the edge of a field but 'outside it,' the field shows itself as belonging to such-and-such a person, and decently kept by him."[48] We understand the owner not by means of reflection, but in our bearing that attests to his presence, in our "circumspective" care not to trespass on his property.

Equipment ready-to-hand thus carries within itself a totality of references— to other equipment, to nature (the things of the earth and sky), and to Dasein. These references are not properties of equipment, as if they could be removed one by one, leaving the thing itself intact. To understand equipment in this way would be to mistake it for something present-at-hand such as Descartes's ball of wax—a physical thing occurring in space to which contingent properties accrue—color, hardness, shape, and so on. By contrast, the references of equipment constitute its very *being*. Detached from the network of references, the equipment would not be what it is.

This totality of references is a first approximation of what Heidegger calls the *world*. From this initial sketch, we can begin to distinguish the world from the concepts of "culture" and "social context." First of all, as the reference to nature suggests, the world is more comprehensive than either of the former terms. For when we speak of "culture" and "society," we typically imply the human world in contrast to the natural. Heidegger's conception of the world undermines this contrast. Furthermore, although Being-in-the-World implies being-with-others, and is in this sense a *public* way of being, such publicness does not imply rigid conformity to social norms. The way in which Dasein, in each case, uses equipment toward its purposes and ends may conform to the typical "way things are done" in its society, but such use may also reflect Dasein's own take on life for which no cultural template exists. Heidegger

47. Ibid., 158.
48. Ibid., 153.

does, of course, suggest that the meaning of any action is shaped by its relation to what one might *typically* do in the given circumstance. And what
one might typically do, is, of course, shaped by culture.[49] But this suggestion does not imply that action as such conforms to some cultural mold. On
the contrary, Heidegger regards the tendency of action to slide toward such
conformity as the *inauthentic* dimension of Dasein. So to understand what
Heidegger means by the world, we should set aside the familiar notions of
culture and social context and follow Heidegger's own terms. Stated simply
and in summary, the world is a totality of things ready-to-hand, which always
involves some way of being of Dasein. We can imagine a number of such
totalities, but the only way to get a firm handle on what Heidegger means is
to consider the totality of one's own life.

Dasein's "absorption in references or assignments constitutive for the
readiness-to-hand of a totality of equipment," even the most basic use of a
hammer or a pair of shoes, embodies a practical understanding of the
world—which is what Heidegger means by "Being-in."[50] The strange phrase
"absorption in a totality of equipment" captures the sense in which Dasein's understanding of equipment, and thereby, the world, is entirely practical. It is not a matter of beliefs, mental contents, or cognition. For what
Dasein "understands" is not some object, but a way of handling things
appropriately. And Dasein does not distinguish itself from the things it
handles. When equipment is being used, when it is ready-to-hand authentically, it "withdraws," thereby veiling even its own being *as* ready-to-hand
within a totality of assignments: "The assignments themselves are not observed; they are rather 'there' when we concernfully submit ourselves to
them."[51]

The phrase "submit ourselves" highlights the unity of Dasein, its work,
and the referential totality (world). Far from being a self-conscious subject
confronted by the object of some task, Dasein *is* its activity. For example,
when a workman hammers at his bench he *is* the activity of hammering.

---

49. See Heidegger's discussion of *das Man*, or "what one typically does," as a fundamental
dimension (or "existentiale") of Dasein (*Being and Time*, ¶27). The concept of *das Man* and its relationship to inauthenticity are treated later.

50. Heidegger, *Being and Time*, 107.

51. Ibid., 105.

But the activity of hammering is never a mere activity; it points beyond itself to Being-in-the-World, to the articulated whole of life in which the workman is immersed. Thus, Being-in-the-World is a mode of "knowing" expressed entirely in Dasein's action, or comportment. It is not the relation of a subject to an object, and, for the most part, its character *as* Being-in-the-World remains hidden from view. This "remaining hidden" does not, as such, denote a vague or deficient understanding. It refers, rather, to the *mode* of understanding, which, as entirely practical, is largely implicit.[52]

The explicit character of Being-in-the-World can emerge only when there is some disruption in Dasein's concernful activity. The tool, for example, might break, and "when its unusability is thus discovered, equipment becomes conspicuous." This conspicuousness "presents the ready-to-hand equipment as in a certain un-readiness-to-hand."[53] In becoming conspicuous, the equipment becomes present-at-hand insofar as it emerges explicitly *as* something. But its presence-at-hand "is still not devoid of all readiness-to-hand whatsoever," as if it were "just a Thing which occurs somewhere," a mere object whose properties we might examine. The equipment is still bound up with our concern; it becomes something explicitly *unusable*, something we need to fix or else shove out of the way.[54] But in emerging as deficient, it emerges as something whose proper nature is to be useful for a certain task. Readiness-to-hand shows itself, "and it is precisely here that the worldly character of the ready-to-hand shows itself too."[55] For what appears is not simply the particular item of equipment, but that *"toward-which"* the equipment is used: "we catch sight of the "toward-this" itself and along with it, everything connected with the work—the 'whole workshop'—as that wherein concern already dwells." In this way, "the world announces itself," not "as something never seen before, but as a totality constantly sighted beforehand in circumspection."[56] By "seen" and "sighted," Heidegger means "understood." For the most part, our "sight" is practical; it operates beneath our

---

52. The phenomenon of the virtuoso at work attests to how masterful, or certain, one's practical understanding can be.

53. Heidegger, *Being and Time*, 103.

54. Ibid., 104.

55. Ibid.

56. Ibid., 105.

conscious awareness. We can "see" something, in the familiar sense of "perceive directly," only on the basis of our practical "sight."[57]

That the world can "announce itself" and be interpreted attests to the intelligibility of Dasein's everyday absorption in work. Such absorption is not mechanical behavior, mere habit, or aimless activity. It has a *point,* which is ultimately tied up with an understanding of the world. The point becomes explicit as that "toward-which" Dasein works. The "toward-which" refers to a totality of things ready-to-hand and finally to Dasein. For example: "With hammering there is an involvement in making something fast; with making something fast, there is an involvement in protection against bad weather; and this protection 'is' for the sake of [*um-willen*] providing shelter for Dasein—that is to say, for the sake of a possibility of Dasein's being."[58]

This "for-the-sake-of" being sheltered—in a house or under a covered railway platform, for example—is not directed toward something else ready-to-hand. It is an end in itself, a particular way of being that expresses what it means to live well and that organizes the totality of equipment:

> The totality of involvements constitutive of the "toward-which," goes back ultimately to a "towards-which" in which there is *no* further involvement: this "toward-which" is not an entity with the kind of Being that belongs to what is ready-to-hand within a world; it is rather an entity whose being is defined by Being-in-the-World, and to whose state of Being, worldhood itself belongs. This primary "towards-which" is not just another "towards-this" as something in which an involvement is possible. The primary 'towards-which' is a "for-the-sake-of-which." But the 'for-the-sake-of' always pertains to the Being of Dasein, for which, in its Being, that very Being is essentially an issue.[59]

---

57. In this respect, Heidegger follows Aristotle's understanding of *nous* as defined in *Nicomachean Ethics,* bk. 6—a certain eye of the soul that grasps particulars, the things most basic in any deliberation about how to act. This sort of grasp is not that of science *(episteme),* nor is it something attained by reasoning *(logos).* It is a certain type of perception *(aisthesis),* but not that of the senses.

58. Heidegger, *Being and Time,* 116.

59. Ibid., 117.

The "for-the-sake-of" is not defined by its usefulness for some further end; it points beyond itself to a totality of other ways of being, ultimately to Dasein's understanding of life as a whole. The "for-the-sake-of-which" is an entity whose being is defined by "worldhood itself." Just as a "totality of involvements which is constitutive for the ready-to-hand" is "'earlier' than any single item of equipment," so a totality of ways of being is "earlier" than any single way.

Characteristic of his style in *Being and Time,* Heidegger leaps over this point in order to summarize the general structure of the world (rather than to describe any particular world). We should pause, however, to consider what he means—especially since the reference "for-the-sake-of-which" is central to the world's structure, linking the totality of things ready-to-hand to Dasein's self-understanding. (Moreover, as Heidegger himself stresses, what he means by the general existential structures of the world are only intelligible in light of examples.) Heidegger's point, stated simply, is that any single way of being attains its distinctive character—the responsibilities it involves, the feelings it evokes, the claim it makes—only in relation to others. What it means to be a family member, for example, emerges in relation to being a friend, coworker, business partner, fellow citizen, and so on. Detached from some such totality, the role of family member could not exist in any recognizable way. Thus, any way of being presupposes a totality of ways, a certain way of life as a whole.

We might illustrate this point through Hegel's conception of the family, whose "immediate" unity based on love emerges in relation to civil society and the state. One is in the family, Hegel writes, "not as an independent person but as a member."[60] Each is loved and cared for equally, regardless of talent and personality. But the very terms that define such unconditional love, and thus, what it *is* to be a family member, presuppose a realm in which distinctions matter. Love appears in light of civil society—the sphere of production and exchange in which members are valued for their particular roles within the economy—as landowners, businessmen, and civil servants. The roles that define civil society, in turn, are possible only in relation to the state—the institution that gives them public recognition as parts of a

---

60. G. W. F. Hegel, *Philosophy of Right,* trans. T. M. Knox (London: Oxford University Press, 1952), 110.

common good. Without this link to the common good, the roles would melt into an undifferentiated mass of profit-seeking individuals. The distinctions would be lost. In this way, the family refers beyond itself. It presupposes the whole of ethical life *(Sittlichkeit)*. To understand one's self as a family member, in other words, is also to understand one's self as a member of civil society and the state. Without the other spheres of life, the family could not exist in any recognizable way. Hegel's account of ethical life helps to illuminate what Heidegger means by "being-with" others as a defining feature of Dasein. Being-with always points beyond "one's closest" (e.g., one's family), which is why the world is a *public* world.

Hegel's account helps to clarify Heidegger's general point about ways of being. That "for-the-sake-of-which" Dasein works presupposes a totality of possibilities in which Dasein understands itself. In other words, in working "for-the-sake-of" a certain way of being, Dasein has taken a stand on what it *all* means. This has nothing to do with explicitly reflecting on the "meaning of life." Regardless of whether Dasein has ever raised such questions, and in spite of any opinions it might have on the matter, Dasein has an implicit awareness, or understanding, of the whole.

More precisely, Dasein *is* its understanding of the whole. Any possibility that Dasein lives out at any moment is part of a larger story; anything "for-the-sake-of-which" Dasein works carries within itself all the other possibilities that Dasein is taking up and passing by. The referential totality of things ready-to-hand, and of Dasein in its manifold ways of being, coheres as a story. The "relation" of one way of being to another is never simply a formal, logical, or analytic link—such as "even implies odd." The relation always involves a kind of enacted "plot line." For example, the relation of family member to citizen involves how one is balancing the claims of each role in light of the other, ultimately in light of the twists and turns of one's life as a whole. We confront the narrative character of relations whenever we attempt to express the meaning of a significant event or person in our lives. When we attempt to elicit such meanings, we find ourselves telling a story about the whole way of life in which they fit. We find ourselves saying something of our world.

But the story of the world is distinctive in this sense: it lacks a fixed meaning. In this crucial respect, the story of the world diverges from Hegel's account of ethical life, whose point is the realization of Spirit. According to Heidegger, there is no single, fully realized story that Dasein embodies. His point is simply that any way of being presupposes some understanding of the whole, however trivial or deep. The far-reaching implications of the world's unfinished character will be treated in the following chapter.

To recognize that a totality of things ready-to-hand always "goes back" to Dasein's way of being is to recognize the unity of Dasein and the world.[61] The world coheres only in relation to Dasein's self-understanding—that "for-the-sake-of-which" things are ready-to-hand:

> The "for-the-sake-of-which" signifies an "in-order-to"; this in turn, a "towards-this"; the latter, an "in-which" of letting something be involved; and that in turn, the "with-which" of an involvement. These relationships are bound up with one another as a primordial totality; they are what they are as this signifying. . . . This is what makes up the structure of the world—the structure of that wherein Dasein as such already is.[62]

But only insofar as there is a world can Dasein "be" in any way. Existing "for-the-sake-of" being sheltered would be impossible without houses, covered platforms, and the network of equipment they imply. Along with Dasein's being, "a context of the ready-to-hand is already essentially discovered."[63] Moreover, any particular "for-the-sake-of" presupposes a totality of possibilities in which it makes sense. In this way, human life is the world it sustains.

Thus emerges the justification of Heidegger's term "Dasein": not only does "Dasein" ward off subjectivist understandings of human life (for we exist "first and foremost" as beings absorbed in what we do), but it also captures the sense in which our nonreflective activity—our absorption in "having to do with something, producing something, making use of something, giving something up and letting it go, undertaking, accomplishing"— presupposes a horizon, or *world* to which we already belong. Human life is

61. For an illuminating account of how Dasein is inseparable from its world, cf. Dreyfus, "The Interdependence of Dasein and World," in *Being-in-the-World*, 96–99.

62. Heidegger, *Being and Time*, 120.

63. Ibid.

defined by "Da-sein," "being-there," or "Being-in-the-World." It is never the activity of an isolated self, whether conceived as a "thinking thing" (Descartes) or as a boundlessly creative individual.

Heidegger adds a further, crucial point: Dasein's Being-in-the-World is by no means broken when Dasein "steps back" from its activity and gives an explicit account of the relations that constitute Being-in-the-World (i.e., when Dasein does philosophy, or "fundamental ontology"). It might be supposed, he acknowledges, that "inasmuch as Relations are always 'something thought,'" that worldhood has been "dissolved into 'pure thinking.'" But although the "context of assignments or references, which . . . is constitutive for worldhood, can be taken formally in the sense of a system of Relations," one must note "that in such formalizations the phenomena get leveled off so much that their real phenomenal content may be lost":[64]

> The phenomenal content of these 'Relations' and 'Relata'—the "in-order-to," the "for-the-sake-of," and the "with-which" of an involvement—is such that they resist any sort of mathematical functionalization; nor are they merely something thought, first posited in an 'act of thinking.' They are rather relationships in which concernful circumspection as such already dwells.[65]

In other words, the involvements constitutive of the world are implicit in Dasein's action, and as such are not discovered for the first time in the interpretation that points them out. The interpretation simply articulates what Dasein already understands in practice. The articulation, moreover, is no substitute for the involvements *themselves,* whose meaning must be lived out.

For example, simply indicating the involvement of "making something fast" in "providing a shelter for Dasein" does not by itself represent, or capture, what it means to build "for-the-sake-of" being sheltered. To understand this, one would need to understand the situations in which being soaked by rain is

64. Ibid., 121.
65. Ibid., 121–122.

undignified, which in turn dictate what sort of shelters get built. In other words, what counts as building a *shelter* ("in-order-to"), rather than an inappropriate covering, requires a practical understanding of being sheltered ("for-the-sake-of"), which means knowing when to seek protection from bad weather and when to remain outdoors. Getting drenched while waiting for the train is undignified. Braving the elements while running a marathon is part of the sport. Covering a railway platform would thus make sense as "building a shelter," whereas covering a marathon route would not. In the latter case, the cover would not be a shelter at all, but an impediment to the sport.

So to consider Heidegger's interpretation of the world an act of pure thinking or cognition would be to misunderstand it entirely. Only in light of the actual relationships to which it points does the interpretation make sense. Rather than a representation of the world, the interpretation is a sort of torch that illuminates it—that reveals the general structure of the articulated whole to someone who already lives within it. The schematic interpretation is no substitute for *what* it illuminates. The words on the page come to life only in virtue of our lived experience, in virtue of the concrete world we inhabit.

The *world* is Heidegger's first formulation of the *whole,* of the all-encompassing situation in which particular entities "within-the-world" emerge. In terms that Heidegger later adopts, and that define perhaps the most crucial distinction in his thought, the world is a first approximation of the Being of beings. Especially in his latter essays, Heidegger uses "Being" to denote the origin or the source of beings, the basis on which beings appear: "Things are, and human beings, gifts, and sacrifices are, animals and plants are, equipment and works are." But "that which is, the particular being, stands in Being."[66] Only Being "grants and guarantees to us human beings a passage to those beings that we ourselves are not, and access to that being that we ourselves are."[67]

As the condition for the possibility of beings, Being is more than the totality of things to which it gives rise; it is "prior," "more fundamental,"

66. Heidegger, "Origin of the Work of Art," 51.
67. Ibid.

"more primordial," or "more fully in being," than beings—all terms which Heidegger at different points uses to express the contrast. Although Being, thus described, would appear to be the first (or "final") *cause* of all beings, "cause" is misleading. For we typically understand "cause" as separate from *effect*—as when we think of a god who creates the world of his own will (God is one thing, the world another). Being is not a cause in this sense.[68] It is not some transcendent principle floating above and beyond the beings it makes possible. If it were, it would be another being among beings (albeit a special one) and not Being (the whole). Being always resides, so to speak, *in beings,* which Heidegger demonstrates concretely in his account of equipment, of how the world "announces itself" in the hammer or the pair of shoes. That is to say, Being, or the world, is an *articulated* whole—composed of different *kinds,* each of which embodies the whole in its own way.

The relationship of the world to entities within the world, Being to beings, whole to part, emerges in light of Heidegger's concrete examples. A hammer, as we have seen, refers beyond itself to the world. It is the distinctive being that it is only as part of the world; otherwise it could not exist. The same, however, is not true in the reverse. The world can be without any particular thing, such as a hammer. But nevertheless, the hammer is not a mere part or fragment of the world and nothing more. It is a point at which the world comes into focus in a unique way. (This "coming into focus," what it implies for the world's identity, and how it rounds out the relation between Being and beings, can be appropriately addressed only in light of Heidegger's interpretation of Being-in-the-World as "thrown-projection," treated in the following chapter.) In summary, the world must also be considered as "Being," or "the whole," which, on the one hand, is distinct from "entities within-the-world," or "beings," or "parts," yet, on the other hand, is related to them in the way so far outlined.

The Meaning of Prejudice in Light of the World

Let us pause to consider how Heidegger's conception of Being-in-the-World clarifies the situated conception of understanding. By the terms "situation,"

---

68. Furthermore, the concept of temporal succession implied by cause and effect is made possible by Being and its special temporality, which is treated in Chapter 3.

"life circumstance," and "prejudice writ large," I mean something like Heidegger's conception of the world. To recognize understanding as "situated" is to see its practical, or existential, character, what Heidegger calls "Being-in-the-World." The "practical" nature of understanding means that understanding is embodied in our activity, in our "concernful circumspection" (dealing with equipment) and "solicitous being-with" (sharing commitments). Such understanding is irreducible to principles or to any sort of mental content; it is never the understanding of a subject related to an object. In understanding the world, or its situation, what Dasein understands is nothing other than its very self. Dasein *is,* in a sense, its world, which means that situated understanding is always *self-understanding.*

This description captures situated understanding from the standpoint of Dasein, that is, in terms of *Dasein's* understanding of the world. But "situated understanding" could likewise be described from the standpoint of the world itself. For the identity of the world—its very being—is inseparable from Dasein's understanding of it. The world thus embodies an understanding; it *is* a situated understanding—an *intelligible whole.*

We can see how far this notion of "situation" takes us from the concept of "social context," or mere habit and custom. Our "situated understanding" is our comprehensive awareness of the world. And our awareness of the world is inseparable from the world itself—from its being. The being of the world, moreover, is the Being of beings—the source of everything that is. As a meaningful whole, irreducible to any of its parts, including the many instances of human being (Dasein), Being has a certain *divine* character. It is internally divided into different ends (the manifold possibilities of Dasein), which all presuppose the whole. The world must therefore be understood as a sort of text. However—and this is essential to Heidegger's thought—the text lacks a final meaning. The meaning of the whole is open to question, which means that the whole is incomplete. The whole is a partial whole, which, nevertheless, cannot be reduced to a part.

But despite its incompleteness, the world is by no means "a mere collection of the countable or uncountable, familiar and unfamiliar things that are just there," and neither is it "a merely imagined framework added by our representation to the sum of such given things."[69] Thus Heidegger

69. Heidegger, "Origin of the Work of Art," 43.

explicitly rejects the view that meaning originates in the subjective con-sciousness. The world is itself a destiny, however veiled.

This interpretation finds support in a line from Heidegger's essay on *The Origin of the Work of Art:* "Through Being there passes a veiled destiny that is ordained between the godly and the counter-godly."[70] Although this sen-tence leaves much in darkness, it illuminates the divine character of the world (here reinterpreted by Heidegger as "Being"), defining the basic terms in which the story must be told. The story is a "veiled destiny," something always already understood but simultaneously discovered. This phrase de-fines the "how" of the story, that is, the way in which the story unfolds. "Between the godly and counter-godly" defines the "what," or the essence. Being transcends particular instances of human action; it is by no means the product of a willing subject. All striving and creating presupposes the world. Human life is the story it enacts.

So Heidegger's "worldly" philosophy is far from "this-worldly," if that means anthropocentric in contrast to theistic. The study of Being, Hei-degger claims, is the key to a true conception of the divine: "the holy, which alone is the essential sphere of divinity, which in turn alone affords a di-mension for the gods and for God, comes to radiate only when Being itself beforehand and after extensive preparation has been illuminated and expe-rienced in truth."[71] Heidegger's point is simple: all conceptions of "the holy," of "the gods," or of "God" presuppose a certain understanding of *being*. Take the well-known statement "the Lord is One." The very word "is" reflects a certain understanding of the manner in which the Lord exists as one. Until such an understanding has been worked out, however, until it has been con-sidered alongside alternatives and shown to be comprehensive, the concep-tions that emerge from it—of God and his attributes—hang, so to speak, in midair. Heidegger seeks to initiate a study of being that can put theology on firm footing. In what sense "is" God one? As a unitary subject? As the sole cause of the world? As a single entity present-at-hand above all others? As "one" in a different sense altogether? Only in light of such questions, insists Heidegger, can we clarify the nature of God and divinity. But for the most part, he suggests, we in the West have neglected these questions. As a result,

70. Ibid., 51.

71. Heidegger, "Letter on Humanism," in *Basic Writings*, ed. David Farrell Krell (New York: Harper & Row, 1977), 218.

we possess a truncated conception of God—a conception supplied primarily by a certain reading of the Bible and based implicitly on the subject-object worldview. By kindling the question of being and working toward an answer, Heidegger intends his "fundamental ontology" to reinvigorate theology.

But Heidegger's ontology is not merely preparatory work. It can be understood to outline a certain worldly theology of its own—one that locates God here and now. This suggestion would seem blasphemous, Heidegger points out, only from a particular view of this world, namely, as broken, fragmented, and in need of escape. To envision the divine as detached from this world, as somewhere else, suggests Heidegger, is to cast an unjust verdict on our own lives and their meaning. Heidegger's philosophy seeks to illuminate the divinity of this world. As we will see, the theological dimension of situated understanding emerges more clearly in Heidegger's discussion of death, conscience, destiny, and time.

At this point, however, we can say the following: Heidegger's conception of the world undermines the notion that our life circumstance is a *mere* prejudice that perverts our understanding. Although a kind of prejudice, our life circumstance, as the very term *world* suggests, is not some subjective "cave," but a comprehensive perspective shared with others—a perspective, moreover, that grants us access to all things. Although we speak of particular life perspectives, or, in Heidegger's terms, particular understandings of the world, each is in principle intelligible from within another. By getting to know someone else, for example, we can bring ourselves within his or her perspective. That one's own world, which is also to say one's own Dasein, may be unintelligible to certain people, or misinterpreted by them, simply reflects their failure to adequately grasp it. Although there is never any guarantee of mutual understanding or the realization of a shared perspective, there is no inherent limit to it. This is what Heidegger establishes by replacing the subject with Dasein.

To state this insight another way: despite the articulation of Dasein into various ways of being, each is a more or less comprehensive understanding of the whole. Because this understanding is not subjective, but expressed in the way each person lives, the understanding is "with" others and more or less intelligible to them. Dasein is, in each case, a point at which the same world shines forth in its own way.

Finally, the double sense in which I have used "prejudice"—sometimes to denote one's whole perspective ("prejudice writ large") and other times to denote particular preconceptions, commitments, traditions, and practices— corresponds to the distinction between Dasein's understanding of the world and of particular entities "within-the-world." Each way of being pre- supposes an understanding of the world, of the whole of life. At the same time, each way of being can itself be considered its own window onto the whole. In this sense, what I have called particular "prejudices" (following Burke's use of the term) are understandings that emanate from one's compre- hensive life perspective. They are not mere sentiments, blind dispositions, or "pleasing illusions" as Burke believes.

The Situated Character of Supposedly Detached Judgment

Heidegger undermines the ideal of detached reflection by interpreting it as a mode of Being-in-the-World. Such reflection is not, Heidegger shows, a procedure by which a subject transcends its "cabinet of consciousness" to attain knowledge of nature in itself, the "object." The kind of "knowing" (*Erkennen*) that is typically considered "objective," or "context-free," is, rather, a modification of our "concernful circumspection" (practical understanding) that has "strayed into the legitimate task of grasping the present-at-hand."[72] But although "legitimate," or unimpeachable as such, this task is in many ways limited. Although it may allow Dasein to predict and control certain phenomena, it by no means reaches the "deeper truth" of nature. To "know" something present-at-hand, to study, for example, its properties, one must abstract from its being ready-to-hand. Before examining how Heidegger puts detached reflection in its place, we should recall Bacon's and Descartes's idealized version of it.

As we have seen, they argue that grasping nature in itself, as it really is, requires abstracting from the way it charms us or draws us in—the way it strikes us as beautiful, threatening, useful, and so on. Human longing and valuing, according to Bacon and Descartes, are merely subjective projec- tions onto the brute facts of the world. Understanding the "deeper truth of nature" (Bacon) requires detached reflection guided by sound method. Only

72. Heidegger, *Being and Time*, 194.

in such a manner does the world first become *known* rather than experienced in a haphazard or mythical way.

An analogous view of the social world informs the moral theories of Smith and Kant. They consider the institutions, practices, roles, and commitments that define society to be contingent arrangements, meaningless in themselves. They embody no intrinsic good but owe their worth to the human subjects who value them. Although certain roles and commitments tend to command our allegiance (just as certain aspects of nature strike us as beautiful or purposeful), such allegiance is ultimately based on our subjective feelings, not on reason. Judging how to act thus requires stepping back from the influence of one's society, or life circumstance, from one's loyalty to family, friends, and country, and reasoning in a detached manner. The prejudice-free ideal of judgment thus governs both modern ethics and science.

"Austere," a term that Charles Taylor invokes, is an apt way of describing the modern scientific and moral attitude.[73] It powerfully captures the sense in which, according to this attitude, sound understanding and judgment requires *discipline*. As Bacon, Descartes, Smith, and Kant all observe, prejudice exerts a strong pull, especially, they claim, when crusted over by habit and custom. The problem is not simply that people fall into error, but that they tend to resist the truth, to be seduced by their own hopes and fears into misunderstanding or poor judgment.

This explains Bacon's extensive indictment of the "idols" of the human mind, which he develops before he outlines his scientific method. It also explains Descartes radical doubting, which is step one of his "rules for the direction of the mind." The elimination of all prejudice and the revelation of how the will leads the intellect into error are the conditions for reconstructing knowledge piece by piece.

In this way, Bacon, Descartes, and all those who considered themselves "enlightenment thinkers," interpreted their mission first and foremost as illuminating darkness, smashing the idols of the past. Of course, they also saw themselves as founders of science. But their negative, or destructive, project is what they tended to highlight. A clear example, as we have seen, is how Kant defines Enlightenment as "the emancipation from prejudices

73. Taylor, *Hegel*, 6.

generally."[74] Enlightenment is not the acquisition of knowledge (although so much is implied), but the struggle against human prejudice, the fight for a detached standpoint from which sound understanding can begin.

The ideal of a detached standpoint is based on the assumption that meaning, or value, originates in the minds of subjects who face a world that is meaningless in itself. Considered from the standpoint of modern natural science, the world is a collection of bodies that have no proper place. The action of such bodies and their mutual relations must be explained in terms of contingent laws. Considered from the ethical standpoint, the world is a set of social facts whose value is given by human subjects. According to this interpretation of the world, the perspective shaped by our desires, aims, practices, and commitments appears to be a *mere* prejudice—a "pleasing illusion" that hinders the rational understanding of nature and leads to uncritical moral judgment. It is precisely this assumption that Heidegger's conception of the world challenges.

Dasein, he argues, is not a self-conscious subject who stamps things with value. The world is not a collection of meaningless objects or contingent social facts. What we typically construe as human "values" presupposes the subject-object distinction, which the notion of Being-in-the-World is meant to undermine. "Values," for Heidegger, are not subjective dispositions, but the ways of being "for-the-sake-of-which" Dasein exists. Such ways of being are not merely human values. Their meaning comes not from the subjective consciousness but from their place in the world. The world is the basis for taking up, questioning, or revising any particular practice. As an intelligible whole, the world is inherently meaningful; it can be understood as a certain kind of text (although essentially unfinished).

To emphasize that the source of value, or better yet, *meaning,* is not human subjectivity, but the world, Heidegger calls his philosophy "antihumanist." By this he does not mean that human life is unimportant or subordinate to some other being of greater force. After all, the Being of beings—the world—"is" only through Dasein. The point of "antihumanism," writes Heidegger, is that human life is never the action of a value-conferring subject set over against a meaningless world: "In the determination of the humanity

74. Immanuel Kant, *The Critique of Judgment,* trans. James Creed Meredith (Oxford: Oxford University Press, [1790] 1952), §40, 152.

of man . . . what is essential is not man [understood as a subject or isolated individual] but Being."[75] Heidegger reiterates:

> [Man] is never first and foremost man on the hither side of the world, as a "subject," whether this is taken as "I" or "We." Nor is he ever simply a mere subject which always simultaneously is related to objects, so that his essence lies in the subject-object relation. Rather, before all this, man in his essence is *ek-sistent* into the openness of Being, into the open region that lights the "between" within which the "relation" of subject to object can "be."[76]

Corresponding to his antihumanism, Heidegger rejects the very term "value" as a term for things worthy, meaningful, or significant:

> It is important finally to realize that precisely through the characterization of something as "a value" what is so valued is robbed of its worth. That is to say, by the assessment of something as a value what is valued is admitted only as an object for man's estimation. But what a thing is in its Being is not exhausted by its being an object, particularly when objectivity takes the form of value. Every valuing, even when it values positively, is a subjectivizing. It does not let beings: be. Rather, valuing lets being: be valid—solely as the objects of its doing.[77]

Returning to the question of nature: according to Heidegger's conception of Dasein and the world, meaning is not a subjective imposition on "nature" understood as the "objective order." "Nature" in the proper and comprehensive sense, Heidegger shows, is the world—the origin of all being. And the world is inherently meaningful. As parts of the world, the things of the earth and sky that we typically class misleadingly as the "natural" things, appear as meaningful in their own ways. In Dasein's "concernful circumspection," its basic way of Being-in-the-World, "nature" appears as "the Nature which 'stirs and strives,' which assails us and enthralls us

75. Heidegger, "Letter on Humanism," 213.
76. Ibid., 229.
77. Ibid., 228.

as landscape."[78] Such characteristics are not merely ways of "taking" nature, "as if some world-stuff which is proximally present-at-hand in itself were 'given subjective coloring' in this way."[79] These terms define nature *in itself.*

Heidegger highlights the difference between his and Descartes's account of nature as follows: Descartes "prescribes for the world its 'real' Being, as it were, on the basis of an idea of Being whose source has not been unveiled and which has not been demonstrated in its own right—an idea in which Being is equated with constant presence-at-hand."[80] This leads him to consider the "world," or nature in itself, to be the extended body *(res extensa).* All beings independent of the intellect, he claims, are intelligible as modifications of extension. Extension becomes the basis of material reality *(res corporea),* the substrate upon which everything else is built. The ontological priority of extension implies that "quantitative modifications of the modes of *extensio* itself" would "provide the footing for such specific qualities as "beautiful," "ugly," "in keeping," "not in keeping," "useful," "useless."[81] If one is oriented primarily by *extensio,* "these latter qualities must be taken as non-quantifiable value-predicates by which what is in the first instance just a material Thing, gets stamped as something good." But all the while, this orientation assumes *"that goods have pure presence-at-hand as their kind of being."*[82] It overlooks the phenomenon of "readiness-to-hand," and therewith, the world.

Of course, writes Heidegger, " 'Nature' itself can be discovered and defined simply in its pure presence-at-hand," as a mere thing with properties, for example, or as formed matter. But to interpret such discovery as reaching the "deeper truth of nature" by transcending everything "subjective" or "artificial" is a mistake.

For such discovery to be possible, "there must first be a deficiency in our having-to-do with the world concernfully" such that things appear as present-at-hand:

When concern holds back [*Sichenthalten*] from any kind of producing, manipulating, and the like, it puts itself into what is now the sole re-

78. Heidegger, *Being and Time,* 100.
79. Ibid., 101.
80. Ibid., 129.
81. Ibid., 131–132.
82. Ibid., 132.

maining mode of Being-in, the mode of just tarrying alongside . . . [*das Nur-noch-verweilen bei* . . .]. This kind of Being towards the world is one which lets us encounter entities within-the-world purely in the *way they look (eidos)*, just that; *on the basis* of this kind of Being, and as a mode of it, looking explicitly at what we encounter is possible.[83]

For example, the hammer a workman grabs might be too heavy so that his work is interrupted. The hammer now appears as something present-at-hand, which can be defined by the way it looks and by other properties detached from its function ("in-order-to"). Such definition is impossible while the hammer functions as ready-to-hand and is not perceptible. But in light of the disruption, it now shows itself as a theme of reflection. Having been grasped as such, it can furthermore become the topic of an assertion: "The hammer is heavy," which is to say, "This thing—a hammer—has the property of heaviness."[84]

Assertion, Heidegger points out, has often been considered the locus of "objective" truth, of things as they really are, detached from everything subjective.[85] For Bacon, assertion is just that. The "form or true definition" of a given "nature," such as heat, he claims, be captured in a list of qualities sufficient to produce it. This list, he claims, defines heat as it really is—relative "to the universe and not to the sense."[86] But this way of thinking, Heidegger shows, is mistaken: "Assertion is not a free-floating kind of behaviour which, in its own right, might be capable of disclosing entities in general in a primary way: on the contrary it always maintains itself on the basis of Being-in-the-World."[87] Specifically, what Dasein grasps in the assertion is one way of understanding the hammer, made possible by Dasein's *withholding of concern*, a stance that conceals far more than it illuminates.

When Dasein thus "directs itself toward something and grasps it, it does not somehow first get out of an inner sphere in which it has been proximally encapsulated" such that now and for the first time it begins to understand the thing itself. Dasein's "primary kind of Being is such that it is 'outside'

83. Ibid., 88.
84. Ibid., 200.
85. Ibid., 198.
86. Bacon, *New Organon*, 135.
87. Heidegger, *Being and Time*, 199.

alongside entities," that is, absorbed in things that it understands as ready-to-hand within a totality of involvements.[88] This understanding is precisely what gets covered over in the assertion, which restricts the hammer to being present-at-hand in a specific way:

> If this entity becomes the "object" of an assertion, then as soon as we begin this assertion, there is already a change-over in the fore-having. Something *ready-to-hand with which* we have to do or perform something, turns into something *"about which"* the assertion that points out is made. Our fore-sight is aimed at something present-at-hand in what is ready-to-hand. Both *by* and *for* this way of looking at it [*Hin-sicht*], the ready-to-hand becomes veiled as ready-to-hand. . . . Only now are we given any access to *properties* or the like. When an assertion has given a definite character to something present-at-hand, it says something about it *as* a "what"; and this "what" is drawn *from that* which is present-at-hand as such. The as-structure of interpretation has undergone a modification. In its functioning of appropriating what is understood, the 'as' no longer reaches out into a totality of involvements. . . . The 'as' . . . dwindles to the structure of just letting one see what is present-at-hand, and letting one see it in a definite way. This levelling of the primordial 'as' of circumspective interpretation to the "as" with which presence-at-hand is given a definite character is the specialty of assertion. Only so does it obtain the possibility of exhibiting something in such a way that we just look at it.[89]

Thus, "assertion cannot disown its ontological origin from an interpretation which understands . . . circumspectively."[90] What assertion articulates, in other words, is not some pure perception of the thing itself. What gets seen in the first place, and how it gets seen, is directed by Dasein's concernful circumspection.

In light of this practical understanding, moreover, assertion, or any supposedly detached "knowing," must be interpreted as a special mode of *engagement,* namely as a *deficient* mode, that is, "holding back," *"not* caring,"

88. Ibid., 89.
89. Ibid., 201.
90. Ibid.

which, as such, is *no less value-laden* than putting things to use and discovering them as ready-to-hand. By "deficient," Heidegger does not mean "inappropriate." He simply means lacking a certain type of concern. His point is that even the "purest theoria" presupposes a certain practical stance, or attitude, toward the thing being examined: "even when we look theoretically at what is just present-at-hand, it does not show itself purely as it looks unless this theoria lets it come towards us in a *tranquil* tarrying alongside."[91] Even what appears to be the most detached scientific reflection remains relative to Dasein's concern. As Heidegger puts it, "any cognitive determining has its existential-ontological Constitution in . . . Being-in-the-World."[92] In this sense, it is a situated kind of understanding.

But what about scientific statements that appear to be unconditionally true? What about the statement "the earth revolves around the sun"? Does this not describe nature "in itself," independent of any particular life perspective? Does it not state a truth that is valid for any rational being anywhere? No, claims Heidegger. The statement presupposes that the sun and the earth appear in a special way, namely, as present-at-hand. More precisely, the statement assumes that the sun and the earth appear as two bodies abstracted from their place in a meaningful whole. As such, their regular motion vis-à-vis each other is an anomaly that must be explained. On the basis of this present-at-hand conception of the earth and the sun, the questions can arise: which revolves around which? does the visible movement of the sun deceive us? But this conception obscures our understanding of the earth and sun as ready-to-hand. Like all things ready-to-hand, each is defined by its proper place in the life of Dasein.

The assumption that the modern astrophysical account of the relation of earth to sun might reach the "true being" of nature, in contrast to our human impression of it, presupposes that nature is given, first and foremost, as a meaningless heap of objects, which later acquires its "value" from the subjective terms we attach to it—"useful," "good," "harmful," "beautiful," and so on. From this viewpoint, it makes sense to abstract from nature as it appears to us, to abstract from everything "subjective" in order to reach nature "in itself"—the "object." But as Heidegger shows, the modern scientific

91. Ibid., 177.
92. Ibid.

understanding of nature rests on nature's appearing as present-at-hand. In this sense, modern science is situated. For the present-at-hand itself rests on the ready-to-hand, which, in turn, rests on the world.

So the statement "the earth revolves around the sun" turns out to be true only conditionally. For the very words "earth" and "sun" contain a remnant of their original nature, an interpretation of what is at stake in these beings, of what relates them and marks them off as distinctive parts of the world. Whether the earth revolves around the sun, and whether each being even admits of "revolution," can be determined only by a comprehensive analysis of what they *are,* by a sufficient account of their being, which would begin from how they first appear. Bacon's science does not attempt such an account. It starts from a faint, unacknowledged, lived awareness of the sun—of the sun as it first breaks into our world in speech and everyday practice—and, from there, begins to investigate properties of the "sun." All the while, it leaves the original being of the sun veiled in darkness.

A sufficient account of the sun would address what marks it off from and relates it to other beings, ultimately, to Being, or to the whole. Such an account would require a return to the sun as it first appears as ready-to-hand in the context of our daily lives. For only on this basis—which is the condition of science—can we begin to clarify the being of the sun—to trace it to its roots in Being itself.

The problem, of course, is this: like all beings, the sun first "appears" as a fragment of the truth, as a commonsense understanding. The task of thought is to develop this initial awareness. How might we begin? The sun first appears as the sunny side of the house, the street lights lining our neighborhood, the lawn chair positioned in the shade. In all these instances—when we build a house facing south, walk along the illuminated road at night, or seat ourselves in the shade-covered chair—we "take note" of the sun without explicitly reflecting upon it.

But these understandings of the sun mark it off from other natural beings only faintly. What distinguishes the sun is the way it guides our daily routine. We set our clocks to its course, we wake up by its first rays, eat lunch at its height, and go to bed in its absence. Precisely because the sun is reliable, we do all these things without reflecting on it explicitly. The stable character of the sun, its guiding influence, marks it off from other natural beings, and especially those which disrupt the rhythm of our daily lives—lightening, storms, and earthquakes.

In this way, we begin to define the sun. But this understanding remains far from sufficient. For in the "sun as our guiding light" we grasp it, for the most part, as connected to our "lives" in an *ordinary,* everyday sense—our "lives" understood as "the daily routine." We grasp the sun as tied to a significant yet superficial sense of "life," a sense that still lacks the unity of Being-in-the-World. And yet, this everyday account of the sun gestures toward a more comprehensive one. In serving as our guiding light, the sun has a special place in the whole. We might articulate its place in many ways, but all would have to somehow connect the being of the sun to Being itself. We find a memorable example of such an attempt in Plato. The sun, he teaches, is nothing less than a reflection of Being itself, a "child of the good," to whom the "good gave birth in its own image." Just as the sun grants being and vision to everything that appears to sight, so the good gives rise to everything that appears at all. The good is the cosmic whole, of which the sun is a special part. The sun, in its own way, reflects the whole: in its illuminating the phenomena of the world, the sun mirrors the relationship of Being to beings. It models the very connection of whole to part that defines the universe itself. We may ask, of course, to what extent Plato's account of the sun is comprehensive. But the kind of account he gives, connecting the sun, as a particular being, to Being, is the sort of comprehensive account that fundamental ontology, according to Heidegger, demands.

3

Situated Agency

The Implication of Being-in-the-World for Freedom

As we have seen, the case against prejudice arose not only out of a concern for the truth. It was motivated, in large part, by a certain conception of freedom, a conception that came to its fullest expression in Kant: to be free is to be guided from within, "to make use of one's own understanding without direction from another."[1] By contrast, to be influenced by prejudice of any sort—whether human authority, tradition, common opinion, or custom—is to be slavish. According to Kant, freedom requires detachment from the perspective of one's upbringing and even from one's own desires.

Heidegger's conception of Being-in-the-World undermines this ideal of freedom insofar as the ideal depends on the possibility of detachment. Even when we try to think and judge detachedly, we never break free of our situation. But we are never enslaved to our situation either. Dasein is "subordinate," so to speak, to a world it sustains. The world *is* only in relation to Dasein's self-understanding. This reciprocal accord of Dasein and the world undermines any distinction of master and slave. Moreover, as I will argue in

---

1. Immanuel Kant, "An Answer to the Question: What Is Enlightenment?," in *Practical Philosophy,* trans. and ed. Mary J. Gregor (Cambridge: Cambridge University Press, [1784] 1996), 17.

this section, Being-in-the-World implies a conception of human agency that preserves the Kantian ideal of self-direction while liberating that ideal from the difficulties associated with Kant's conception of pure reason. In other words, we should understand Heidegger not simply as an opponent of Kant or of the ideal of self-direction, but actually as its savior.

The Kantian ideal of detachment from all prejudice presents two difficulties. First, as Heidegger argues, the ideal cannot succeed. It is impossible to be detached from all prejudice. But second, even if such detachment were possible, if pure practical reason could be sovereign, this very ideal is in tension with Kant's conception of freedom as autonomy. For autonomy means *self-direction,* which put negatively, means freedom from dependence on another. But according to Kant, such freedom can be won only by presupposing a subject of pure practical reason whose identity is fixed and given. If this is so, freedom is, in a sense, at odds with the very ideal of autonomy. Who I am is entirely beyond my control; I remain the same regardless of any stance I take toward myself. Whether I pursue this desire, this role, this way of being, my identity remains unaffected. Now, of course, from Kant's point of view, this immutability is just the point. The subject, being the presupposition of experience, is not transformed by experience. But one could argue that this way of conceiving the self unduly restricts the self-direction of which a truly autonomous self is capable.

To be sure, Kant offers a powerful conception of autonomy: to be free from every influence external to one's self. But the ideal falls short in this respect: the autonomous self lacks the capacity to effect any fundamental *change,* to develop its identity. This lack, moreover, represents a shortcoming of autonomy itself, which Kant formulates precisely in terms of "self-rule" and "self-direction." But is self-direction not, in a certain sense, empty if it completely lacks power over the self that does the directing? To be sure, giving the moral law to myself implies a certain "positive" conception of freedom, but this self-legislation still never touches my identity. It remains an act of self-respect that merely lives up to who I already am and always will be.

Furthermore, freedom, as Kant conceives of it, comes at the price of individuality. Insofar as human beings are free, they are members of an undifferentiated, unitary subject. Only as empirical selves who pursue particular desires do they achieve any distinction. Even granting that Kant does not mean to *denigrate* the empirical self who pursues happiness in its own way, the empirical self is not *autonomous*. More precisely, the desiring and striving self is free only insofar as it remains capable of abstracting from all desiring and striving, capable of attaining a standpoint shared with everyone else. Although there is something appealing about the unity of all rational beings, there is something at least unsettling about the notion that our individuality consists in nothing more than our contingent impulses and desires.

Finally, the Kantian subject lacks agency in a sense that points beyond the capacity to shape its own identity: it is utterly incapable of changing the way things *are,* of having any responsibility for nature, which, as Kant maintains, is the realm of necessity. The complication, to be sure, is that this necessity lies in the knowing subject itself. The mind, or the transcendental subject, prescribes to nature its laws. But insofar as the categories of the subject are fixed, so too is nature. Nature obeys a strictly necessary course in the face of which human beings are powerless. From the standpoint of human agency, nature is something *alien,* something to overcome through detachment. Insofar as we are free beings capable of autonomy, we exist in *opposition* to nature. Human agency can strive for what *ought* to be only in contrast to what *is.*

My suggestion is that Heidegger's notion of Being-in-the-World involves a more powerful kind of agency than Kant's ideal of pure practical reason. Being-in-the-World aspires to a deeper sense of self-definition and individuality than the Kantian subject is capable of. Moreover, unlike the Kantian subject, who is responsible only for itself and for what *ought* to be, Dasein is responsible for the world—for what *is*. If plausible, this view of agency would dissolve the second pillar of the case against prejudice. It would show that situated understanding, not detached reason, is what makes true freedom possible.

The notion of freedom connected to Being-in-the-World can be understood to fall within the tradition that conceives freedom as *independence*. This tradition, shaped notably by Rousseau, Kant, Hegel, and Marx, can be distinguished from the tradition typically attributed to Hobbes, Locke, and Hume, which conceives freedom as the ability to act on one's desires unimpeded. Freedom, conceived as independence, requires more than the absence

of obstacles to one's action. It involves independence from everything external to the self.

The thinkers who develop this conception of freedom give, broadly
speaking, two different answers to the question of how we achieve independence. The first, which comes from Kant, is that we achieve independence
by abstracting from everything external to ourselves and reasoning, so to
speak, "from within." But Kant's successors, most notably, Hegel and Marx,
argue that this ideal of abstraction is misguided. Human life, they maintain,
is inextricably dependent on nature and society. To neglect this dependence,
moreover, is to miss an essential dimension of ourselves. Not only is the
ideal of detached reason impossible; it also *alienates* us from our desires and
the world in which we realize them.

Hegel and Marx thus seek to replace the Kantian ideal of detachment
with a rival version of independence: the ideal of *integrating* the objective
world into one's very self, of coming to recognize what is "other" as ultimately one's *own*. For Hegel, independence is coming to recognize the objective world as ultimately the expression of subjectivity, as posited by a
cosmic spirit who attains self-knowledge through human action and understanding. For Marx, who rejects Hegel's notion of spirit, human independence involves transforming nature and society in order to reflect back to
man his own "species being." In both cases, independence requires overcoming alienation from the surrounding world, or as Hegel puts it, "being
one's self in one's other."

Common to these different versions of independence is the idea that
freedom is ultimately of a *subject* or involves the dialectical overcoming of
an alien, "objective" world. Achieving freedom means either abstracting
from what is alien (Kant) or integrating it, coming to see it as an expression
of one's self (Hegel and Marx). Heidegger's replacement of the subject with
Dasein significantly alters the problem of freedom. It shifts the issue away
from overcoming external influences and toward extricating ourselves
from submersion in what lies *closest* to us.

As Being-in-the-World, Dasein *belongs* to its world, and, in this sense,
faces nothing alien. The threat to Dasein's independence comes not from
some external source, but rather, from its own tendency to become absorbed in the details of life in a way that obscures the whole. Instead of living out its roles understandingly, with a certain eye to the unity of its life

and with a view to clarifying that unity, Dasein performs them in a formulaic manner, guided by the way in which "others" do it, without a sense of nuance or of what the situation may call for. Heidegger calls this tendency toward blind conformity the "inauthenticity" of Dasein. He stresses that the "others" to whom Dasein conforms are not *"definite* Others" who stand out as separate from my own Dasein and to whom I consciously compare myself: "What is decisive is just that inconspicuous domination by Others which has already been taken over unawares from Dasein as Being-with. One belongs to the Others oneself and enhances their power."[2] The others are not "this one, not that one, not one's self *[man selbst],* not some people *[einige],* and not the sum of them all." They are "the neuter, the *"they" [das Man]."*[3]

Heidegger's concept of *das Man,* awkwardly translated as "the they" is meant to capture Dasein's tendency to succumb to "the way *they* do things" or "the way things are typically done":

> We take pleasure and enjoy ourselves as *they* [*man*] take pleasure; we read, see, and judge about literature and art as *they* see and judge; likewise we shrink back from the "great mass" as *they* shrink back; we find "shocking" what they find shocking.[4]

To reiterate that Dasein's submersion in *das Man* does not involve explicitly looking toward others and away from one's self, Heidegger notes that such submersion often drives Dasein into "the most exaggerated 'self-dissection', tempting itself with all possibilities of explanation" so that Dasein becomes *"entangled [verfangt]* in itself."[5] Such excessive self-scrutiny (reflected in the culture of psychoanalysis) masquerades as a genuine way of unearthing Dasein's "true self," but in reality, it plunges Dasein further into the depths of self-delusion. For to assume a "true self," or core, beneath some "culturally constructed" facade, entirely misses the basic character of human life. Dasein is neither a subject who defines its identity nor an object buffeted to and fro by society.

2. Martin Heidegger, *Being and Time,* trans. John Macquarrie and Edward Robinson (Malden, MA: Blackwell, [1927] 1962), 164.
3. Ibid.
4. Ibid.
5. Ibid., 222–223.

In losing itself in the details of its life—in this or that role, activity, attitude, or some collection thereof—and in thus falling victim to what "they" do, Dasein tends toward a generic *type,* what Heidegger calls the "inauthentic" self. This self is inauthentic in two, ultimately connected, senses. First, the inauthentic self is dispersed into anonymous "others," bearing no mark of its *own.* It carries out its life as if it were, so to speak, replaceable by anyone else with the same curriculum vitae. Second and above all, this self is inauthentic in that it conceals the very essence of Dasein. For Dasein is defined by Being-in-the-World, by its situated understanding of the whole, and not by its being this or that. In its everyday preoccupations, inauthentic Dasein loses itself "among beings," thereby forgetting its fundamental relation to Being, or to the whole of life.[6] This forgetfulness is the source of Dasein's lack of self-possession. For Dasein's awareness of the whole is what affords it a critical standpoint from which to assess its particular activities, from which to see them in the right proportion, undistorted by the superficial understandings of *das Man.*

Heidegger interprets Dasein's tendency toward self-dispersion as "falling" into the world and "away from itself."[7] "Falling" is meant to evoke a downward free fall, a plunge into some narrow, bottomless, pit of the world. But furthermore, it evokes the biblical notion of Adam's "fall"—the notion of his original sin against God. Heidegger interprets Dasein's falling as its sin against the world—as its "falling away" from Being. A key mode of falling, moreover, at least in modern times, is the rise of a certain kind of *knowledge*—the very self-conscious sort of knowledge that defines Adam's sin. Insofar as "knowledge," conceived as detached reflection, masquerades as a way of reaching the depths of the world, it blinds Dasein to Being and constitutes its sin.

"Falling," Heidegger makes clear, is not the tendency of a subject to become submerged in an object called the "world." Falling is a mode of Being-in-the-World, which, as it were, conceals the very *character* of the world. One *way* of falling is to become submerged in the subject-object interpretation of the world, to mistake presence-at-hand, one stance toward the world, for the world itself. In a sense, Dasein's falling is the opposite of the predicament

6. Martin Heidegger, "What Is Metaphysics?," in *Basic Writings,* ed. David Farrell Krell (New York: Harper & Row, [1929] 1977), 106.

7. Heidegger, *Being and Time,* 220.

facing a subject confronted by an alien world of objects. To remedy the latter involves recovering a certain communion, whereas to remedy the former involves winning a certain distinction. Both predicaments, however, can be interpreted as a kind of alienation, or loss of self-possession. Falling Being-in-the-World, writes Heidegger, is "alienating."[8] It conceals Dasein's basic relation to Being and, thereby, the possibility of being something of its *own*.

Authenticity, Anxiety, and the Call of Conscience

To win independence is to exist authentically, to overcome one's tendency toward falling and to recognize one's self as Being-in-the-World. This recognition does not require that Dasein *conceptualize* Being-in-the-World as such; it requires only that Dasein live its life in a way that embodies an *awareness* of Being-in-the-World. The key feature of this awareness is a certain reflective distance from beings, or particular activities and roles, such that they no longer crowd in on Dasein's identity. This distance is attained not through detachment, or abstraction from beings, but through understanding their place in the whole of one's life, their place in the *world*. Dasein must come to recognize the world, or Being, rather than beings, as the source of its identity. In other words, what defines Dasein is not this or that detail, or some collection thereof, but its lived awareness of the whole.

This interpretation of authenticity, which relies on the distinction between Being and beings, better captures Heidegger's meaning than familiar accounts that emphasize Dasein's choosing its life rather than passively living it. The latter finds expression in Richard Polt, who writes that I exist authentically when "I truly choose this identity [of mine], instead of just letting it happen."[9] "Choosing" versus "letting it happen" is misleading insofar as Dasein's authentic "choice" still involves a certain passivity. The origin of choice, according to Heidegger is not the will of a self-sovereign subject. Dasein's "choice" is always within the *world*. The passive dimension of choice implies that even authentic Dasein's life, in a sense, "happens" to it.

8. Ibid., 222.
9. Richard Polt, *Heidegger: An Introduction* (London: Routledge, 1999), 79.

In other words, to conceive of authenticity simply in terms of "choosing" still leaves in darkness the *basis* of choice. In fairness to his interpreters, Heidegger himself is notoriously vague on the basis of authentic choice. He insists that the basis is "indefinite" and that "only the resolution [authentic choice] itself can give the answer."[10] But if we keep clearly in view the relation of Being to beings, we can offer at least a general answer to the nature of authentic action: its mark is clear-sighted decision on the basis of Being, on the basis of one's lived understanding of the whole, rather than on this or that detail of life.

In this sense, Dasein achieves a certain independence. Dasein is conditioned, as Heidegger puts it, by *nothing*. This "nothing" is not to be confused with the mere negation of everything that is, nor with some abstract ideal of pure reason. "Nothing," moreover, does not imply the emptiness of existence, as if, in Dreyfus's terms, "nothing is grounded and there are no guidelines for living."[11] "Nothing" captures the sense in which Being, or the whole, is irreducible to any of the beings it makes possible.[12] In other words, Being cannot be understood as a thing or collection of things; Being is quite literally *no-thing*. Expressed in terms of a narrative, Dasein's life story is irreducible to any of the events, projects, and relationships it involves. The story as a whole is the source of any and all its details. In being conditioned by nothing, Dasein is "individualized *as* Being-in-the-World."[13]

Being thus individualized, Heidegger stresses, does not mean becoming a "free floating" individual who turns away from its particular activities and commitments or who surveys and assesses its life as if from a bird's-eye view: "Authentic Being-one's-Self, does not detach Dasein from its world, nor does it isolate it so that it becomes a free-floating 'I.' And how should it, when . . . authentic disclosedness, is *authentically* nothing else

10. Heidegger, *Being and Time*, 345.

11. Hubert L. Dreyfus, *Being-in-the-World: A Commentary on Heidegger's* Being and Time, *Division I* (Cambridge, MA: MIT Press, 1991), 38.

12. Heidegger, "What is Metaphysics?," 110. In a general sense, and at a more comprehensive level, Heidegger's conception of being dependent on "nothing" recalls Rousseau's notion of being dependent on the "general will" rather than any particular will. Of course, for Heidegger, the "nothing," or "Being," is an articulated whole rather than the sort of unitary whole suggested by the general will. (And, of course, "Being" reaches far beyond the bounds of politics.)

13. Heidegger, *Being and Time*, 233.

than *Being-in-the-World*"? Authenticity "brings the Self right into its current concernful Being-alongside what is ready-to-hand, and pushes it into solici-tous Being with Others."[14] The difference is that authentic Dasein lives out its commitments in a new spirit, recognizing them as parts of a lived narrative—a "fate," or "destiny." Authenticity, writes Heidegger, "snatches one back from the endless multiplicity of possibilities which offer themselves as closest to one—those of comfortableness, shirking, and taking things lightly—and brings Dasein into the simplicity of its fate *[Schicksal]*."[15] To signify that this "fate" is one that Dasein, in each case, shares with others, Heidegger calls it a "destiny" *(Geschick)*.[16]

In light of its destiny, Dasein comes to see its relationships, activities, and aims no longer as generic roles, as objects of fanatic devotion, or as what one typically does, but as distinctive points at which its life as a whole shines forth. Having thus recovered its particular loyalties from the depths of *das Man* and recaptured them within its own life, Dasein gains a personal stake in them. In this sense, Dasein no longer "takes things lightly," but is "pushed into solicitous Being with Others"—pushed into a clear-sighted loyalty to those with whom its destiny is bound.[17]

Agency involves an awareness of this destiny and a simultaneous recog-nition of Dasein's own responsibility for it. The world, or destiny, to which Dasein is subordinate, itself depends on Dasein. For the world, as we have seen, is structured by the possibilities "for-the-sake-of-which" Dasein *lives*. And through Being-in-the-World, through living out its life, Dasein simulta-

---

14. Ibid., 344.

15. Ibid., 435.

16. Ibid., 436.

17. This conception of authenticity may be contrasted to Dreyfus's. According to his view, authenticity means realizing that "no possibilities have intrinsic significance, i.e., that they have no essential relation to the self, nor can they be given any." In light of this insight, which wipes out "all intrinsic meaning and so all reasons for doing things," Dasein adopts a certain stoic indiffer-ence to life, living an "empty, open spontaneous way of Being-in-the-World" (Dreyfus, *Being-in-the-World*, 316, 321). This notion of authenticity fits with Dreyfus's view that the world is a contin-gent network of shared practices. He therefore understands authentic Dasein as an empty locus of ultimately unguided activity that understands itself as such. For his description of authentic Das-ein's spontaneous action and indifference toward its own desires; cf. Dreyfus, *Being-in-the-World*, 323. This description presents a contrast to the conception of authenticity that I derive from Hei-degger. Far from being "indifferent" to its desires, authentic Dasein, according to my reading, pursues them all the more tenaciously.

neously *develops* itself and its world, reshaping, or, better yet, clarifying, *the basis* of its own being. Dasein, and, thereby, its world, is never fixed once and for all. Insofar as the world is the Being of beings, as Heidegger maintains, Dasein's agency reaches beyond self-responsibility. Unlike Kant's subject of pure practical reason, who is responsible only for its own actions and what *ought* to be, Dasein, is responsible for the world, for what, in the most basic sense, *is*.

Before deriving Heidegger's conception of situated agency, we should consider a puzzle that he addresses. If Dasein tends to exist inauthentically, as a fallen "they-self," submerged in its circumstance, how does Dasein in the first place become aware of its inauthenticity and seize upon its potential for agency? The task seems especially difficult in light of this predicament: the defining feature of inauthentic Dasein is its lack of self-awareness. In the depths of its "downward plunge," inauthentic Dasein believes itself to be leading "a full and genuine 'life,' . . . for which everything is 'in the best of order' and all doors are open."[18] As Dasein plunges into "the groundlessness and nullity of inauthentic everydayness," this plunge "remains hidden from Dasein by the way things have been publicly interpreted, so much so, indeed, that it gets interpreted as a way of 'ascending' and 'living concretely.' "[19] How does Dasein free itself from this fix?

The root of the answer is that "inauthentic" Dasein is still *Dasein*. In other words, in existing inauthentically, Dasein does not become something else. It becomes dominated, rather, by a specific mode of being—one that *covers over* its true nature:

> On no account "do the terms 'inauthentic' and 'non-authentic' signify 'really not,' " as if in this mode of Being, Dasein were altogether to lose its Being. "Inauthenticity" does not mean anything like Being-no-longer-in-the-world, but amounts rather to a quite distinctive kind of Being-in-the-World—the kind which is completely fascinated by the "world" and by the Dasein-with of Others in the "they."[20]

18. Heidegger, *Being and Time*, 222.
19. Ibid., 223.
20. Ibid., 220.

Heidegger is careful not to claim that some people are thoroughly authentic and others thoroughly inauthentic.[21] Inauthenticity is rather a tendency of Dasein in each and every case. Human life is strung between an authentic relation to Being and a falling away from it. For the most part, we relate to each other and to the things around us in a superficial manner. We fall into conventional patterns of behavior. We spend our day following what's expected of people in our circle. We do our job as anyone else in our position would do it. We enjoy what "they" establish as pleasant and take pain in what "they" say is burdensome. But even the most extreme instance of Dasein's falling contains the seed of authenticity.[22] (In other words, even the most extreme conformism is never wholly thoughtless; it always involves some understanding of how to balance commitments in the situation at hand. To be "entirely" inauthentic would be to live a wholly mute and unintelligent life, to be something other than Dasein.) Although Dasein may, for the most part, remain buried in what "they" do, its authentic self has a way of surfacing in certain unpredictable moments.

Throughout his work, Heidegger gives different accounts of such moments. In *Being and Time,* he speaks of the fundamental experience of "anxiety" *(Angst),* which he elaborates as the "call of conscience."[23] Precisely

21. Although some interpreters read Heidegger as thus dividing human beings (Dreyfus, for example, refers to "the transformation from inauthentic to authentic existence" as a "gestalt switch"; cf. Dreyfus, *Being-in-the-World,* 317), the notion that some people are thoroughly authentic and others thoroughly inauthentic would undermine Heidegger's firm claim that Being-in-the-World is the basic mode of *all* human life. For if some people were thoroughly inauthentic, they would no longer exist as Being-in-the-World. They would behave in a purely predictable, formulaic way and thus would no longer be *Dasein.* If this were the case, moreover, a switch to authentic existence would be impossible. For no appeal to live authentically would have purchase with those who entirely lacked a sense for the shortcoming of their lives.

22. Mulhall thus interprets the "seed" of authenticity as the *"repressed but not extinguished* capacity for genuine individuality" (emphasis added; Stephen Mulhall, *Inheritance and Originality: Wittgenstein, Heidegger, Kierkegaard* [New York: Oxford University Press, 2001], 276). He likewise interprets inauthenticity as "the self which is in eclipse" (277).

23. Cf. Heidegger, *Being and Time,* ¶40, ¶54–60. As one might expect, "conscience," for Heidegger, is not some inner moral voice that commands certain actions. It is the call of Being-in-the-World, a call "which *we ourselves* have neither planned nor prepared for nor voluntarily performed." But "the call undoubtably does not come from someone else who is with me in the world." The call "comes *from me* and yet *from beyond me*" (Heidegger, *Being and Time,* 320). It speaks, moreover, without voice, conveying no particular command. And how could it, when it calls Dasein to nothing else than Being-in-the-World? If the call is to be interpreted as saying anything, writes Heidegger, it says only one word: "Guilty!" Dasein as Being-in-the-World, writes Heidegger, is essentially guilty—not because it has done something wrong, but because, whether

what experience these terms are meant to capture is notoriously vague, and Heidegger seems to have abandoned the concepts in his later writings. He turns instead to the way in which experiencing works of art and, in particular, poetry reveals to Dasein its authentic relation to the world.

But common to all of these fundamental experiences is that they reveal Dasein as defined by its relation to Being. Recognition of this basic relation is the key to Dasein's liberation from "fallenness" *(Being and Time),* "the public superficies of existence" *(What Is Metaphysics?),* or "captivity in that which is [i.e., beings]" *(The Origin of the Work of Art).* Anxiety, for example, brings Dasein face-to-face with itself *as* Being-in-the-World, thereby shaking it loose from the clutches of those entities in which it is prone to lose itself. Unlike fear, which is always fearful in the face of something threatening, anxiety, in Heidegger's special sense, is anxious in the face of nothing in particular: "Nothing which is ready-to-hand or present-at-hand within the world functions as that in the face of which anxiety is anxious."[24] Rather, *"the world as such is that in the face of which one has anxiety."*[25]

Anxiety thus brings us before our Being-in-the-World. It "tells us that entities within-the-world are of so little importance in themselves that on the basis of this *insignificance* of what is within-the-world, the world in its worldhood is all that still obtrudes itself."[26] The key insight is the insignificance of entities *in themselves,* that is, entities considered in abstraction from their place in the whole. Contrary to a familiar reading, "anxiety" does not reveal entities "within-the-world" as without intrinsic worth, as if our particular loyalties and commitments no longer mattered. Heidegger makes this clear: "If concern and solicitude fail us [in anxiety] this does not signify at all that these ways of Dasein have been cut off from its authentically Being-its-Self. As structures essential to Dasein's constitution, these have the share in conditioning the possibility of any existence whatsoever."[27] What anxiety reveals is that Dasein is always *more* than the totality of its concerns and commitments. This "more" is not some other entity, separate from the totality

---

consciously aware of it or not, Dasein, in its very mode of existence, is responsible for a world that it has not chosen or created. Living authentically involves owning up to this guilt.

24. Heidegger, *Being and Time,* 231.

25. Ibid.

26. Ibid.

27. Ibid., 308.

of one's involvements, but the world itself, the whole story in which one's family, friends, country, vocation, have meaning at all.

Anxiety, in other words, brings Dasein before the *nothing* of its existence. Nothing and no one in particular can teach Dasein how to live. Only Dasein's own self, its own destiny, can serve as guide. Thus emerges the sense in which the "call of conscience," the call to authentic life from the depths of anxiety, says nothing. The call, Heidegger writes, says *"nothing which might be talked about, gives no information about events."*[28] It says nothing *"currently useful about assured possibilities of 'taking action' which are available and calculable."*[29] And yet, the call does not convey an empty, meaningless "nothing," as if, in Dreyfus's terms, anxiety "wipes out all reasons for doing things"[30] so that "nothing is grounded and that there are no guidelines for living."[31] The call says nothing in that it calls Dasein to the single destiny that defines the totality of its life. Destiny itself, Dasein in the whole of its being, is *"at the same time* both the caller and the one to whom the appeal is made."[32] For this reason, the call "does not come from someone else who is with me in the world." The call "comes *from* me and yet *from beyond* me."[33] The call is therefore to be understood in sharp contrast to a private call that comes from the depths of my "inner conscience," "my conscience" in contrast to the word of "another." Kant interprets conscience in the latter sense—as the voice of pure practical reason in contrast to nature, society, or any external influence. To conceive of conscience in this way is to fall victim to the subject-object interpretation of the world. To say that the call comes from *me* is to say that it comes from my own Dasein, from Being itself, and not from the superficial understandings of *das Man:*

> When the they-self is appealed to [by the call], it gets called to the Self. But it does not get called to that self which can become for itself an "object" on which to pass judgment, nor to that Self which inertly dissects its "inner life" with fussy curiosity, nor to that Self which one has in mind when one

28. Ibid., 325.
29. Ibid., 340.
30. Dreyfus, *Being-in-the-World*, 316.
31. Ibid., 155.
32. Heidegger, *Being and Time*, 320.
33. Ibid.

gazes "analytically" at psychical conditions and what lies behind them. The appeal to the Self in the they-self does not force it inwards upon itself, so that it can close itself off from the "external world." The call passes over everything like this and disperses it, so as to appeal solely to that Self which, notwithstanding, is in no other way than Being-in-the-world.[34]

Although the call comes essentially "from me," its focal point, or messenger, could very well be another Dasein—a friend, for example, or a loved one. Heidegger does not overlook this possibility by placing the call in one's own Dasein. For Heidegger defines "one's own" ("individual") Dasein in contrast to *das Man,* not in contrast to others or to "external" influences. Heidegger's point is that the "messenger" of the call, whoever or whatever it is, acts strictly as an intermediary of Being—of the destiny that defines my own life and yours. What Heidegger's conception of the call forbids is that the caller be "another" who simply gives instructions to the person called—as if the caller's function were simply to implant some novel insight in the person called. In this case, the call would, indeed, be something alien. It would come from someone *else,* not from me.

That the call of Being may come through an intermediary, such as a friend, reflects that Dasein's own destiny, its guiding light is not "individual" in the sense that I have one and you have another: "Destiny is not something that puts itself together out of individual fates, any more than Being-with-one-another can be conceived as the occurring together of several Subjects. Our fates have already been guided in advance, in our being with one another in the same world."[35]

By revealing the world but not anything within it as the ultimate condition of Dasein and as the source of all meaning, anxiety pulls Dasein out of its absorption in what "they" do, bringing it "face to face with its Being-free for . . . the authenticity of its Being, and for this authenticity as a possibility which it always is."[36]

The full sense in which Dasein's authenticity comes with a certain agency rests on the relation of Dasein to the world. This relation is one of mutual dependence. On the one hand, Dasein is subordinate to Being. As Heidegger

34. Ibid., 318.
35. Ibid., 436.
36. Ibid., 232.

writes, "Being's poem, just begun, is man."[37] On the other hand, Being unfolds only through the action of Dasein. In this sense, "man is the shepherd of being."[38] This conception of human agency is perhaps best captured in Heidegger's reformulation of Being-in-the-World as *thrown-projection*.

Dasein as Sufferer and Author of Its Destiny

What might appear, at first glance, to be a piece of baffling jargon is a carefully chosen term of art. To understand what Heidegger means by "thrown-projection," we should consider each part in turn. To be "thrown" is to be acted upon, as when a ball gets thrown or a person gets shoved from behind. The passivity of "being thrown" captures the sense in which we find ourselves "always already" in a world, situated in a web of meanings that we have not created or chosen. But "thrownness" is not an event that we suffer at one point in time. It does not mean being cast, or "thrown," into a given society at the moment of birth. For when we speak in this way, we imagine an individual subject who must piece together its identity from a unique cultural "starting point"—from within the range of social options available to it. "Thrownness," thus understood, is a kind of mark, or alien influence on one's identity, that remains more or less prominent throughout one's life. Heidegger means something different. Thrownness is not an event that I have suffered in the past and that has left me with some lingering aftereffect. It defines my being *with equal force at any possible moment*. Dasein in each case "has *always already* been thrown" (emphasis added).[39] To be thrown means to lack sovereign power over one's own identity. It reflects the way in which any freely chosen stance toward one's own being is possible only in relation to the *unchosen*, in relation to a totality of involvements always already given. The moment we have any awareness of ourselves as thinking and acting beings, we are already participants of a shared destiny that none of us has created.

The meaning of being thrown emerges in light of the question: Who or what throws us? Properly speaking, the answer is no one and nothing. We

---

37. Martin Heidegger, "The Thinker as Poet," in *Poetry, Language, Thought*, trans. by Albert Hostadter (New York: Harper & Row, 1971), 4.

38. Martin Heidegger, "Letter on Humanism" (1947), in *Basic Writings*, 210.

39. Ibid., 236.

are thrown into the world by the *world*. Heidegger thus speaks of Dasein's being thrown by Being, or, what amounts to the same, being thrown by nothing (for Being is irreducible to a thing or collection of things). Dasein is thrown by nothing into nothing.

The complement to thrownness is "projection." It has to do with driving forward, as when we "project" a cannon ball or set out on a "project." Although "always already" thrown, Dasein is, at the same time, the "thrower," or author of its destiny. Projection captures the creative and dynamic dimension of Dasein. In virtue of its power to "project," Dasein's identity is open, never exhausted by any given structure. For any expression of Dasein's thrownness is at every moment shaped by how Dasein lives it out. Projection reflects the interpretive power of Dasein to transform its world.

As the hyphenated phrase "thrown-projection" indicates, "thrownness" and "projection" must be taken as two sides of the same phenomenon. Each defines the whole of Dasein. Roughly speaking, "thrownness" denotes the passive dimension of Dasein and "projection" the active. But this distinction demands qualification: although splitting the phenomenon is helpful for the sake of analysis, the halves must be reunited in the final interpretation. Neither thrownness nor projection can be understood without reference to the other. Moreover, even to speak of an active and a passive dimension of Being-in-the-World is somewhat misleading. The full force of thrown-projection, I believe, is that Dasein is entirely passive and entirely active. Because Dasein is defined by this contradiction, each term must be stated with full force, only to be negated by the other, and then, finally, comprehended together. Furthermore, the conception of agency that I aim to highlight would be lost if projection were simply equated with freedom and thrownness with its lack. It is not as though Dasein is partly determined (thrown) and partly free (projecting). Thrownness is just as essential to Dasein's agency as projection. Moreover, each term taken in isolation would, in its own way, imply a total lack of agency.

By highlighting the entirely passive, entirely active character of agency, I hope to read Heidegger in a way that avoids two familiar extremes—what we might call the "existentialist" interpretation of his thought, on the one hand, and the "communitarian" interpretation on the other. The "existentialist" reading neglects the implication of thrownness and maintains that Dasein is self-creative—defined, ultimately, by its own choices and actions rather than tradition or any enduring source.[40] This way of taking Heidegger finds its most famous expression in Sartre but also figures prominently in contemporary Anglo-American literature. Richard Polt, for example, suggests that according to Heidegger, "taking a steadfast stance [i.e., choosing to act resolutely] is the only sort of constancy that we can achieve."[41]

By contrast, the "communitarian" reading of Heidegger highlights the passive dimension of Dasein, relying on a certain construal of thrownness while overlooking projection. According to the communitarian reading, human beings are moved by large impersonal forces, whether the spirit of their times or some mysterious collective fate. At moments, at least, and especially in his later work, Heidegger himself appears to adopt this sort of fatalistic view. He slides most infamously toward denying human agency in his suggestion that the Nazis were not really responsible for their own actions but simply swept up in the "will to power," a certain mode of being that had come to dominate modern life, quite beyond human control, in the form of technological society and the "conquest of nature." But a balanced examination of Being-of-the-World reveals a more complex account of agency than either the "existentialist" or "communitarian" reading admits.

Not surprisingly, many interpreters advance a conception of Dasein as partly free, partly constrained, which appears to incorporate both projection and thrownness. In this vein, Polt qualifies what I have called his "existentialist" reading with the suggestion that "we are free, but our freedom is necessarily limited; our possibilities have to be drawn from our own heritage."[42] Hoffman similarly maintains that Dasein is free to choose, but "only within a certain spectrum of values and traditions."[43] Although the partly free, partly constrained notion of Dasein seems to acknowledge both pro-

---

40. Another version of this "existentialist" reading is that Dasein, although driven by circumstances beyond its control, still acts spontaneously, unburdened by any tradition or destiny. Without any reason for acting one way or another, Dasein instinctively responds to its current situation. In this sense, Dasein is radically free, in Dreyfus's terms, a "self-defining set of factors" (Dreyfus, *Being-in-the-World*, 300.)

41. Polt, *Heidegger*, 95.

42. Ibid., 103.

43. Piotr Hoffman, "Death, Time, Historicity: Division II of *Being and Time*," in *The Cambridge Companion to Heidegger*, ed. Charles B. Guignon (Cambridge: Cambridge University Press, 2006), 239.

jection and thrownness, it actually commits the same oversight as the existentialist and communitarian readings. It fails to recognize that projection and thrownness are two sides of the same phenomenon, not conflicting aspects of human life. To say that we are free *but only* within our "heritage" or "tradition" is to interpret thrownness as a limit to freedom rather than its source. According to the interpretation I offer, thrownness and projection are complementary dimensions of Dasein's situated agency.

Thrownness denotes the passive dimension of Being-in-the-World, that Dasein "is and has to be."[44] To state this necessity with full force: who I am, as this particular being, is determined in advance of any stance I might take toward myself. Nothing I do—no activity I assume, no role I take up, and certainly no belief I come to hold—will ever change my identity. To be thrown means "never to have power over one's ownmost Being from the ground up."[45] This "facticity" of Dasein, "that it is and has to be," recalls, in a general sense, the Kantian notion that the self is prior to the ends it pursues—that personal identity precedes any possible innovation or act of choice. However, there is a great difference that we should reiterate: Dasein's identity, its structure, has nothing to do with its being a *subject*. According to Heidegger's account, the *world* replaces the subject as that which unifies experience. Thrownness expresses the basic fact that any way of realizing my identity—in "concernful circumspection," "solicitous being-with," or explicit self-reflection—presupposes my Being-in-the-World. To state the same in terms of understanding: any way of understanding myself, at any moment, presupposes an understanding of the world, of *a way of life that I have not created or chosen*. My life, which is also to say the world in which I am engaged, inevitably precedes and conditions anything I might do to change it. Thrownness thus denotes Dasein's "fate" or "destiny," which is why it makes sense to recast my "Dasein," or "Being-in-the-World," as my life story.

For this reason, thrownness must be sharply distinguished from a sort of limit to one's options given the cultural or historical circumstances. According

44. Heidegger, *Being and Time*, 174.
45. Ibid., 330.

to this view, what we might call the sociological account, an individual gets "thrown," or born, into a "world," such as twentieth-century America, and then must piece together its identity from a certain range of activities. At first, the influence of habit and custom may direct the choice, but eventually, the individual may come, of its own, to prefer certain life options. Moreover, it may eventually create new options and thereby change, at least bit by bit, the culture in which it lives. This freedom qualified by cultural limits is precisely the sort of partly free, partly determined conception of human life that Heidegger rejects. Dasein is not some present-at-hand individual, or center of self-consciousness, that gets thrown into a present-at-hand "culture." Human existence is never the mutual interaction and compromise of two such entities. Any notion of the "individual versus culture" itself presupposes being-thrown into a world in which that distinction has some meaning.

Thrownness denotes the "submission" of Dasein to its world. Dasein *is* its world, and as a unity of meaning, its world is its destiny. All willing, acting, or making can do nothing more than realize what Dasein already *is*. We might begin to express the nature of this passivity by means of the following example: Consider someone who must write the final chapter of a book; or better yet, "part two." Imagine also that he did not himself write "part one," but that the book somehow fell into his hands. Now, if we imagine the author's freedom, at a given point in time, to accept or reject authorship, the example is imperfect. It will suffice, however, if we assume that, for reasons beyond his control, the author *must* write the next chapter. (He is so struck by the book's beauty, let us assume, that he is compelled to keep writing it.) In this situation, the author is clearly not free to write whatever he desires. Insofar as he must continue the story, any addition, any new creation, is determined by the standard of story itself, by the unity of meaning that the text expresses. The addition, even if we speak of it as a wonderful enhancement, is nothing other than the story *itself*. It would be a mistake, in other words, to consider each successive addition as a creative act that alters the original—as if one alien item after another got tacked onto the story and eventually contorted the original into something no longer itself. Each addition, whether the first, the tenth, or the hundredth, brings forth the same unity of meaning.[46]

46. This process should be obvious to any author or interpreter. (Ronald Dworkin, for example, has expressed this basic idea with respect to legal interpretation. In *Law's Empire* [Cambridge, MA: Belknap Press, 1986], he compares judges to authors of a chain novel.)

"Being-thrown" means that Dasein, at every moment, is a conditioned author of this sort. The fundamental difference, however, is that the unfinished text is Dasein *itself* expressed in everything it does, in its very way of life. Unlike the imaginary author who could relinquish the book he happened to find, Dasein has no choice but to live as the text that it always already is. At no point in time did Dasein choose the text of its life. As soon as Dasein can choose anything at all, it chooses on the basis of this text (whether conscious of it or not). Any attempt to detach itself from the story and to "rationally" dissect and determine its life from the "outside"—as an "impartial spectator," for example—is *itself* a part of the story. For once we come to see the so-called objective standpoint as simply one mode of rationality, rather than its primary realization, we must consider it a part of life, which, like all parts, attains its sense in light of the whole. Any particular act of "narration," any deed or new insight, whether explicitly intended to change Dasein's story or not, nevertheless presupposes the entire narrative— the "meaning of it all." This is especially conspicuous in cases where Dasein's action is unfitting—as when Dasein tries to transform its identity by adopting a radically new style. The "outstanding" character of such action— the "shock value"—emerges precisely in *contrast* to Dasein's "former" identity. This is to say, of course, that the "former" is not "former" at all. It constitutes the very being of the "new," which is really just a mirror image of the old—the old reflected in a shocking new guise. Such attempts of Dasein to create itself anew bring its thrownness all the more obtrusively to the fore. They indicate the way in which agency is not the mere exercise of will. To be an agent involves owning up to a pre-given destiny.

In what does this "owning up" consist? It means facing up to one's destiny but also *making* it one's own. Thrownness means that Dasein can only become what it already (implicitly) is. But despite its necessary structure, Dasein is at the same time undetermined, a "potentiality-for-being," the author of its fate. Dasein's potentiality-for-being is rooted in "projection"—the active, or creative, dimension of Being-in-the-World.[47]

To interpret projection, let us return, once more, to the example of the imaginary author. In defining the author's fidelity to the text (thrownness), we had to use terms such as "part two," "addition," "creation"—all of which

---

47. Heidegger, *Being and Time*, 185.

imply a capacity to bring about something new, to *"project."* Although the given text as a whole constrains what the author can write, its meaning remains open. The standard to which any addition must comply, the meaning of the whole, is never captured by a set of rules that could dictate the book's end in advance, or even prescribe a definite range of endings. The authority of the text still leaves to the author a *boundless responsibility*. The book's fate lies entirely in his or her hands. For each addition inevitably transforms the whole, however imperceptibly. To be sure, the addition must take its direction from the whole, but through the addition, the whole resonates in a new tone. The nature of a dramatic plot twist, the climax, or the denouement makes clear this part-whole interdependence and highlights the potentially radical character of a particular change. From the standpoint of the peak, everything looks different. Certain events fade into obscurity, others emerge as significant, and the meaning of it all finally comes forth, as if a curtain veiling the action had suddenly been torn aside. Such instances make obvious the transformative power of the author, despite his or her fidelity to the given text.

At every moment, Dasein, as thrown, is also projecting. Just as it has no choice but to be the text it always already is, so too does it have no choice but to write the next chapter.[48] Dasein is constantly "writing" simply in virtue of living its daily life, which, for the most part, has nothing to do with reflecting on *what* to write (i.e., how to live well). In this sense, the comparison to the imaginary author may be somewhat misleading. Insofar as Dasein is always projecting, whether aware of it or not, projection belongs to thrownness: "Dasein is thrown into the kind of Being which we call 'projecting.'"[49] As thrown, Dasein is subordinate to the lived story (world) in which it is immersed. Any action Dasein takes for the sake of any way of being is conditioned by the world. But the world (and thereby Dasein) is characterized by the same openness as the unfinished text in the example just given. In "projecting" itself upon a particular way of being, Dasein transforms the whole.

All understanding, Heidegger shows, is projective. Its nature is to develop itself, to move beyond what it achieves, and to redefine its condition

48. With respect to this responsibility emerges the sense in which Dasein is fundamentally guilty. Whether aware of it or not, Dasein has a boundless responsibility for its own, unchosen, destiny.

49. Heidegger, *Being and Time*, 185.

(the world). The most basic kind of understanding, of which all other kinds are modifications, is the practical wisdom involved in "'being able to manage something', 'being a match for it', 'being competent to do something.'"[50] Such understanding, as Heidegger shows, always pertains to a certain way of being—that "for-the-sake-of-which" Dasein "manages," "manipulates," or "puts to use." Understanding of this sort, Heidegger elaborates, has the character of a *possibility:* "Dasein is in every case what it can be . . . it is its possibility."[51] The meaning of such possibility must be distinguished from "possibility" in the familiar sense:

> Being-possible which Dasein is existentially in every case, is to be sharply distinguished both from empty logical possibility and from the contingency of what is present-at-hand, so far as with the present-at-hand this or that can "come to pass." As a modal category of presence-at-hand, possibility signifies what is *not yet* actual and what is *not at any time* necessary. It characterizes the *merely* possible.[52]

An example of what Heidegger calls the *"merely* possible" would be "I could cast a ballot in today's election primary, just as I could go (instead) to the grocery store or take a trip to China." These "possibilities" are actions that I relate to as present-at-hand, as mere options with no difference in meaning. They might as well be called options "x, y, and z." Moreover, the standard of their completion is something of which I'm consciously aware and treat as known (putting the ballot in the box, walking through the entrance, setting foot on Chinese soil). But since all of the possibilities lie ahead of me, there is no necessity that I realize any of them. In this sense, they are *"merely* possible."

Dasein's manifold ways of being are "possibilities" in a very different sense. On the one hand, they are not "free-floating;" they make a certain claim on Dasein in relation to other possibilities. They are not possibilities that Dasein could take up or let go with indifference. (It means something that one casts a ballot instead of making a grocery run.) On the other hand, the possibilities of Dasein are far more open than empty logical possibilities. For

50. Ibid., 183.
51. Ibid.
52. Ibid.

no fixed standard, or "plan," as Heidegger puts it, could define their completion. Understanding possibilities "has nothing to do with comporting one's self toward a plan that has been thought out, and in accordance with which Dasein arranges its Being."[53] Knowing how to be a family member or how to fulfill a vocation is not something that I fully grasp at some point and thereafter just apply to my actions—as if now I know it and merely have to decide whether to continue. Such "knowledge" is *itself* attained only through being applied, or lived out. The standard of its "validity," one might say, emerges through the activity itself—much in the same way as the standard of virtue, according to Aristotle, emerges through practice.

Thrownness implies that any way of being is defined by a standard, a certain structure that marks it off from other ways. The standard is given by the world, by the relational totality of possibilities and the ready-to-hand contexts to which they are linked. Although the standard is seldom the theme of explicit reflection, and never reducible to rules, it can be indicated in speech. As Hegel demonstrates, for example, one can give a definition, a *logos,* of what it means to be a family member by articulating the bond of immediate unity, distinguishing it from the bonds of civil society, and so forth. One could deepen the definition by pointing to examples of people who display the excellence of the role, who balance the competing claims of other spheres in a manner befitting of a "family man." Hegel's analysis shows that the family has a certain form, or basic character.

But according to Heidegger's account, the form itself is never fixed once and for all. It is always open to reconsideration in light of new situations, which require adaptation. Such adaptation inevitably comes to reshape the form.[54] So although living out a certain role means, in a sense, "applying" a

---

53. Ibid., 185.

54. For this reason, Dasein's various ways of being cannot be considered generic roles. The projective dimension of existence implies that any way of being is open to transformation; it bursts all cultural molds toward which it may tend. Nowhere does Heidegger suggest that authentic Dasein "must take over the average for-the-sake-of-whichs one has in one's culture, just like everyone else" (Dreyfus, *Being-in-the-World,* 157). When Heidegger writes that *das Man,* or "the they," is a fundamental dimension of Dasein, he means simply to point out that any way of being attains its full meaning in relation to how one might typically act. In other words, part of the significance of an action is the way in which it creatively diverges from what one would typically do in the situation.

given understanding to the concrete circumstance, the understanding is itself enriched by the application—enriched such that it can really be considered a "new" understanding. The new understanding, in turn, is itself open to further development. In this sense, understanding is "projective"—the working out of a possibility that is not extinguished, but kept open, maintained as a possibility, even in being actualized: "projection, in throwing, throws before itself the possibility as possibility, and lets it *be* as such."[55]

Although projection is most conspicuous in extraordinary situations that give rise to radically transformed understandings, Dasein is always projecting, even in moments that appear banal. As Heidegger constantly emphasizes, the simple act of maintaining a possibility, even in the most routine manner, means letting others pass by: Dasein "always stands in one possibility or another: it constantly is *not* other possibilities, and it has waived these in its existentiell [individual] projection."[56] Such "letting pass by" is not a simple rejection of one option in favor of another. For the very act of "letting pass by" redefines the possibility taken up. The latter is now something to which Dasein "holds on" in the face of "so and so." The new terms inevitably give the possibility a different cast, redefining its very being. Perhaps now it is something to be preserved all the more, perhaps something to be rejected.

Through projection, Dasein develops its possibilities—the various ways in which it can be. But in doing so, Dasein simultaneously develops its world: "With equal primordiality the understanding projects Dasein's Being both upon its "for-the-sake-of-which" and upon . . . the worldhood of its current world."[57] From the perspective of a significant transformation, Dasein's entire life (the world) rings out in a new voice. The particular transformation lights up and gathers together all the essential events and relationships, letting everything merely accidental fade away: "Wherever those decisions of our history that relate to our very being are made, are taken up and abandoned by us, go unrecognized and are rediscovered by new inquiry, there the world worlds."[58]

55. Heidegger, *Being and Time*, 185.
56. Ibid., 331.
57. Ibid., 185.
58. Heidegger, "Origin of the Work of Art," 43.

In such moments, the world, and thereby Dasein as a whole is clearly transformed, not simply altered as if Dasein had seized a new possession, tossed it in its hopper of capacities, and moved on as the selfsame being "plus one." As Gadamer puts it, Dasein is "suddenly and as a whole something else . . . in comparison with which its earlier being is nil."[59] This radical transformation comes with the awareness that Dasein's identity, what it now *is* cannot possibly be deduced or predicted from anything that has come before. The transformation reveals that any "before," any past, was without the terms that now define Dasein. Projection thus expresses the revolutionary dimension of Dasein's being, its capacity to lead rather than follow, to reshape its own identity—the world itself.

But what the world thereby becomes is nothing other than what Dasein has always already understood, however hazily. Or in other words: The sense in which an act is truly revolutionary, truly creative, depends on its ability to highlight a dimension of our world hitherto unnoticed. We're unable to say whether an act is creative until we can place it within the whole of our familiar orientations and show how it reveals that whole in a new light. What projection brings about is a new understanding of thrownness: "Projection is the opening up or disclosure of that into which human being as historical is already cast."[60] In this statement, the two terms emerge as one: thrownness directs projection, which, in turn, reveals thrownness. For this reason, Dasein's thrownness, or, its fate, is not a condition that pushes it from behind. The meaning of the world emerges only through Dasein's writing it.

We now can see how Dasein is at once entirely passive and entirely active. Thrownness and projection each characterize the whole of its Being-in-the-World. Thrownness does not simply express the constrained part of Dasein and projection the free. To think in these terms is to misconceive thrownness as something like the range of cultural options and projection as the ability to act and adapt within that range. Many interpreters conceive of thrownness and projection in this way, overlooking their fundamental unity. Hoffman, for example, writes that to recognize thrownness is "to acknowledge that my life can express itself [i.e., project] only within a certain

59. Gadamer, *Truth and Method,* trans. Joel Weinsheimer and Donald G. Marshall, rev. ed. (New York: Continuum, 1989), 111.

60. Heidegger, "Origin of the Work of Art," 73.

spectrum of values and traditions. I now realize that I cannot be 'anything and everything,' since my life is bound up with such and such (and not any other) historical roots."[61] But if we consider the world to be an open-ended text, an unfinished unity of meaning in contrast to "such and such" constraining factors, thrownness is not some limit to agency but the source of boundless creativity. It is the ultimate standard of Dasein's projection, the source of freedom. Correspondingly, projection is not simply a creative capacity that struggles to overthrow the given. It is rather a capacity for authorship that unveils a destiny already afoot.

In other words: the radical dependence of human life on fate emerges only in light of Dasein's *creativity*. The creative actor discovers this dependence not in light of his willing and striving being thwarted by external forces, but in light of how a truly creative act is *original*, how it *returns* Dasein to itself.

The unity of thrownness and projection implies that true creativity, and thus true power, the power over one's own Dasein and the world itself, is not to be found in the noisy self-assertive will that seeks to overcome the given and to create the world by its own design. Dasein's thrownness dooms these attempts to failure. What they tend to "create" is nothing but a shocking opposite of what is all too familiar. They leave the world itself essentially unchanged. Such attempts reveal the impotence of the will and the necessity of knowledge—knowledge understood as *interpretation*. True creativity and self-possession, being one's *own* in contrast to the way "they" are, involves *owning up* to the world—discerning one's destiny, which is always already afoot, and living in its light. That is why the call of conscience, the call to authentic life, says only one word: "Guilty!" Unlike Kant's conscience, which can be "guilty" only through a misstep of the will, Dasein's conscience is essentially guilty. For in every step of life, Dasein must bear full responsibility for the world—for a destiny it has not created but must constantly meet. Only in this way can Dasein be said to "create" the world: by writing a "new" interpretation that rings true to the world itself:

> All creation, because it is such a drawing-up, is a drawing, as of water from
> a spring. Modern subjectivism, to be sure, immediately misinterprets

---

61. Hoffman, "Death, Time, Historicity," 239.

creation, taking it as the self-sovereign subject's performance of genius . . . Pure projection [creation] comes from Nothing in this respect, that it never takes its gift from the ordinary and traditional. But it never comes from Nothing in that what is projected by it is only the withheld vocation of the historical being of man itself.[62]

By revealing man's "withheld vocation," projection attests to a memory in Dasein that reaches deeper than any past event or series of world affairs. It attests to a fate that Dasein at once carries out and uncovers—a fate that is, in this sense, *historical*.

Being and Time

Heidegger thus reinterprets thrown-projection as the "historicity"[63] of Dasein—that Dasein is at every moment handing itself down (projecting) a destiny (thrownness). Here emerges the fundamental connection between Being and *time*. Being, the world, Dasein—three ways of expressing our situated understanding of the whole (which is identical with the whole itself)— must be understood in terms of *time*. Heidegger concludes that Being itself *is* time. The claim is radical. Throughout the western tradition, at least, being has typically been understood in contrast to time. "To be," we tend to assume, means "to be always," to admit of no change, to be "eternal." But where is such being to be found? In a stone, or a diamond? After millions of years, won't even these things crumble? Even the most durable parts of the visible world seem ultimately fragile. More profoundly does human life. The very awareness that today will become yesterday, that what I do now, in the present, will become the past, seems to prove the utter futility of human action, the sovereignty of becoming, the rule of time and its covetousness. Being must be found elsewhere—in some place detached from the visible world and the realm of human affairs, detached from the sequence of

---

62. Heidegger, "Origin of the Work of Art," 73.

63. Macquarrie and Robinson render *Geschichtlichkeit* as "historicality," reserving "historicity" for Heidegger's less comprehensive term *Historizitat*, which refers to the study of history. But as "historicity" is the translation of *Geschichtlichkeit* that we find in most other translations of Heidegger, and in Weinsheimer and Marshall's edition of Gadamer's *Truth and Method*, I will use it here.

events that we call "world history." Being must be found in a God that stands apart from the world, in the immutable laws of nature, or in a realm of "things-in-themselves." Heidegger's claim that being itself is time challenges these traditional notions of being. It challenges the equation of being with motionless self-identity, with timelessness. Heidegger's claim also challenges our traditional notion of time. It challenges the equation of time with a sequence of moments, from past to future, in which things arise and perish. By interpreting being as the world and the world as the historicity of Dasein, Heidegger attempts to reconcile being with becoming, eternity with time.

His claim that being itself is time is crucial to his vision of human agency. It reveals that time is not some alien force to which Dasein is subject. Time must be understood in terms of Dasein's basic way of being. Time, in other words, answers to the question of *What* and *How* Dasein is. As we have seen, Dasein's "What" and "How" come together in thrown-projection. Time, as Heidegger understands it, is a reinterpretation of these terms. The reinterpretation is meant to correct the familiar view of time as a river that carries us, inexorably, from past to future. Understood in this way, time is an obstacle to our agency, indeed, the ultimate stumbling block. For despite our efforts to resist its current, time thrusts us forward. It wears us down, carries us to old age, and in the end, brings us to death. The flow of time thus appears to be the ultimate challenge to human agency. Heidegger attempts to show that it isn't. He does so not by denying the flow of time, but by interpreting it as superficial. Time flows from past to future, he shows, only in virtue of Dasein and its *own* "temporality." By locating time in Dasein's "temporality," Heidegger recaptures it as an expression of human agency.

Perhaps the best way of articulating Dasein's temporality, the time that defines Being and that drives the *flow* of time, is by considering Heidegger's claim that Dasein "*is* its past, whether explicitly or not."[64] To say that Dasein "*is* its past" certainly seems paradoxical in terms of our common conception of time. For when we say "past," we typically mean what was but no longer *is*—then, not now. Although the past may, of course, be preserved in memory, we consider it nevertheless separate from the current state of affairs, what is real, here and now, that is, the present.

---

64. Heidegger, *Being and Time*, 41.

In light of this conception of the past, we are liable to mistake Heidegger's novel claim for a familiar genetic account of human life—that Dasein "is" its past only in the figurative sense that its current identity is the end result of a sequence of past transformations. Each transformation, according to this account, brings Dasein one step further from its origin and one step closer to its present identity. Although such genetic accounts place great emphasis on "history" for understanding human life, they conceive of "history" as something separate from what exists here and now—as a sequence of past events leading up to the present but in no sense identical to it. Such accounts, in other words, conceive of history as a "thing of the past," as *dead*. Although we may, of course, remember history, and even, in a figurate sense, "relive" it, history is what *was* but now *is not;* it has no being, except for a sort of sham, shadowy being in the form of memory or imagination. According to such thinking, human life is a *product* of its past, but, strictly speaking, is not identical with its past. Even if the "past" is understood as a past event or sequence of events that continues to affect Dasein's present, this conception still fails to capture the sense in which Dasein, in the whole of its being, is defined by the past. For if the past is understood as an event with lingering aftereffects, then, in principle, at least, the past is escapable. Just as one can always rectify a bad start to the day, one can transcend the effect of any event considered as a particular occurrence.

To understand the sense in which the past is inescapable, the sense in which it defines Dasein's being at every moment, one must consider the past to be a reinterpretation of fate, or the text of one's life as a whole. The "past," as Heidegger conceives of it, is a reinterpretation of thrownness in terms of *time*. To say that Dasein "is its past" is another way of saying that Dasein is the world to which it belongs. The past is the unmovable stone of fate, the necessary structure of existence, the sense in which Dasein "is and has to be." In Heidegger's initial account of thrownness, the past is implicit in the phrase: "Dasein has always *already* been."[65] The "already" does not denote some former state that Dasein now is not. It expresses the fact that anything Dasein does here and now, in the present, presupposes a world that Dasein has not made or chosen. The past is the presupposition of Dasein's present activity. It "precedes" Dasein not in the sense of lagging

---

65. Heidegger, *Being and Time,* 236.

behind, but rather, in the sense of *predetermining* any innovation or new experience.

Heidegger's special sense of the "past" emerges in its unity with the *future*. Just as the past is not something lagging behind Dasein, the future is not something yet to happen. Both the past and future define the (present) moment *(Augenblick)* of Dasein's existence. The "future" is Heidegger's temporal reinterpretation of projection, which appears implicitly in the phrase "being-*ahead*-of-itself."[66] What Heidegger means by this crucial phrase emerges in contrast to our familiar understanding of "ahead" as "lying in front but not yet present." We say, for example, "don't get ahead of yourself," thereby warning that a future hope may not come to be. In this sense, we separate the future from the present. We understand the future not as constitutive of the present, but in terms of hopes and expectations to be actualized at some latter date.

By contrast, Dasein is "ahead of itself," or defined by the future, in the radical sense of being *essentially incomplete,* open to question, always "on the way." This incompleteness is tied to the creative dimension of action—that whatever I am doing in the moment, here and now, is inevitably reaching beyond the task or accomplishment, redefining my identity as a whole—my past, or thrownness. Although most action is relatively inconsequential, every moment is potentially transformative. Thus, to be "futural," in Heidegger's sense, is to be *at every moment* emerging, and hence "possible," to be above and beyond what I can possibly know, foresee, or be aware of: "The persistent endurance of Dasein's possibility is what we call *to be futural.*"[67]

But Dasein's movement beyond the past is at the same time a movement toward it. Any "new" creation is a repetition of the old—the ringing out of the past in a new voice. The future is grounded in the past; the past is grounded in the future. Heidegger prefers the latter formulation, but according to his conception of time, both are equally true. The advantage, however, of the latter is that it wards off the familiar, genetic sense of "historical"—that Dasein's present condition and future possibilities have been determined, or shaped, by a series of past events, each distinct from the former.

66. Ibid.

67. Martin Heidegger, *The Concept of Time*, trans. Ingo Farin with Alex Skinner (New York: Continuum, [1924] 2011), 48.

To say that Dasein's past is grounded in the future makes clear the special sense of "past" and "history" that defines Being-in-the-World. In the words of Krzysztof Michalski, we can understand this "past" as a past that has *never happened*. It is a past whose necessary complement is a future that will never be.[68] As the unity of past and future, Dasein is *historical:* Dasein is perpetually in motion, but moving toward no goal external to its very *self*.

Dasein's historical mode of being defines it as *simultaneously finite and eternal*. Given the traditional sense of "eternal," as unchanging and independent of human concern, Heidegger highlights Dasein's *finitude:* Dasein is finite in that it *becomes*. To become means never to reach a single identity that comprehends the whole of Being. Dasein is always, in each case, an open *perspective* on Being—a situated understanding of the whole and never the whole itself. Dasein's particularity, moreover, is not some deficiency that could somehow be filled. Dasein is always a particular "clearing," a *window* onto the whole, in virtue of its *future*—a future that Dasein itself tears open as it projects upon possibilities. In each and every instance of projection, in even the most subtle preservation of tradition (which is always preservation against other possibilities and thus transformative), Dasein is transcending itself. And every moment of transcendence, every step of Dasein's projection, harbors a magnificent possibility—a sunburst, which suddenly, in the twinkling of an eye, initiates a new world. Dasein is, in this way, the engine of its own finitude. Its becoming is a *power* and not simply a fate that its suffers.

But Dasein's becoming, its finitude, is impossible without *eternity*. Dasein is eternal in virtue of its *past,* in virtue of the fact that it always becomes *itself*. Any transformation, any change of identity, is such only as a *revelation:* to shatter the structure of one's "former" world is always to recapture it within a "new" whole. The "new" thus contains the old; it *is* the old, which means that the old never really "passes." "The oldest of the old follows behind us in our thinking and yet *it comes to meet us*" (emphasis added).[69] The past is inescapable. It defines the very possibility of the future. In each and every instance of becoming, and most clearly in moments of dramatic change, Dasein *repeats* itself anew. In this moment, in every moment, the

---

68. I take this formulation from Krzysztof Michalski's *The Flame of Eternity,* trans. Benjamin Paloff (Princeton, NJ: Princeton University Press, 2012). The book offers an illuminating account of Nietzsche's conception of time, which I have found of great aid to understanding Heidegger.

69. Heidegger, "Thinker as Poet," 10.

past returns. What comes back is not some event or series of events—as if, during a certain interval, the world runs its course and then begins once more, as if what I did today will, at some point, and endlessly, recur in the same order. To think of the past "returning" in this way is to mistake Heidegger's special sense of time, of the past and future that define Being, for a past that lags behind and a future that lies ahead. But *past* and *future* are not primarily points along a line. They define *each and every possible point*. Dasein is always *at the same time,* its past and its future. The past that returns is not an event or series of events but what is basic in everything that happens. What eternally comes back, ever anew, is the destiny of Being—the story in which events and sequences appear at all.

Death as the Key to Authentic Life

The unity of finitude and eternity defines Dasein's *mortality,* the essence of its situated understanding. Dasein is mortal in that it *dies.* But in what sense? Clearly "death" can only "befall" Dasein in a special way. For if Dasein dies, and if Dasein is nothing other than Being-in-the-World, then *the world itself* must somehow "die." The world, we must remember, is not a way station through which Dasein, with its own, independent course of life, passes—as if "Dasein" were a being who entered the "world" at birth, were "present" in that world for a time (the span from birth to death), and then departed to some other realm. Dasein *is* the world; and if Dasein dies, so too must the world. The phenomenon of death does not simply characterize this or that instance of human life; it inheres in the world, in the world's historical movement, its *becoming.* Heidegger's analysis of death is an extension of his analysis of thrown-projection, of the sense in which Dasein is at once the sufferer and author of its destiny. By finding death in the basic structure of Dasein, Heidegger recaptures death within life. He undermines the conception of death as an event that someday befalls us. Death is not primarily an event, but a way of being. At every moment, as Being-in-the-World, Dasein is dying (and returning to life).

Each term—finitude and eternity—is necessary for understanding death. If human life were "purely eternal," in the sense that in each and every moment it maintained a motionless self-identity, it could not be said to die. For what would it mean to die without being transformed? If, by contrast, human life were "purely finite," in the sense that in each moment it were something other, it could not be said to die either. For perpetual flux is simply the mirror image of stability. Change at every moment would be the endless repetition of the same, disconnected, meaningless nothing. Dasein can die only because its structure persists through change, only because it partakes, at the same time, of eternity and finitude.

In existing as "Being-in-the-World," as "thrown-projection," as eternal and finite, Dasein is "Being-toward-Death" *(Sein-zum-Tode)*. The death "toward" which Dasein moves is not an event that will someday occur. It is not (simply) the moment at which the body breaks down such that Dasein no longer shines forth in the eyes and gestures of a particular person. Such cases of "death," which Heidegger calls "demise" *(Ableben),* are expressions of death in the fundamental sense—the sense in which Dasein is *always* dying.

But does this "fundamental" sense not dissolve the phenomenon of death into something *abstract* in contrast to which the everyday experience of death, conceived as demise, is *concrete?* No, claims Heidegger. We might see things this way only because "the most concrete" is so deeply ours that it lies, for the most part, beneath our range of view. In reality, death, understood as "demise," becomes concrete, or something that we can experience as we do, *only on the basis of Being-toward-Death:* Dasein "can [meet a] demise only as long as it is dying. . . . In any 'typology' of 'dying', as a characterization of the conditions under which a demise is 'Experienced' and of the ways in which it is 'Experienced', the concept of death is already presupposed."[70] Being-toward-Death is the condition for the possibility of demise. As such, it is not a rival account to what we typically call "death," but the *source of its intelligibility.* Just as Heidegger undermines the subject-object relation by exposing it as a mode of Being-in-the-World (the relation of Dasein to something present-at-hand) so too does he undermine our familiar interpretation of death. Our familiar interpretation is not false, but partial. We mistake the partial understanding for the comprehensive precisely because the latter is so deeply ours. We "know" it in the way we live, but our ability to *explicitly identify it* lags behind.

In relation to Dasein's Being-toward-Death, the event of demise at once loses its distinctiveness and gains its meaning. The demise I might someday

70. Heidegger, *Being and Time*, 291.

meet is no different, in principle, from every moment of my life. For every moment is a potentially transformative step, a leap beyond what I can imagine or foresee, a turning point at which the world shines forth in a new light. And what more could my demise be? To think of it as the extinction of my consciousness, as its restoration in a new realm, as a dreamless sleep, is to make it *all-too-familiar*. Demise may involve any one of these things, but beyond all of them, demise is *death*. To think of death only in the terms just given is to envision the mere absence of particular stances we take toward the world and thus to *deprive death of its radical character*. Death permeates the whole of our lives, which is precisely what our familiar accounts overlook.

To think of death as lying ahead, moreover, is to deny death its *certainty*. Death, Heidegger insists, is certain. Common sense also admits a "certainty" to death, but it fails to sufficiently justify it. Everyone divines that "death is certain." But according to common sense, death is "certain" only *empirically*. By experiencing cases of "death" in *others*, we deem death "inevitable." But as with all such empirical claims, this so called certainty assumes that the "objective" order observed today will persist to the next, that tomorrow will be like yesterday, that the future will be like the past. But once Dasein conceives of the future as *separate* from the past, it destroys any basis for this assumption. For all you or I know, we could be the first cases of someone whose body never decays and who never experiences demise. "Death," conceived as something yet to come, is *uncertain*.

To be sure of its death, Dasein must *already* be dying. The future "I will someday die" must be happening *now*. Each moment, on this account— "each instant (and not just that one, as yet unknown, next Friday, or one hundred years from now) conceals within itself a potential end, a limit, an edge, a closing of the world as it is—and of a new beginning, of a departure beyond the borders of what is and can be known, the potential for a world that is radically new."[71]

Death is not an event but a *way of Being*, a way "which Dasein takes over *as soon as it is*" (emphasis added).[72] Death is thus a *possibility*—not a remote "possibility" that may or may not come to pass—something potential in contrast to actual—but a possibility *already afoot*—a possibility upon which

71. Michalski, *Flame of Eternity*, 64.
72. Heidegger, *Being and Time*, 289.

Dasein projects in every step of life. Death is Dasein's *basic* way of being, the way that defines its life as a whole.

In this sense, death is a special possibility: it is not the possibility of being this or that (being a father, a workman, a philosopher, a citizen), but *the essence of possibility itself*.[73] Death expresses how Dasein drives the movement of the world, how Dasein holds the world *open*. Death is thus "a possibility in which the issue is nothing less than Dasein's Being-in-the-World." Death "is the possibility of no-longer-being-able-to-be-there"; for Dasein always belongs "somewhere" else. Its "there"—or present situation—is always on the way, always moving beyond its structure.[74]

Heidegger's special conception of death must be distinguished from familiar interpretations that reduce death to an oncoming event. Heidegger does not, of course, deny the significance of the event of death (or, in his terms, demise). One's impending death, in this sense, might shake one loose from the clutches of *das Man* and be the occasion for authentic life. Richard Polt points to this possibility: "The sense of impending death is known for making one's life flash before one's eyes: in this moment one reviews one's life-story as a whole."[75] But the event of demise, however meaningful, does not reach the sense of "death" in "Being-toward-Death." Polt reduces the latter to the former in reading "Being-toward-Death" as living every day as if you might die *tomorrow*:

> If you knew that this was the last day of your life, what would you do? Look for pleasures? Rob your neighbor's house? Spend time with your family? Pray? Write poetry? Read Heidegger? The answer to this question says a lot about who you are—what you care about the most and how you really want to live. . . . As long as readers keep in mind this phenomenon of facing up to mortality, they will be able to follow Heidegger's meticulous analyses [of death].[76]

However descriptive of demise and its significance, this passage overlooks Heidegger's conception of death in two key respects. First, it reduces the es-

---

73. Ibid., 294.
74. Ibid.
75. Polt, *Heidegger*, 86.
76. Polt, *Heidegger*, 85–86.

sence of life, "what you care about most and how you really want to live," to an explicit *account* you might offer in response to a hypothetical scenario. (This reduction runs contrary to Polt's own instructive account of how Dasein is not defined by its explicit awareness.) Second, it conceives of "death" primarily as an oncoming event. Being-toward-Death, according to Polt, means facing up to the possibility that "death," in the sense just given, could materialize at any moment—that the possibility lurking "out there" could become actual here and now. His reading overlooks Heidegger's claim that "dying is not an event,"[77] and that Dasein, whether explicitly aware of it or not, "is dying as long as it exists."[78]

Furthermore, Polt's understanding of "Being-toward-Death" does not find expression in Heidegger's preceding analyses of Being-in-the-World and thrown-projection. And as Heidegger insists, Being-toward-Death is nothing but a reinterpretation of these preceding terms.[79] According to Polt's reading, Being-toward-Death is just one stance toward life among others, not the essence of Dasein in each and every moment. According to Heidegger, death permeates the whole of Being-in-the-World.

Piotr Hoffman similarly interprets Heidegger's conception of death as an event lurking out ahead of Dasein. His interpretation is striking in that it likens Heidegger's conception of death to Descartes's "evil demon": "For both philosophers [Descartes and Heidegger], the human individual is thrown back upon his own self by a sense of total powerlessness and vulnerability in the face of an ultimate threat (of, respectively, the evil demon and death)."[80] In likening Heidegger's notion of death to Descartes's evil demon, Hoffman conceives of death as something decisively *alien* to Dasein. And from this conception of death, Hoffman derives Dasein's "total powerlessness." Hoffman's connection of death to lack of power is a sharp contrast to the interpretation I suggest: that death, for Heidegger, is the very essence of authenticity and freedom.

The possibility of death, in Heidegger's sense, emerges in anxiety. Death "*is* essentially anxiety," a reinterpretation of anxiety, which highlights the

77. Heidegger, *Being and Time*, 284.
78. Ibid., 295.
79. Ibid., 293.
80. Hoffman, "Death, Time, Historicity," 226.

dynamism of Dasein (emphasis added).[81] Death is the flash in which one's life as a whole shines forth as *inexhaustible,* as always *more* than one can possibly know. Death is thus the key to authentic life. It pulls Dasein out of its submersion in beings, revealing its fundamental relation to Being, to the whole, to *nothing.*

Being-toward-Death means stepping into the nothing of existence. Heidegger's conception of nothing does not signify the mere absence of structure. Least of all does it signify the empty "nothing" of which we conceive by removing the totality of things around us, by imagining pitch dark, a dreamless sleep, a "night in which all cows are black." To imagine nothingness in this way is to imagine the *absence* of all things present-at-hand, which is really just the mirror image, or formal opposite of their presence. The "nothing" that defines death is not presence or absence or emptiness. Nothing reflects the relation of Being and beings, of our destiny and its particular expressions. Nothing thus admits of being spoken, even if no account will ever say it all.

To authentically project one's self upon death is to *recognize and live up to* the sense in which Dasein is responsible for the destiny of Being—a destiny that unfolds through Dasein's own action. For the most part, Heidegger points out, we relate to death *inauthentically.* We treat death as an event that will someday befall us, but not now. By deferring it to a future detached from the present, we keep death at arm's length. We act as if death were like any other event (present-at-hand) for which we might prepare. In our attempts to postpone it or to arrange properly for its arrival, we lapse into an excessive concern about death—one that masquerades as being "responsible," but which, at bottom, is an *evasion* of one's "ownmost" responsibility for the world—for the destiny of Being and its boundless possibility. When we defer death to "sometime later, but not now," we forget that the meaning of anything we might plan for today could, in the blink of an eye, be dissolved in the historical whirlwind of the world.

Authentic Being-toward-Death is nothing other than a genuine response to anxiety, a response to the call of conscience that summons Dasein to be

---

81. Heidegger, *Being and Time,* 310. Heidegger's discussion of thrown-projection, which explicitly deals with the dynamism of Dasein, decisively prepares his analysis of death. It is no accident, therefore, that his treatment of death appears on the heels of his analysis of thrown-projection.

itself—to be primarily unsupported by this or that role or relationship, but rather by its own life as a whole:

> [Authentic Being-toward-Death] *reveals to Dasein its lostness in the they-self, and brings it face to face with the possibility of being itself, primarily un-supported by concernful solicitude, but of being itself, rather, in an impas-sioned* **freedom toward death**—*a freedom which has been released from the Illusions of the "they," and which is factical, certain of itself, and anxious.*[82]

Death rescues us from submersion in the distracted, formulaic way in which "they" act, revealing our relation to Being, to the standard of authentic ac-tion: "When one becomes free *for* one's own death, one is liberated from one's lostness in those possibilities which may accidentally thrust them-selves upon one; and one is liberated in such a way that for the first time one can authentically understand and choose."[83]

Heidegger thus presents a revolutionary conception of death. What is typically viewed as an event that we all suffer in the end, as a limit to our self-possession—as the *ultimate* limit—is actually the expression of our agency, the possibility of authentic *life*. To die, writes Heidegger in a later essay, is "to be *capable* of death as death" (emphasis added). Death is a capac-ity and not simply an event that we suffer: "Mortals dwell in that they initi-ate their own nature—their being capable of death as death—into the use and practice of this capacity."[84] Death is not merely an end but a moment of redemption from fallenness, a moment of *rebirth:* in Being-toward-Death, "Dasein guards itself against falling back behind itself . . . It guards itself against 'becoming too old for its victories' (Nietzsche)."[85]

To fall "behind itself" and into the world is the persistent affliction of Dasein. To "fall behind" is to experience how the moments that once reflected the world itself, that brought us to our knees before the majesty of Being, dwindle to past events within a sequence that we mistake for our biography. To "fall behind" is to suffer today's becoming yesterday, to suffer the flow of time in which we grow "too old" for our victories. As much as

---

82. Heidegger, *Being and Time*, 311.
83. Ibid., 308.
84. Martin Heidegger, "Building Dwelling Thinking," in *Poetry, Language, Thought*, 148.
85. Heidegger, *Being and Time*, 308.

we long for their return, and as much as we attempt to "relive" them in memory, they slip further away. Even our longing *itself,* the more intense and sentimental it grows, becomes all the more half-hearted and empty. For the things we remember and long to recover retain only a shadow of their original being. We "recover" them not as living possibilities, not as the shimmering moments they once were, but as pale representations, as nothing more than lifeless relics of a past that lies behind. From this predicament, death redeems us. In a flash, it brings us face to face with the nothing of our life as a whole; it reveals the eternal source of the events that run their course in time and thus restores the past.

The Moment Is Now

In authentic Being-toward-Death, suggests Heidegger, we gain access to primordial *temporality*—the unity of past and future that defines the world as historical. For the most part, however, we experience time in a different way, as split into "past," "present," and "future," each separate from the other. We spend "today" looking forward to "tomorrow," with a backward glance, here and there, at "yesterday." The present moment—today—is all that really *is,* but we spend it preparing for tomorrow, for a future not yet actual, but "in the works." What guides our activity *today* (our vision of the future) is something decisively separate from it—something that concerns us, but not immediately. Today is an "investment" in the future but not the future itself. The future has yet to come, and our investment may or may not yield fruit.

Today is similarly detached from yesterday. What we are up to right now, in our planning for the future, may be limited (or enabled) by yesterday's deeds, but "to dwell on the past is pointless." For the past is *gone.* It won't come back, and we should not brood over it lest we paralyze our current plans. We look back on the past as a source of inspiration for the future, but we otherwise forget about it and move on. Thus, we experience the flow of time—as a cycle of expectation, achievement, and forgetting that ends, finally, in death—the last event in the sequence of one's biography.

Authentic Being-toward-Death reveals this sequential understanding of time as *superficial.* We come to see that time is more than a passage from one moment to the next. That time flows is not, of course, an illusion that conceals some other "real" time. Time does flow, and we experience its passage as meaningful. It makes a difference that the first inning of a ball game moves to the second, that we finish the race before the next guy, that we grow "too old" for our victories. Heidegger does not suggest that we cease to keep time or to pay attention to its passage. But what he does seek to point out is that time's passage would not happen without time in a *deeper sense*—a sense that, for the most part, remains hidden. We could not look forward to a future and backward at a past without understanding time—past, present, and future—as a *unity*—as the answer to how the destiny of Being unfolds.

By pointing out this unity, Heidegger seeks to reorient our practice. He seeks to shift our attention from the familiar cycle of expecting, planning, and forgetting to its *basis*—to the destiny of Being for which we, as its authors and sufferers, are responsible. Heidegger seeks to remind us that time does not flow independent of us, independent of how we live our lives.

That Dasein drives the flow of time is the ultimate expression of human agency. It implies that how we live today—here and now—in this moment—the one and only—is the most urgent question. And only on the basis of a thoughtful answer, one that will always be provisional, unsettling, and in need of improvement, can we plan wisely for tomorrow.

In pointing to the time that defines Dasein, Heidegger seeks, in particular, to curb a certain attitude familiar in our times: the obsession with planning for the future, drawing up blueprints, and living for tomorrow. The attitude is well captured by our feverish attempts to extend life, to discover a "fountain of youth" that will stall the body's decline, to find a new diet that we can trade for another twenty years of breath—as if life could be measured in breaths or days or months or years. Once we define the clock of our life in such terms, our goal must be *never* to "die." For conceived as a sequence of moments, time is in principle infinite. In relation to the infinite expanse of time, what difference do ten years make, a hundred, a million? The longing for any addition short of infinity is ultimately pointless. And the very longing for "infinity" has no rational basis. For to separate past and future is to destroy any guarantee that the order which has preserved our life today, will persist tomorrow. (For all we know, some unforeseen event—a meteor smashing the earth to pieces—could destroy everything we took to be secure.) The longing for life extension is self-defeating.

But the longing is misguided in a far deeper and altogether different sense—a sense to which Heidegger alerts us. Even assuming that we *could* "live forever," in the sense that our bodies remained impervious to harm, impervious, even, to earthquakes, lightning, and meteors, *we could not outstrip death.* For death defines the whole of life. In our feverish attempts to postpone the event of demise, we distract ourselves from Being-toward-Death. We flee the necessity of coming to grips with our "ownmost possibility." Life, Heidegger insists, is *too short* for such postponement. Life is too short because *there is no time*—no time, at least, that could be counted or measured, spent wisely or wasted. "The time is at hand."[86] Right now, the past and future are happening. Destiny is calling, and whether we choose to or not, we must somehow hand it down.

Stepping back, we might restate the difference between the time that defines Dasein and time as we typically understand it as follows: we typically think of the "present" as a certain interval in time, for example, the year 2012. (In principle, the interval is infinitely divisible, but the unit of a year may serve as an example.) Lagging behind this interval is an infinite sequence of intervals in the "past" (2011, 2010 . . .), and going ahead of it is an infinite sequence to come. When we speak of "a long time ago," in this sense, we mean many years back. "Long" in this context denotes a large quantity of time that has elapsed. We can thus speak of the "temporal distance of 2,500 years" between our society and ancient Athens.

By contrast, the time that defines Dasein is the sort of time captured in expressions such as "the time is at hand," or "there is no time." Time in this sense denotes the character of a situation rather than some measurable interval within a boundless sequence. "Past," "present," and "future," as structural elements of Dasein, are dimensions of time in what we might call the

86. Michalski, *Flame of Eternity*, 62. A remarkable account of this conception of time, as interpreted by Nietzsche, and in relation to the Apocalypse, is offered by Michalski in his Chapter 5, "The Time is at Hand." His account of time, as derived primarily from Nietzsche, has been a profound influence on my reading of Heidegger.

"situational" sense. Heidegger teaches that Being-in-the-World must ultimately be understood in terms of this sort of time.

We should consider how situational time admits of its own kind of
"temporal distance." For example, when we speak of "a world change," or
"revolution," we imply a certain gulf between the world now (in the present) and what it once was (in the past). This distance clearly transcends any
quantification and can be experienced without any awareness of measurable time having passed. The greatest changes, we might say, happen in the
"twinkling of an eye."[87] Moreover, the notion of "having passed," and
hence, the possibility of measuring *how much* time has passed, emerges
only in light of such a measureless rift in situational time. Once I become
aware of a "world change," I can conceive of a past and go about measuring
the interval of time that has since elapsed. If it turns out, however, that I
was mistaken about the change, and that the world has, in fact, maintained
its identity, I would no longer have any basis for asserting that time had
gone by.

Heidegger's temporal interpretation of thrown-projection is a special
conception of situational time, namely the unity of past and future that
defines any possible moment. Dasein's historicity—the basic being-in-
motion of human life that defines every moment as the unity of past and
future—is the condition for the possibility of representing the "past," that
is, conceiving of a sequence of events. As Heidegger puts it: Dasein's "historicity" is "prior to what is called 'history' . . . only on the basis of [Dasein's
historicity] is anything like 'world history' possible or can anything belong
historically to world history."[88] In other words, only in light of Dasein's
destiny and how it unfolds does it become possible to conceive of something "having happened," to draw distinctions among events, to place
them in order, and thereby to articulate a "world history." Such a history,
moreover, is always precarious, always open to realignment in light of Dasein's essentially temporal existence. In the terms of Michalski, the force of
human life, in its endless, self-propelled motion, tears the past from the

87. The German *Augenblick,* or "moment," which literally means "the twinkling of an eye,"
well captures this sense of time. It should be clear, moreover, by reference to our everyday absorption in action. When, at some point, a distraction directs us toward the clock, our awareness refutes the number of hours gone by. It denies the very flow of time.

88. Heidegger, *Being and Time,* 41.

future ever anew. In every moment, Dasein is reordering what has been and redefining what can be.

The unity of throwness and projection, of past and future, emerges in Heidegger's own interpretation of the world. On the one hand, Heidegger's philosophical statement depends for its meaning on what is given, namely, the world itself—the world as experienced "preontologically" in Dasein's everyday life. Only on the basis of this practical awareness can Dasein articulate the world in terms of relations that make sense. In abstraction from the actual world, Heidegger's terms such as "with-which," "in-order-to," "for-the-sake-of," and so on, would fall flat. The interpretation, one might say, is entirely predetermined by the phenomenon of the world itself.

Although Heidegger's interpretation is a sketch of what is pre-given, it is also more: in pointing to the world, Heidegger not only represents it as best he can, but, at the same time, transforms it. By finding the right words to characterize the world, the Being of beings, words that had never before been spoken, Heidegger's interpretation paves the way for a new stance toward things, thereby transforming the world itself. Consider, for example, how his philosophy might transform the practice of someone stuck in the framework of detached reason. We might imagine a person who attempts to live by the standard of utility or Kantian morality and spends an excess of time calculating, reckoning, or scrutinizing his motives. Upon reading Heidegger and realizing that his everyday loyalties are intelligible parts of his world, not sentiments formed by blind habit, such a person could not help but pursue them in a new spirit, to consider them potential sources of guidance rather than parochial impediments to judgment. In thus assuming a new stance toward life, one gains a new perspective on the whole—a turning point from which to view the world in a new light. In this way, Heidegger's own philosophical interpretation is determined by thrown-projection. It presupposes an understanding it brings to be.

The unity of throwness and projection is the key to understanding Heidegger's account of human agency. It is helpful to consider how agency would be lost if human life were characterized by only one of the two terms. "Pure throwness," for the sake of argument, would mean something like complete subordination to a destiny written in the stars. In this case, human beings would live meaningful lives, and perhaps distinctive ones, but they would be the mere playthings of the gods and in no sense free.

"Pure projection" would, in a sense, reverse matters. It would imply an utterly chaotic universe upon which human beings would impose all order. In such a world, human beings would be free from any transcendent standard of action, but life would be wholly meaningless. Without any standard to guide willing and creating, human life would collapse into an endless spiral of the same spontaneous action, each deed as fleeting and insignificant as the next. In such a world, human beings would lack any self-possession. They would be the focal points of arbitrary deeds and in no sense agents.

The conception of Dasein as thrown-projection avoids each of these two extremes. As thrown, "every Dasein has been factically submitted to a definite 'world'—'its world.'"[89] This "submission," however, means that Dasein has a guiding light, a destiny, a standard for action. But the destiny emerges only though Dasein's attempts to fulfill it. Human life simultaneously partakes of making and discovering. Through its own action, Dasein brings to light the source of its being. In this sense, Dasein is truly self-directed.

Heidegger and Situated Understanding

In Heidegger's different formulations of Being-in-the-World—as thrown-projection, Being-toward-Death, the unity of past and future—emerges the phenomenon of *situated understanding*. The "life circumstance" from which we understand, judge, and act—the *situation* from which we can never detach ourselves—is not any particular community, or culture, or set of customs, but the *world*. The world, as we have seen, takes us far beyond the concept of "social context," for which "situation" might easily be mistaken. The world is the Being of beings. It answers to the question of why there is something rather than nothing. For only as parts of the world do the things with which we deal and the things on which we reflect exist as the things they are. As the source of beings, and as irreducible to any of them, the world is, in a sense, *nothing*. The world is nothing we can see or touch or

89. Heidegger, *Being and Time*, 344.

experience before our conscious gaze. It is not "the tangible and perceptible realm in which we believe ourselves to be at home."[90] The world is the destiny of Being expressed in the way we live. The world is thus a meaningful "nothing"; it is a "nothing" that we can (and must) interpret. And in the very act of interpreting the world—in our words and actions—we bring it to be. Through our interpretations, we discover that the world is not some fixed destiny written in the stars, but a destiny that we *unfold*. The unfolding of the world is *history* in the essential sense. History is not, primarily, a series of events, one after the next, but the circular movement of Being and beings, of our destiny and its particular expressions. Only as parts of this movement do events and sequences emerge at all.

In light of Heidegger's notion of the world, our situation might seem to be a strange place. The world he describes is not a location in three-dimensional space. It is nothing we can see, touch, or imagine. It is not any particular practice, custom, or tradition. It unfolds temporally but never passes. How can Heidegger defend this conception against the testimony of our lives? Is the "real world" not the one extended in space, the world we can see with our eyes and grasp with our hands? Is it not the world of our everyday occupations and roles and projects? Is it not the world of our bodies and their limitations—not least their being vulnerable to demise? Does not the gradual decline of our bodies attest to the passage of time, to the world's unfolding in a sequence of moments that we can measure? In light of these undeniable features of our experience, we might suppose that Heidegger's world is an abstraction. But to draw this conclusion would be to miss his claim. Heidegger does not mean to deny the sensible "world," the significance of our everyday commitments, the presence of our bodies, or the flow of time. All of these are parts of the world. But they are only parts. As such, they presuppose the whole. Detached from the world, claims Heidegger, none of these parts could be. And this is his radical claim. It is radical in relation to our misinterpretations, which mistake parts of the world, such as things present-at-hand, for the whole. Heidegger's conception of the world seeks to dispel such confusion. It does so by showing that what we take to be the whole is really part of a more comprehensive awareness. The "more comprehensive" is such in that it makes better sense of the parts than rival accounts. So despite appearance, Heidegger's conception

90. Heidegger, "Origin of the Work of Art," 43.

of the world is by no means abstract. It makes sense of the many articulations of life that we call "concrete."

Stepping back, we may spell out the situated conception of understanding as follows: take any human activity—from the most basic use of a hammer or a pair of shoes, to the most rigorous scientific analysis of things present-at-hand. Whatever the activity may be, one can say that it points beyond itself to a certain way of life as a whole—to the world, to our situation writ large. Although a way of life is, for the most part, lived unconsciously, that is, without explicit reflection upon its ultimate point, it nevertheless embodies an *understanding*. This understanding is revealed by the simple fact that when our absorption in life is interrupted, when something goes wrong, or perhaps when someone asks us what we are up to, we can give an account in terms of purposes ("in-order-to"), ends (for-the-sake-of"), and ultimately, a certain story ("our world"). Although the account will never fully represent the nuances of the story as actually lived, the account will still make sense to those who are there, living *with us,* or to those who can relate to similar concrete experiences. The basic implication of Being-in-the-World is that our more or less comprehensive understandings of life, in light of which our particular activities make sense, are not subjective or cognitive but embodied in life itself.

Because any particular activity points to some such vision of the whole, any activity can be questioned, revised, or developed in light of that vision. And by revising or developing any particular understanding, we thereby develop our understanding of the whole that oriented us in the first place. According to Heidegger's account of thrown-projection, we are at every moment developing our particular understandings, simply in virtue of living out certain ways of being and letting others pass by. Through such "projection," we are continuously working out the comprehensive understanding into which we are (always already) "thrown." This development may be for the better or for the worse. It may be an expansion of our horizon or a contraction. Prudence would say that we never can know for sure which horizons, or perspectives, are superior to others. Without any fixed criteria in hand, evaluation is difficult. It must be added, however, that once we become aware that our horizons embody a certain story and that the story is essentially open, we come to recognize that any transformation must be understood in terms of a better or worse articulation of the whole. In light of this recognition, we place

ourselves in a position to discriminate intelligently among competing interpretations of the world and to offer more illuminating ones ourselves.

The implication of thrown-projection is that any world change is either
a revelation or concealment of the same. In response to Nietzsche's suggestion that all truth is human creation, that all world views are arbitrary con-
structions of the will to power, which throws up horizons and tears them
down, Heidegger conceives of truth as "unconcealment."[91] Although he
admits a creative, or "projective," dimension of understanding and thereby
maintains that truth is not merely the reflection in speech of a fixed order,
Heidegger insists that creation is a sort of midwife that allows an implicit
truth to emerge. Thus "truth" has a double meaning: truth of the particular
being and truth of Being. It is notable that Heidegger connects "unconceale-
ment" to the Greek *aleitheia*—the common word for "truth," but also signify-
ing "un-forgetfulness," or, less awkwardly, "recollection."[92] Thrown-projection
implies that "thinking holds to the coming of what had been, and is remem-
brance." This insight points to a sense in which situated understanding is
consistent with universal truth—an idea that Gadamer develops and that
we will take up in the following chapter.

91. Heidegger, *Being and Time*, ¶44.
92. Ibid.

4

The Role of Prejudice in the Study of History

Gadamer on Past and Present

Perhaps the most striking aspect of Gadamer's *Truth and Method* (1960) is his defense of prejudice *(Vorurteil)*. In attempting to revive prejudice from its disparaged status, Gadamer seems to follow in the footsteps of Burke. On the surface, the similarities between the two thinkers are remarkable. Both use "prejudice" to denote the influence of tradition. Both defend prejudice against those Enlightenment thinkers who impugn its legitimacy. But Gadamer, unlike Burke, connects prejudice to reason. Prejudice, Gadamer writes, is a "condition of understanding," and certain prejudices are "productive of knowledge."[1] Whereas Burke defends prejudice in terms of "sentiment" and "pleasing illusion," Gadamer defends it in terms of *truth*.

In connecting prejudice to truth, Gadamer's real predecessor is not Burke but Heidegger. Although Heidegger uses the term "prejudice" *(Vorurteil)* rarely and without fanfare, he tends to use it with positive emphasis— typically as a synonym for "presupposition." Gadamer takes up and develops this meaning. He does so with particular reference to Heidegger's account of

---

1. Hans-Georg Gadamer, *Truth and Method,* trans. Joel Weinsheimer and Donald G. Marshall, rev. ed. (New York: Continuum, [1960] 1989), 280.

thrown-projection. As "thrown," Dasein always interprets itself (or any other entity) in light of what Heidegger calls a "preunderstanding," or "fore-having," which is what Gadamer means by "prejudice." But this "preunderstanding," or "prejudice," is constantly being worked out as Dasein "projects" itself upon it—whether explicitly, in thematic interpretation (e.g., Heidegger's study of being), or implicitly, in the course of everyday life. Following Heidegger's distinction between the world and entities within-the-world (or Being and beings), Gadamer uses "prejudice" in a double sense. He sometimes speaks of one's comprehensive "prejudice," or *horizon,* and other times, of one's particular "prejudices." Any act of understanding involves working out both layers of prejudice—our preunderstanding of the particular entity, and our preunderstanding of life as a whole. As our understandings are inseparable from the things themselves, "prejudice," for Gadamer, is an ontological concept. The to-and-fro movement of our particular prejudices and our comprehensive prejudice (horizon) is the play of reality itself, what Heidegger calls the "historicity" of Dasein.

This fundamental movement is what Gadamer means by "hermeneutics," a term traditionally confined to the interpretive understanding of texts (in particular the Bible). The familiar principle of literary hermeneutics, as summarized by Gadamer, is that the meaning of a text as a whole "guides the understanding of the particular passages: and again this whole can be reached only through the cumulative understanding of the passages."[2] The "anticipation of meaning in which the whole is envisaged becomes actual understanding when the parts that are determined by the whole themselves also determine this whole."[3] Although Gadamer is interested in how to understand texts, his primary aim is not to develop the method of literary hermeneutics. His aim is rather to point out the "hermeneutics" of human existence. "Hermeneutics," for Gadamer, expresses the sense in which *life itself* is the unfolding of a certain understanding of Being:

> Heidegger's temporal analytics of Dasein has, I think, shown convincingly that understanding is not just one of the various possible behaviors of the subject but the mode of being of Dasein itself. It is

2. Ibid., 176.
3. Ibid., 291.

in this sense that the term "hermeneutics" has been used here. It denotes the basic being-in-motion of Dasein that constitutes its finitude and historicity, and hence embraces the whole of its experience of the world.[4]

The Relation of the Human Sciences to the Self-Understanding of Dasein

In *Truth and Method,* Gadamer demonstrates how the hermeneutics of Dasein plays out in the human sciences, particularly in the study of historical tradition. His basic question is the following: How does historical research relate to the fundamental "historicity" that defines Dasein? How does such research draw upon and affect "the totality of our experience of [the] world?"[5] More specifically, in what sense does understanding the meaning of a historical event, a work of art, or a text involve prejudices drawn from our lives, and ultimately, the comprehensive prejudice, or horizon, that defines our life as a whole?

Behind this question is Gadamer's awareness that contemporary historical study tends to conceal its tie to our own lives. It tends to neglect its relationship to the living history that defines our Being-in-the-World and that grounds the sequence of events we call "world history." Our attitude toward the past, writes Gadamer, has become "strangely detached," and in two senses.[6] The first we might call the "practical," the second the "methodological." Neither, shows Gadamer, does justice to our actual practice of historical study.

The "practical" sense of detachment has to do with the relationship between history and ourselves. It captures the tendency to view historical tradition as a collection of relics rather than a guide to our own practice. Gadamer remarks that people used to study the classics of philosophy, literature, and art with great personal interest, seeking to learn truths relevant to contemporary life. In this sense, they were engaged with their objects of study. Properly speaking, their "objects" were tied to their self-understanding,

4. Ibid., xxvii.
5. Ibid., xxii.
6. Ibid., xxiii.

and thus not objects at all. Today, however, a tendency has emerged to study the classics in an antiquarian manner—not out of a desire for instruction, but to learn "how they lived back then." The antiquarian approach, we might say, is a highly developed mode of the attitude we typically take toward museum exhibits. We seek to experience a great civilization of old but do not expect guidance from it.

But however entrenched this attitude might be, argues Gadamer, it misunderstands itself as wholly antiquarian. Whenever we consider a historical relic—a work of art, the ruins of a temple, an ancient text—insofar as it provides a glimmer of insight into how "they" lived, we can never quite silence its claim on our own lives. Quite beyond our control, we will incorporate the experience of its meaning into "the totality of our self-understanding."[7] What we take to be a mere relic will inevitably give us new terms in which to understand our own commitments and concerns. It would be difficult to make sense of the interest we take in history without reference to its effect on us.

The "methodological" sense of detachment has to do with the way we understand history as scholars. It is tied to a certain notion of "correct" or "scientific" historical analysis: In order to recover the meaning of a historical event, a text, or a work of art, we must step back from our own understandings (i.e., our own concerns). We must step back to avoid interpreting the past in terms that were foreign to *its* way of thinking. According to this view, historical works must first and foremost be understood as products of their own age, as products of the context in which they were written. To grasp what they are about, we must escape our "contemporary" historical situation and return to the past's way of thinking. We must put our own thoughts aside and consider instead the "worldview" of the author; we must reconstruct the linguistic usages of his time, the literary forms that prevailed, and so on. By doing so, we can recover the "original" meaning of the text—the meaning it had when it first took shape within the author's historical situation.

This conception of detached historical research is what Gadamer calls "historicism"—an intellectual movement whose origin he attributes to the romantic period (Friedrich Schleiermacher), and which blossomed in

7. Ibid., xxvii.

nineteenth-century German thought (Wilhelm Dilthey). Historicism calls for detachment in that it teaches us to flee our "contemporary" situation, or "prejudice," and to thereby "return" to the past in an uninvolved manner. This "return" is supposed to reveal the prejudice-free, "original" meaning of the work—the one "true" meaning, fixed once and for all, untainted by contemporary bias.

Historicism, or "methodological" detachment, we might say, represents a more extreme rift between historical study and ourselves than does the antiquarian attitude. For according to historicism, the only way of gaining genuine access to history, to the meaning of an ancient text, for example, is through suspending its relevance to our own lives. Whereas the antiquarian attitude simply neglects to explicitly consider what history might teach us, historicism denies the very possibility of learning anything from history—at least until detached historical inquiry has revealed history's "true" meaning. Historicism assumes a radical difference between present and past that requires special methodological effort to overcome. In short, it enjoins us to treat the past as dead. Any "life" that the past may appear to have is deemed "contemporary bias."

Gadamer argues that historicism has matters reversed. Only in light of our own horizon can we draw distinctions among epochs, or "worldviews," and determine the true meaning of historical works. Despite the claim of historicism to provide an "objective" analysis of history, its very "objects" are constituted by the prejudices of the interpreter—by understandings drawn from the interpreter's own horizon.

To historicism, Gadamer opposes his own "hermeneutics," which seeks to illuminate the inescapable role of prejudice in historical study. There is no such thing, Gadamer argues, as the "original" meaning of a historical event, a work of art, or a text—if by "original" we mean something that can be uncovered without reference to our own prejudices. Whenever we try to understand the past, we do so from within our own horizon. More specifically, our own understandings—our own "prejudices"—animate our historical inquiry, determine what themes we select for research, and shape how we interpret those themes. Properly speaking, there are no historical "objects" separate from our preconceptions of them.

But this does not imply that we are confined by whatever understandings we may begin with. Although certain prejudices may distort the meaning of a historical work, other prejudices, he argues, can illuminate it. They can be "productive of knowledge." When we attempt to attain a detached understanding of history, to abstract from our own perspective and to think purely as people "back then" thought, we not only fail, but we "more or less forget half of what is really there—in fact, we miss the whole truth of the phenomenon."[8] The "phenomenon," Gadamer maintains, is, in a certain sense, the original meaning of the historical work—its meaning untainted by contemporary *bias* (or *distorting* prejudice). He insists that there is such a truth to be discovered—a truth that is not merely relative to the interpreter's own fancy. But paradoxical though it may sound, we recover this original meaning, Gadamer argues, not simply by imagining how *they* thought, but by considering the relation of the text (or the work of art, or the event) to our *own* lives.

Although Gadamer is well aware that certain features of our own lives, certain contemporary prejudices, may hinder our understanding of the text, he maintains that other prejudices may enable it. By considering the text within our own perspective, we can actually reveal layers of its original meaning that its author or initial recipients did not explicitly recognize. According to Gadamer's view, the original meaning of a text cannot be captured in a single account that would be intelligible to anyone anywhere. It unfolds only in light of certain prejudices. But even though the original meaning "unfolds," and thus is never fixed once and for all, it unfolds into *itself*, realizing its very identity through change. The task of critical reason, therefore, is not to escape prejudice as such, but to separate the "*true* prejudices by which we *understand*, from the *false* ones, by which we *misunderstand*."[9] "Hermeneutics," as Gadamer intends it, describes the process of this separation.

Gadamer's rehabilitation of *prejudice* might appear to be a polemical defense of what might otherwise be called the "situated," "perspectival," or "engaged" character of understanding. All of these terms describe what Gadamer is get-

8. Ibid., 300.
9. Ibid., 278.

ting at, and he often employs them. But his use of "prejudice" is not simply a shocking formulation of what he could have stated otherwise. For "prejudice," as we have seen, is the very term used by prominent Enlightenment thinkers to denote custom, tradition, particular commitments, perspectives, insofar as they predispose our understanding and action. Gadamer seeks to defend precisely what Enlightenment thought discredits. In speaking of "prejudice," Gadamer consciously adopts the Enlightenment's own term and reinterprets it, revealing prejudice as a feature of reason rather than its opposite. His defense of prejudice appears shocking only because we have been so thoroughly influenced by what he calls the "prejudice against prejudice,"[10] the ideal of "the absolute self-construction of reason,"[11] that the word "prejudice" now has a decisively pejorative meaning.[12]

But before the Enlightenment, Gadamer points out, "prejudice" did not have "the negative connotation familiar today." It simply meant "a judgment that is rendered before all the elements of a situation have been finally examined." For example, "in German legal terminology, a 'prejudice' is a provisional verdict before the final verdict is reached." As such, it has a "positive validity, the value of the provisional decision as a prejudgment, like that of any precedent." Only in light of the ideal of detached reflection did "prejudice" come to mean a baseless judgment—a judgment influenced by tradition, habit, custom, and not reason.[13] Gadamer seeks to rehabilitate the older notion of "prejudice" associated with "prejudgment" and "precedent." His novel twist, of course, is to give "prejudice" ontological significance and to connect it to historical understanding.

10. Ibid., 273.

11. Ibid., 278.

12. And only once it acquired its negative meaning could it later be used to describe genuinely deplorable attitudes such as racial hatred.

13. The German *Vorurteil*, continues Gadamer, "like the English 'prejudice' and even more than the French prejuge, seems to have been limited in its meaning by the Enlightenment critique of religion simply to the sense of an 'unfounded judgment.' The only thing that gives a judgment dignity is its having a basis, a methodological justification (and not the fact that it may actually be correct). For the Enlightenment the absence of such a basis does not mean that there might be other kinds of certainty, but rather that the judgment has no basis in the things themselves—i.e., that it is 'unfounded.'" (Gadamer, *Truth and Method*, 273).

Gadamer's Critique of Historicism

Let us review the historicist premise that Gadamer challenges. According to historicism, all thought belongs to a unique "historical situation," or "worldview," which denotes something like the comprehensive background of meanings, or terms of description, available to a given age. Central to the concept of "worldview" is that it does not merely describe a set of beliefs, or propositions, or claims to truth, where "truth" means the conformity of a statement to its object. The defining feature of a worldview is that it sets the bounds of truth; more precisely, it determines what counts as *relevant* truth, what commands the concern of a given age. A worldview, then, is equivalent to what we might call "truth" with a capital "T," as distinct from the many truths to which it gives rise. Insofar as a "worldview" dies, so too do its "truths." They may still be "correct," i.e., in conformity with their objects, but this correctness becomes meaningless, no longer part of any whole to which a sensible person would subscribe.

According to historicism, history presents us with a sequence of worldviews, the rise and fall of standards of truth that define different epochs. History thus teaches that there is no transhistorical truth, no standard that persists throughout the ages, that would allow us unmediated access to the past's way of thinking. Strictly speaking, the persistence of a worldview would deny the existence of the "past" in the decisive sense of an epoch distinct from the present.[14] Because history consists of a sequence of worldviews, historical understanding requires a special sort of effort: it requires that we leap out of our own worldview, which is a *mere* prejudice, and "transpose ourselves" into the worldview of the epoch under consideration. We must think in terms of "its ideas and thoughts" and thus advance toward historical "objectivity"—toward a decisive statement of "what *they* thought."[15]

Gadamer credits historicism with divining the situated character of thought insofar as it admits the belonging of thought to a "worldview" or

---

14. This view, ultimately, was Hegel's. Although he ascribes a sequence, of sorts, to history, the "sequence" is really a repetition of the same epoch on a higher level. For example, the Greek world of art expresses hazily the same Spirit that is realized in conceptual thought at the end of history. Thus, the Greek world has "passed on" only in a sense. In the end, it is preserved at a higher level.

15. Gadamer, *Truth and Method,* 297.

"horizon." But he corrects historicism's mistaken assumption that our own "present" horizon can be separated from the "past," that human life can be torn asunder in this way, split into a sequence of separate "horizons." Gadamer asks rhetorically:

> Are there really two different horizons here—the horizon in which the person seeking to understand lives and the historical horizon within which he places himself? Is it a correct description of the art of historical understanding to say that we learn to transpose ourselves into alien horizons? Are there such things as closed horizons, in this sense?

His answer is "no." In positing a sequence of horizons, or in speaking of horizons as "closed," or in tearing "present" from "past," historicism misunderstands the very meaning of "horizon." It assumes that its "own" horizon can become an object of detached knowledge, that it can be defined with sufficient clarity so as to separate it from "horizons" of the "past." This separation is impossible. For to be situated within a horizon "means that we are not standing outside it and hence are unable to have any objective knowledge of it."[16] The sort of knowledge of our horizon we can acquire is inescapably engaged and always partial: "throwing light on it is a task that is never entirely finished."[17] Our own horizon, or comprehensive self-understanding, directs every attempt to express its limits and every attempt to separate it from a "past" horizon:

> *To be historically means that knowledge of one's self can never be complete.* All self-knowledge arises from what is historically pregiven, what with Hegel we call "substance," because it underlies all subjective intentions and actions, and hence both prescribes and limits every possibility for understanding any tradition whatsoever in its historical alterity [i.e., difference].[18]

The thought that separates epochs, that, for example, distinguishes between our worldview and that of ancient Greece—is *itself* embedded in our own,

16. Ibid., 301.
17. Ibid.
18. Ibid.

all-encompassing horizon—and questionable in light of it. Any such separation may, in fact, turn out to be unwarranted. Perhaps what we consider to be "our" worldview is, upon proper reflection, basically the same as the worldview of the Greeks. Perhaps what we consider "theirs," is a *clearer* expression of our own. Perhaps what we take "ourselves" to be and, thus, what we take "them" to be is merely a foreground estimate, a distinction drawn on the basis of inessential concerns that occupy the forefront of our attention. Gadamer's point is simply that we can never know in advance and we can never know decisively. Historicism assumes a radical separation of worldviews that is unjustified. Without warrant, it denies the possibility that our own understandings might illuminate the meaning of the historical tradition we study and that the understandings of that tradition might illuminate our own lives.

The notion that any distinctions we might draw between present and past are questionable in light of our own, all-encompassing horizon is a key point for Gadamer. As an example of how such distinctions can be effectively questioned, we may examine Gadamer's own argument against the separation of the "age of Enlightenment," from the "age of myth." Gadamer is especially interested in this separation for the following reason: not only does he consider it to be a misstep that still exerts undue influence on contemporary thought; he also identifies it as the *very origin of the historical consciousness itself*—the consciousness accustomed to driving a wedge between the present and past, between "today" and "back then." By showing how this particularly fateful distinction of epochs is mistaken, Gadamer achieves two things: he exemplifies how all such distinctions can be questioned, and he accounts for our very tendency to assume them uncritically.

Gadamer argues that the distinction between the "age of Enlightenment" and the "age of myth" is founded on the false distinction between reason and prejudice. We have already examined how that distinction defines the self-understanding of the Enlightenment. People saw themselves as part of a new age—an age in which reason and not prejudice would be the ultimate source of authority. No longer would people allow tradition, habit, or custom to shape their understanding. All matters would now be decided "before the judgment seat of reason."[19] In the preceding chapters, we have considered examples of how the crusade against prejudice featured in seventeenth-century natural philosophy (Bacon and Descartes) and Enlightenment ethics (Smith, Hume, Kant). The same way of thinking dominated the study of traditional texts, and in particular, the Bible. The "real radicality of the modern Enlightenment," observes Gadamer, is that "it must assert itself against the Bible and the dogmatic interpretation of it." As with any claim to truth, the teaching of the Bible must be verified by detached analysis:

> Thus the written tradition of Scripture, like any other historical document, can claim no absolute validity; the possible truth of the tradition depends on the credibility that reason accords it. It is not tradition but reason that constitutes the ultimate source of all authority.[20]

But the very distinction between "tradition" and "reason," argues Gadamer, is misguided. So too is the more general distinction between "reason" and "prejudice." What the Enlightenment defines as "reason," is only a narrow species of understanding. By limiting reason to method, the Enlightenment neglects the practical understanding embodied in everyday life, what Heidegger explicates as Being-in-the-World. Gadamer credits Heidegger with presenting the phenomenon of reason, or understanding, in its true proportion: "Before any differentiation of understanding into the various directions of pragmatic or theoretical interest, understanding is Dasein's mode of being insofar as it is 'potentiality-for-being' and 'possibility.' "[21] What the Enlightenment deems sources of "prejudice"—tradition, custom, commitment to one's own—are actually "possibilities" of Dasein— understandings, which, as such, are open to question and constantly evolving. Without warrant, the Enlightenment relegates these understandings to the categories of "sentiment" and "rote habit."

Gadamer reiterates this point with respect to tradition—the paradigmatic "prejudice." What determines the Enlightenment understanding of

19. Ibid., 274.
20. Ibid.
21. Ibid., 250.

tradition, writes Gadamer, is its antithesis to reason: "Whether one wants to be revolutionary and oppose it or preserve it, tradition is still viewed as the abstract opposite to free self-determination, since its validity does not require any reasons but conditions us without our questioning it."[22] But this view, he continues, is a mistake:

> There is no such unconditional antithesis between tradition and reason. . . . The fact is that in tradition there is always an element of freedom and of history [i.e., movement or evolution] itself. Even the most genuine and pure tradition does not persist because of the inertia of what once existed. It needs to be affirmed, embraced, cultivated. It is, essentially, preservation and it is active in all historical change. But preservation is an act of reason, though an inconspicuous one. For this reason, only innovation and planning appear to be the result of reason. But this is an illusion.[23]

Despite all appearance and without explicit "innovation and planning," tradition is constantly in motion. What might seem to be blind perpetuation of the old, or mechanical habit, always has a "projective" dimension. Handing down tradition really means adapting it to the current circumstances, maintaining it in the face of other possibilities. And through such preservation, tradition is constantly being redefined: "affirmed, embraced, cultivated." Although this process operates, for the most part, unconsciously, it is nevertheless critical. The distinction between tradition and reason is ultimately unfounded.

Nevertheless, the distinction is assumed uncritically and leads to the impression of a vast gulf between present and past, between the "age of reason" and the "age of myth." Such a rift in time, writes Gadamer, was previously unimaginable. For centuries before the Enlightenment, people had related to historical tradition as a counterpart to the current times. One need only consider how theologians such as Thomas Aquinas studied the texts of Aristotle and Plato. Far from treating the classics as relics of a bygone epoch, they read them with deep personal interest, not as historical documents, but as guides

22. Ibid., 282.
23. Ibid.

to the good life. It was generally understood that the classics were concerned with the same basic questions as the present. The Western philosophical tradition was, in Gadamer's words, a "continuous stream" that lacked a historical sense. Although diverted at moments—by the "latinization of Greek concepts and the translation of Latin conceptual language into the modern languages"—the stream flowed relatively unbroken.[24]

By calling tradition (as such) into question, the Enlightenment prepared historicism. But insofar as the Enlightenment understood itself to have discovered "reason" as the decisive standard of knowledge, its self-consciousness was still unhistorical. Reason, people believed, would now serve as the standard for all time. For the idea of the relativity of epochs to emerge, the Enlightenment's faith in reason had to be shaken. This upheaval took place in the nineteenth century, when *romanticism* at once challenged the standard of reason, entrenched the reason-myth distinction, and led to an interest in the revival of tradition.

Instead of celebrating the advent of reason, romanticism disparaged it, seeking to recover tradition, habit, sentiment, and so on. A notable example, from the very beginning of the movement, is Burke's defense of prejudice. But the romantic critique of the Enlightenment still adopted the Enlightenment's basic premise: the distinction between reason and myth, and the corresponding philosophy of history: "the conquest of mythos by logos."[25] Instead of questioning this history and articulating a vision that could comprehend both "reason" and "myth," romanticism merely "reverses the values"—"seeking to establish the validity of the old simply on the fact that it is old."[26] "What determines the romantic understanding of tradition is its abstract opposition to the principle of enlightenment."[27] Now "the world of myth, unreflective life not yet analyzed away by consciousness, in a 'society close to nature,' the world of Christian chivalry—all these acquire a romantic magic, even a priority over truth."[28]

24. Ibid., xxiii.
25. Ibid., 275.
26. Ibid.
27. Ibid., 282.
28. Ibid., 275.

These "romantic revaluations" entrenched the idea that history consists of radically different epochs, each with its own standard of authority. The "age of reason" can make no privileged claim to allegiance. Although it can appeal to the value of detached reflection, free thinking, and so on, it cannot refute the ages that did not value these things—that instead valued sentimental commitment and respect for traditional authority. The "age of reason" can cite the predictive power of the new natural sciences, but it cannot discredit the ages uninterested in the "conquest of nature," the ages whose teleological science aimed to understand nature in the image of man. Why should the criterion of predictive power be made decisive for knowledge of the earth and sky?

Challenges to reason along these lines seemed all the more compelling in light of the wealth of historical knowledge unearthed by the romantic passion for revival: "the discovery of the voices of the peoples in their songs, the collection of fairy tales and legends . . . the discovery of worldviews implicit in languages."[29] The Enlightenment no longer appeared as a privileged age, but as one unique worldview among others, an island floating on the great sea of history.

Soon arose the view that all ages, including the Enlightenment, could be understood only historically—as ages defined by their own standards. As people began to accept the relativity of their own age, their interests shifted toward historical research. Historical knowledge now seemed to be the type of knowledge *par excellence*, the "liberation of the mind from the trammels of dogma," including the dogma of reason itself.[30] Thus emerged nineteenth-century historicism, the way of thinking that teaches us to forget ourselves and return to the past's way of looking at things.

To summarize the train of events: what set everything in motion was the Enlightenment distinction between reason and prejudice—between the authority of detached, methodical thought, on the one hand, and of tradition, custom, and habit, on the other. On the basis of this distinction arose the perception of two radically different epochs—the present age, whose standard was "reason," and the past, whose standard was "myth." And on the basis of this division of epochs arose the historical consciousness—the

29. Ibid., 276.
30. Ibid., 277.

general sense of a rift between "today" and "back then." Subsequent historical research presumed this rift, which soon became a self-evident point of departure: only by suspending contemporary criteria, the mere "prejudices" of the present times, can we obtain knowledge of how people thought "back then."

The way in which Gadamer interprets the Enlightenment, romanticism, and historicism in light of the "prejudice against prejudice" is itself an example of how a historian's own prejudice can illuminate the meaning of history. Gadamer's prejudice, we might say, is his understanding that the prejudice-reason distinction is misguided and has undue influence on contemporary life. This prejudice, in a sense, belongs to Gadamer's own historical situation. It is shaped, for example, by his study of Heidegger, by his familiarity with the German philosophical tradition, and so on. Nevertheless, Gadamer's own prejudice helps to clarify some key turning points in the history of ideas. His prejudice really does make sense of the Enlightenment, romanticism, and historicism in a way that other historical analyses might overlook.

By explaining the genesis of historicism in terms of the effect of the "prejudice against prejudice," Gadamer helps makes sense of historicism's fundamental ambiguity: historicism assumes the historically situated, or "prejudiced," character of all thought, but inconsistently supposes that we, as historical interpreters, can leap out of "our own" situation and into "another"— and furthermore that this sort of procedure is the proper method of historical research. Historicism falls prey to this confusion because it misconceives the nature of "situation" or "horizon." Biased by the romantic reaction to the Enlightenment, which perpetuates the sharp contrast between "reason" and "prejudice," historicism confuses "historically situated thought" with something like "incompatible standards of thought," "divergent worldviews," "alternative vocabularies," or "closed horizons." To someone who thinks in these terms, it makes sense to teach the suspension of one's own perspective, or set of "prejudices," in order to understand another.

But to think in this way neglects the true implications of situated thought. In supposing that we can leap out of our situation and that we should try to do so, historicism *"is based on the modern Enlightenment and unwittingly shares its prejudices.*"[31] Specifically, it shares the "one prejudice of the Enlightenment that defines its essence . . . the prejudice against prejudice itself . . ."[32] Beneath historicism's "critique of rationalism and of natural law philosophy,"[33] beneath its apparently generous pronouncement of the relativity of all worldviews—itself included—smolders the hubris of a present age that presumes to have mastered itself—that presumes to know its own horizon thoroughly and thus to be able to distinguish it from all the ages that have come before. But as Gadamer reminds us, "It is important to avoid the error of thinking that the horizon of the present consists of a fixed set of opinions and valuations, and that the otherness of the past can be foregrounded [i.e., separated] from it as from a fixed ground."[34]

Properly grasped, our historicity, or Being-in-the-World, denies the possibility of complete self-knowledge and, hence, of analyzing "other" horizons in abstraction from "our own." Our conception of "other" horizons will always rest on a questionable interpretation of "our own," and, in this sense, will involve prejudice. Thus, to understand "other" ages in their own right, undistorted by our own biases, we must attain an adequate understanding of *ourselves*. (This, indeed, is the same principle that Heidegger teaches concerning understanding among instances of Dasein: "Dasein's resoluteness [i.e., authenticity] toward itself is what first makes it possible to let the Others who are with it 'be' in their ownmost potentiality-for-Being.") Although our self-knowledge will always be incomplete—a prejudice open to revision—we can deepen it in many ways. And one significant way, Gadamer points out, is through the very activity of interpreting texts from our historical tradition—not as relics of an alien age or as mirror images of who we take ourselves to be—but as critical sounding boards for our own prejudices.[35] Only through such self-examination can we begin to sort out our relation to so-called past ages.

In other words, the situated character of our thought ensures that the past, insofar as it is intelligible as such, will always, in a sense, *belong* to the present: "Understanding will always involve more than merely historically

31. Ibid., 272.
32. Ibid., 272–273.
33. Ibid., 272.
34. Ibid., 305.
35. Ibid.

reconstructing the past "world" to which the work belongs. Our understanding will always retain the consciousness that we too belong to that world, and correlatively, that the work too belongs to our world."[36] It is a mistake, therefore, to treat the works of our historical tradition—classical texts, works of art, deeds—as parts of an alien age.

Nevertheless, a historical consciousness is illuminating in this sense: it makes us aware that a historical work speaks from a perspective that is not merely identical to our own. It reminds us, all-too-loudly, of the tension between the meaning of the work and the meanings we may uncritically read into it. A historical consciousness thus guards us against the tendency to dig up from a text the prejudices that we ourselves have buried. We always approach a text with prejudices, and if we are to uncover the text's meaning, we must have some awareness of its "otherness"—that it may not conform to the meanings readily familiar to us. Such awareness involves "neither neutrality with respect to the [text's] content nor the extinction of one's self," but the awareness of "one's own fore-meanings and prejudices."[37] Thus, a historical consciousness helps us formulate "the fundamental epistemological question for a truly historical hermeneutics" as follows: "What is the ground of the legitimacy of prejudices? What distinguishes legitimate prejudices from the countless others which it is the undeniable task of critical reason to overcome?"[38]

The Practice of Gadamer's Theory: How to Separate Legitimate from Illegitimate Prejudice

The answer, in a sense, is straightforward: the "legitimate prejudices" make the best overall sense of the "things themselves."[39] In the case of literary interpretation, the "things themselves" are the texts, but more precisely, what the texts are discussing, that is, the subject matter as presented in the texts.

For example, in the case of Plato's *Republic,* the "things themselves" are Plato's accounts of justice, the good, poetry, and so on. The interpreter will approach the text with certain expectations of meaning drawn from his

36. Ibid., 290.
37. Ibid., 271.
38. Ibid., 278.
39. Ibid., 269.

own understanding, certain prejudices, or "fore-meanings" of the "things themselves."

These prejudices may be more or less explicit. For example, the inter-preter may approach the *Republic* with a nuanced account of justice based on previous studies, or he may simply be familiar with how the word "justice" is used in everyday life. In either case, the "prejudices and fore-meanings that occupy the interpreter's consciousness are not at his free disposal." He can-not "separate in advance the productive prejudices that enable understand-ing from the prejudices that hinder it and lead to misunderstandings."[40] The separation "must take place in the process of understanding itself."[41] The process involves testing the prejudices against the articulation of the text, determining whether the prejudices make sense of the text in all its parts:

> A person who is trying to understand a text is always projecting. He projects a meaning for the text as a whole as soon as some initial mean-ing emerges in the text. Again, the initial meaning emerges only be-cause he is reading the text with particular expectations in regard to a certain meaning. Working out this fore-projection, which is constantly revised in terms of what emerges as he penetrates into the meaning, is understanding what is there. . . . A person who is trying to understand is exposed to distraction from fore-meanings that are not borne out by the things themselves. Working out appropriate projections, antici-patory in nature, to be confirmed by "the things" themselves, is the constant task of understanding. The only "objectivity" here is the con-firmation of a fore-meaning in its being worked out. Indeed, what char-acterizes the arbitrariness of inappropriate fore-meanings if not that they come to nothing in being worked out? But understanding realizes its full potential only when the fore-meanings that it begins with are not arbitrary.[42]

How is this circular movement worked out in practice? Let us consider both cases: an illuminating prejudice (or a "fore-meaning" that is "not arbi-

40. Ibid., 295.
41. Ibid.
42. Ibid., 270.

trary"), and a misleading one. How might an interpreter justify the first and overcome the second?

Imagine that our aim is to interpret an ancient text, for example, Plato's *Republic*. We might ask many questions about the dialogue, but let us suppose, for the sake of example, that we wish to discover Plato's view of poetry—specifically, the relationship of imitation *(mimesis)* to truth. In Book 10 of the dialogue, Socrates suggests that such poetry is a lowly art involving deception: that Homer and Aeschylus create only illusions of virtue, vice, and things divine, just as a man holding up a mirror to the world creates an illusion of the animals and plants reflected.[43]

For many thoughtful readers, this condemnation of poetry, or what today we call the "arts," would appear to be unduly severe. Surely poetry can enrich our understanding of virtue and vice by providing new and illuminating terms in which to express it. Does not Homer's Achilles reveal in unforgettable terms both the nobility and narrowness of the warrior ethic? Does not Aeschylus's Orestes help us see the impotence of the human will in the face of fate—the folly of trying to master life as if we were at our own mercy? We recognize all this, and with it, the general power of poetry, in light of the profound reflections on language that emerge from romanticism. We learn, for example, from thinkers such as Johann Gottfried von Herder and Wilhelm von Humboldt that language does not simply label, or mirror, an independent reality, but participates in constituting what it expresses. From their accounts and from subsequent versions of this expressive conception of language, we are disposed to a deeper appreciation of poetry and its connection to truth. We recall, for example, Nietzsche's suggestion that art is the "truly metaphysical activity of man."[44] All of this, we might say, constitutes a sort of prejudice in favor of poetry. When we encounter Socrates's harsh critique, the prejudice gives us pause. Could Plato really mean to liken poetry to a mirror?

Upon closer examination of Book 10, the text yields a more complex account. In light of our prejudice, certain features stand out that actually undermine the mirror-image understanding of poetry and suggest a stronger relationship between poetry and truth. We notice, for example, that Socrates

---

43. Plato, *Republic*, 596c-e.

44. Friedrich Nietzsche, *The Birth of Tragedy*, "Attempt at Self-Criticism," In *Basic Writings of Nietzsche*, trans. and ed. Walter Kaufmann (New York: Modern Library, 2000), §5, 22.

never himself affirms the mirror-image account, but merely proposes it as a possible analogy—specifically the first of three that he offers from 596a to 598c. Although the analogies seem to elaborate the mirror-image account, they actually call it into question. We can summarize them as follows:

(1) The poet is like a man with a mirror (*Republic,* 596c–e):

The man with a mirror "makes" all of the things that each of the craftsmen produce and "makes" all the things of the earth and sky, simply by capturing their reflections. Insofar as the things that the person mirrors are themselves imperfect images of their *ideas,* the person is an imitator of an image. For example, when the person holds the mirror up to a couch, he makes an image of the craftsman's couch, which is itself an image of the one *idea* of a couch (the true, or natural, or god-given couch).

(2) The poet is like a painter who paints a couch (*Republic,*
     596e–598b):

The painter paints the craftsman's couch, and in doing so, necessarily renders the couch from a certain perspective—from the side, or front, or somewhere else. The painter thus imperfectly imitates the craftsman's couch, which is itself only an instance of the *idea* of a couch. The painter is thus far from truth, or in the words of Socrates, "at the third generation from nature."

(3) The poet is like a painter who paints a craftsman (*Republic,*
     598b-c):

Supposedly to emphasize the suggestion that the painter's imitation is "far from the truth," Socrates adds this consideration: "The painter, we say, will paint for us a shoemaker, a carpenter, and the other craftsmen, even though he does not understand any of these arts. But if he is a good painter, in painting a carpenter and displaying him from far away, he would deceive children and foolish human beings into thinking that it is truly a carpenter."

These analogies are all supposed to reveal the sense in which the tragic poet is "third from the king and the truth" when it comes to virtue, vice, and things divine—a mere imitator of images. But in light of our prejudice concerning poetry, we can see that each successive analogy actually moves further from *mirroring* and closer to *illuminating*. Unlike the man with the mirror, who passively and haphazardly reflects the couch as he walks by, the painter must omit and heighten certain features of the couch. The painter's couch, in other words, involves interpretation. Socrates draws our attention to this by noting that the painter must paint from a certain perspective. Although Glaucon (Socrates's interlocutor) assumes that the painter's perspective is a shortcoming, Socrates invites the reader to draw the opposite conclusion: that by rendering the couch from a certain angle, in a certain light, in certain relations, the painter actually participates in clarifying the essence, or "couchness" of a couch. The best painters, we might say, help bring forth the *idea* of a couch itself. At any rate, their paintings are certainly more than mirror images.

Socrates underscores this point by considering the painter who paints a craftsman. If painting a couch involves interpreting, painting a shoemaker or a carpenter involves it all the more clearly. For what defines a craftsman is not his looks or anything that appears to the naked eye, but his characteristic *activity*. To paint a craftsman well, or to even paint one at all, the artist would have to capture, in some way, the craftsmanly work, bearing, attitude. Not just any snapshot, or arbitrary mirror image, would suffice. The painter's ability to render the craftsman would presuppose a certain understanding of craftsmanship—not the technical know-how of a craftsman, as Socrates misleadingly suggests, but knowledge of the vocation: of the attitudes and concerns it involves, of what marks it off from other activities, of how it fits into life as a whole. Don't all skilled painters draw upon some such comprehensive understanding? By highlighting the features of a craftsman in a uniquely fitting way, would they not elicit what a craftsman, in truth, *is?* Insofar as the painting does elicit the truth, it dissolves the sharp distinction between the "real," animate craftsman and the artistic rendition of one. The possibility that the painting might trick a child or fool from afar would not weaken its claim to truth.

Taken together and in sequence, the analogies seem actually to undermine Socrates's initial suggestion that imitative poetry is a deceptive mirror image of the world. Interpreted in light of our prejudice, the analogies edge closer and closer to the idea that poetry participates in bringing forth the very being, or truth, of its theme. As if pushing us to draw this conclusion, Socrates considers the truth of poetry anew: "Or, again," he asks Glaucon, "is there something to what [the praisers of poetry] say, and do the good poets really know about the things that, according to the many, they say well?"[45] If the answer were unqualifiedly "no," and if it simply followed from the previous analogies, why would Socrates pose the question anew? His reiteration of the question indicates a potential link between poetry and truth.

And sure enough, Socrates's final analysis of poetry drops the mirror-image analogy and turns instead to the influence of poetry on the soul. Socrates impugns the poets not for telling lies, but for awakening the soul's desire and thereby provoking *lawlessness*. According to this indictment, poetry is at odds with law *(nomos)*, but not with truth. At least with respect to a certain aspect of the soul, or an important category of "the human things"—with respect to "*eros*, and spiritedness," and "all the desires, pains, and pleasures in the soul," poetry does not simply mirror them, but brings them to life.[46] More precisely, poetry "cultivates and waters" the desires[47]: it evokes their nature, directs them toward certain ends, and thus shapes their influence on human action. This expressive-constitutive power of poetry is precisely what puts it at odds with the law. But if the soul's passionate side, rather than its sober, law-abiding tendency, is the springboard for philosophy (as Socrates consistently intimates), then poetry would be a potential ally in the quest for truth.

The point of this example is by no means to decisively settle the question of Plato's conception of poetry. It is intended, rather, to show how reading an ancient text with a certain "contemporary" prejudice may actually illuminate the text in a way that one might otherwise ignore—especially if one attempts to suspend all prejudice. The prejudice, or preconception, that poetry is tied to truth really does make sense of Plato's account. It fits with the twists and turns of the dialogue.

This is what Gadamer means by "testing" a prejudice and justifying it. We begin with a preconception of the text as a whole, or of a certain theme

---

45. Plato, *Republic*, 599a.
46. Ibid., 606d.
47. Ibid.

in the text as a whole, and we see whether it fits the parts. If it does, we can say provisionally that the prejudice is "productive of knowledge."

The knowledge at stake is always twofold: we understand both Plato's conception of poetry more clearly and also our own. I have emphasized the first insofar as understanding Plato, rather than ourselves, is the explicit goal of historical research. But according to Gadamer's hermeneutics, understanding runs in both directions: our own understanding of poetry reveals Plato's, which in turn, reveals our own. Specifically, Plato offers a distinctive version of the link between poetry and truth by tying it to the doctrine of *ideas*. We cannot begin to develop this relationship here. But in brief, we can say this: if the *ideas* are, in some sense, the eternal truths, as Plato suggests, then poetry is subordinate to what it elicits. Poetry, in other words, is not purely creative. This insight might help to adjust the dominant contemporary accounts of poetry (or, more broadly, art), which tend to emphasize its creative dimension—that poetry constructs reality, or "truth," rather than reflects it. The point is that Plato's distinctive formulation of the link between poetry and truth can serve as a critical sounding board for our own accounts of that link—the very accounts that prejudiced our reading of Plato in the first place. The two combine to express a more comprehensive insight, which is what Gadamer calls the thoughtful mediation of the past with contemporary life.[48]

It would be a mistake, therefore, to call the hermeneutic, or prejudicial, character of interpretation "reading merely our own meanings into the text." First, insofar as our prejudices really do make sense of the subject matter as presented by Plato, they justly belong to the text itself, or to Plato's conception of poetry itself. No amount of empirical historical findings could refute this. A historian of ideas could heap example upon example of divergent usages of "poetry" and "truth" in classical Athens or marshal extensive biographical evidence suggesting that Plato believed that poetry was strictly at odds with truth. None of this evidence would be decisive for reaching the historically accurate meaning of Plato's dialogue until such evidence could be organized into an interpretation of the text that surpassed the one just given by making better sense of the text as a whole.

---

48. Gadamer, *Truth and Method*, 161.

Second, to say that we read our own meanings into the text misses the sense in which we revise our own meanings as we read. Even when our prejudice seems to fit the text with remarkable precision, the very process of having justified the prejudice, of having measured it against the meaning of another, amounts to an increase in knowledge. Insofar as we comprehend the "other" within "our own," we take away more than we came with. In reference to the previous example, our "own" conception of poetry cannot be formed without Plato's.

Having considered an illuminating prejudice, and how it can be justified, let us consider a misleading one, and how it can be overcome. The obvious answer is that we overcome misleading prejudices in the same way as we justify illuminating ones: by testing them against the text. But we confront a difficulty: for the most part, our prejudices are unconscious, which means we cannot test them explicitly. So if they lead to misunderstandings, how do we become aware of our mistake? How, asks Gadamer, "can we break the spell of our own fore-meanings?"[49] Provided that we read with care, they will dissolve of themselves:

> Just as we cannot continually misunderstand the use of a word without its affecting the meaning of the whole, so we cannot stick blindly to our fore-meaning about the thing if we want to understand the meaning of another . . . if a person fails to hear what the other person is really saying, he will not be able to fit what he has misunderstood into the range of his own various expectations of meaning.[50]

Consider, for example, a familiar prejudice that might lead us to misinterpret Plato's comparison of opinion *(doxa)* to knowledge *(episteme)*.[51] As contemporary readers, we might be inclined to mistake Plato's term "opinion" for "subjective belief," and "knowledge" for "objective truth." On this point, the prejudice at play is the subject-object distinction, which, although

49. Ibid., 270.
50. Ibid., 271.
51. Cf. Plato, *Republic,* 477–480.

foreign to Plato's philosophy, exerts a strong and largely unconscious influence on contemporary thought. Originally a novel theoretical distinction drawn by modern philosophers to separate what is produced by "inner consciousness" from what actually corresponds to the "external world," the distinction has since become a familiar and implicit part of everyday discourse. We use the terms "subjective" versus "objective" unreflectively, often as substitutes for "baseless" versus "justified," or "biased" versus "fair." When we read Plato, the subject-object prejudice is liable to shape our interpretation while escaping our notice. We might be wholly unaware of any possible difference in meaning between "opinion" and "subjective belief." How then do we come to recognize Plato's own meaning?

At a certain point, we get "pulled up short" by the text, and our prejudice emerges explicitly. We can no longer reconcile the text with our misinterpretation. For example, we meet the puzzling suggestion of Socrates that "opinion" occupies a space *between* "ignorance" and "knowledge."[52] This tripartition seems to clash with the equation of "opinion" and "subjective belief." For when we speak of "subjective belief," we imply that it has (potentially) *no* relation to knowledge. The clash calls our attention to the possibility that Plato's term "opinion" diverges from our initial expectation.

The divergence becomes all the more apparent in light of Socrates's suggestion that opinion, in a sense, grasps reality, or what *is*. Although it falls short of knowledge, which grasps what *is* "without qualification," opinion does not lay hold of mere illusion, or what "in every way *is not*." Occupying a middle position between knowledge and ignorance, opinion grasps what "at the same time *is* and *is not*."[53] More precisely, opinion grasps a likeness, or an imperfect instance of the *idea*. Thus the text refutes our prejudice that what Plato calls "opinion" means "subjective belief."

In becoming aware of our prejudice, we not only free Plato's meaning from distortion, but we also gain a potentially deeper understanding of Plato's subject matter: the nature of opinion. Upon discovering Plato's claim that opinion divines the truth, or, in his terms, points to the *ideas,* we can no longer uncritically accept our own view that opinion is merely subjective. Perhaps Plato is right. In any case, the encounter with Plato's text provokes

52. Ibid., 477a.
53. Ibid., 478d.

us to question our own understandings. As in the previous example, historical research is simultaneously an exercise in self-knowledge.

The discussion of interpreting Plato is intended to clarify the circular movement between our own "contemporary" prejudice and the meaning of a historical text. I place "contemporary" in quotation marks so as to indicate the possibility that our own prejudice actually makes sense of the historical work and therefore belongs to the past. To make sense of the work means to harmonize its parts: "The harmony of all the details with the whole is the criterion of correct understanding."[54]

In the case of our first example, our prejudice, or anticipation of the whole, is our (provisional) answer to the question: What is the point of Plato's discussion of poetry? Roughly stated, it goes something like this: imitative poetry actually participates in constituting what it imitates, and, therefore, is not a mirror image of the world. In light of this preconception of the whole, certain parts of the text stand out. The parts may affirm the preconception or clash with it. In either case, we revise the preconception of the whole in light of the parts. In the case of a stark clash, we might have to reject the preconception in favor of another. In the case of a neat fit, we might still sharpen our preconception to reflect the whole more adequately. Thus "the movement of understanding is from whole to parts and back to whole."[55]

But even when we revise our prejudice to fit the parts of the text, our understanding remains incomplete. For the fundamental circle at play is not simply the particular circle between our preconception of the whole text and the meaning of its parts. This particular circle, Gadamer reminds us, is part of the comprehensive circle of our interpretations of historical texts, events, and so on, and the whole horizon within which we interpret.

Gadamer's case for prejudice ultimately goes back to the prejudicial or "thrown" character of human life. His point in *Truth and Method* is to play out Heidegger's ontology of Dasein with reference to the human sciences. We always interpret historical tradition from within our own horizon, or world. It "determines in advance both what seems to us worth inquiring about and what will appear as an object of investigation."[56] We attempt, for example, to understand Plato's view of poetry because the question of poetry

54. Gadamer, *Truth and Method*, 291.
55. Ibid., 292.
56. Ibid., 300.

is somehow of concern to us. It appears within our horizon, and in a certain light. But by deciphering Plato's view of poetry, or by discovering the meaning of any historical work, we broaden the horizon that guided our inquiry in the first place. Given that this comprehensive circle never comes to a close, the true meaning of a text (or any topic of interpretation) is never final. As our horizon develops and gives rise to new interpretive prejudices, we may discover unexpected layers of a text's meaning.[57] Indeed, the act of having interpreted a text reshapes our horizon, which, in turn, might reveal a deeper interpretation of that very text. Prejudice thus remains an essential feature of understanding: "[The] understanding of the text remains permanently determined by the anticipatory movement of fore-understanding."[58]

This apparently abstract point is actually quite concrete. What Gadamer means by the essentially prejudicial, or horizon-bound nature of understanding, reveals itself in the familiar experience of rereading a book, or seeing a movie later in life and grasping what it means in greater depth. Consider, for example, reading a novel in high school and then again ten years later. What accounts for the gain in understanding? Is it that we look harder at the text as adults, or that we have keener cognitive faculties? Neither seems to account for the gain. We may have read every word in school and had a quicker mind in many ways—at least concerning things like counting and memorizing. A simpler yet deeper explanation is that ten years later we read the book from a broader, more mature perspective. It is not that we read what "is there" more carefully or with greater brain power but that we see it differently—in light of new interests, concerns, and understandings. Certain themes stand out that before we failed to recognize, that we were unable to recognize because we lacked the relevant terms of expression that come with experience and cultivation.

The gain in perspective that comes with adulthood is a conspicuous example of Gadamer's general point: Our horizons are at every moment evolving, giving rise to potentially deeper interpretive insights. For this reason, "the discovery of the true meaning of a text or a work of art is never finished; it is in fact an infinite process."[59] The infinity reflects the projective character of understanding, its endless potential to develop itself: "Not

57. Ibid., 298.
58. Ibid., 293.
59. Ibid., 298.

only are fresh sources of error constantly excluded, so that all kinds of things are filtered out that obscure the true meaning; but new sources of understanding are constantly emerging that reveal unexpected elements of meaning."[60] Although no account of a text will be final, the best interpretations are still true in a sense that is "universal." That is to say, they really do illuminate the text itself, which remains the same throughout the various interpretations that shed light on it in different ways. The same subject "presents different aspects of itself at different times or from different standpoints."[61]

60. Ibid.
61. Ibid., 285.

5

The Role of Prejudice in Moral Judgment

A Hermeneutic Reading of Aristotle

The situated conception of understanding is not simply an achievement of twentieth-century thought. In a sense, we have always known ourselves to be "situated," even before we were able to express it in such terms. The great achievement of Heidegger and Gadamer was to elicit the situated conception of understanding from the depths of our implicit awareness. In light of this achievement, Heidegger and Gadamer might seem to be torchbearers. Interpreters tend especially to view Heidegger in this way, as a rebel against a tradition of thought distracted by abstract theory and detached from the world. Dreyfus offers one such reading:

> From the Greeks, we inherit not only our assumption that we can obtain theoretical knowledge of every domain, even human activities, but also our assumption that the detached theoretical viewpoint is superior to the involved practical viewpoint. According to the philosophical tradition, whether rationalist or empiricist, it is only by means of detached contemplation that we discover reality.[1]

1. Hubert L. Dreyfus, *Being-in-the-World: A Commentary on Heidegger's* Being and Time, *Division I* (Cambridge, MA: MIT Press, 1991), 6.

Dreyfus goes on to read Heidegger as a corrective to the misguided "philosophical tradition" starting "from the Greeks." But to view Heidegger in this way is a mistake. It overlooks the roots of his thought and therewith the full breadth of his vision.

If Heidegger is right to suggest that we have always implicitly understood ourselves to be situated, we might expect this insight to have found expression at other moments in the Western philosophical tradition. And in a way, it has. In this chapter, I examine one such moment: the philosophy of Aristotle. The distance between Aristotle and twentieth-century hermeneutic thought is less vast than it first appears. For Heidegger and Gadamer were both deeply influenced by his thought. Gadamer cites Aristotle's conception of moral judgment as a model for his situated conception of historical understanding (cf. "The Hermeneutic Relevance of Aristotle" in *Truth and Method*). To this end, Gadamer interprets the basic problem of Aristotle's ethics in the following terms: "If man always encounters the good in the form of the particular practical situation in which he finds himself, the task of moral knowledge is to determine what the concrete situation asks of him."[2]

Moreover, in a fascinating remark in his essay "Hermeneutics and Historicism" (1965), Gadamer acknowledges that his use of Aristotle actually "followed a line that Heidegger began in his early years at Freiburg, where he was concerned with a hermeneutics of facticity [i.e., the "given"], against neo-kantianism."[3] This comment suggests that Heidegger's infrequent and often critical citations to Aristotle in *Being and Time* actually conceal a deep debt to Aristotle's *Ethics*. As Gadamer (who was one of Heidegger's closest students) reveals, Aristotelian philosophy was a springboard for Heidegger's notion of Being-in-the-World: "a real vindicator of [Heidegger's] own philosophical purposes." In particular, Heidegger drew upon Aristotle's "demonstration of the analogical structure of the good and the knowledge of the good that is required in the situation of action."[4] So we see that both Heidegger and Gadamer developed their situated conceptions of understanding by appropriating Aristotle—in particular, by appropriating his conceptions of action, moral judgment, and the good. The situated conception of under-

2. Hans-Georg Gadamer, *Truth and Method,* trans. Joel Weinsheimer and Donald G. Marshall, rev. ed. (New York: Continuum, [1960] 1989), 311.

3. Hans-Georg Gadamer, "Hermeneutics and Historicism" (1965), in *Truth and Method*, 536.

4. Ibid., 536.

standing turns out to be not only a child of twentieth-century Germany, but also of ancient Greece.

To be sure, there is an important difference between Aristotle and Heidegger. Unlike Heidegger, Aristotle does not speak of the "situated conception of understanding." To speak of "situated" understanding and the role of "prejudice" in reason is to assume a tradition of thought that developed long after Aristotle's time. The very term "situated" understanding attains its full meaning only in contrast to "detached" understanding, in contrast to the ideal of abstraction as expressed by Bacon, Descartes, Smith, Kant, and other modern figures. Aristotle, of course, did not contend with this tradition. Therefore, he did not (and could not) define "situated understanding" in Heidegger's terms.

Nevertheless, Aristotle does articulate his own version of situated understanding. By examining his version—implicit in the concepts of action *(praxis)*, the good life *(to eu zein)*, and practical wisdom *(phronesis)*—we gain a firmer grasp of what Heidegger and Gadamer develop explicitly. At the same time, we gain a firmer grasp of Aristotle. By returning to his *Ethics* with the torch of twentieth-century thought in hand, we can make sense of its key twists and turns. By showing how a "contemporary" prejudice (the hermeneutic tradition) actually illuminates Aristotle, I aim to further demonstrate how a prejudice can be, as Gadamer puts it, "productive of knowledge."

Aristotle understands our comprehensive "situation," or "life perspective," in terms of *the good life*. The good *(to agathon)*, he writes, is not some abstract form to which we look for guidance but a concrete end *(telos)* expressed in our action *(praxis)*. Whenever we make things, put them to use, and live out certain roles, our actions aim at the good (whether or not we consciously reflect upon the good *as* our aim). For "the good," Aristotle maintains, is the end of all ends—that "for the sake of which everything else is done."[5] As such, the good is both the aim of our action and its condition. It is the ultimate

5. Aristotle, *Nicomachean Ethics*, trans. H. Rackham (Cambridge, MA: Harvard University Press, 1926), 1097a 15.

end *(telos)* toward which we strive, and, at the same time, the source, or beginning *(arche)*, of all striving.

To make sense of this special conception of the good, we should consider its familiar meaning in Greek. The concept of "good" *(agathos)* is closely tied to the concept of "useful," "fitting," or "suitable for a given end." In this sense, *agathos* is close to our notion of "good" as when we speak of a "good bridle" or a "good horseman." The key is that *agathos* does not carry the moralistic sense that "good" often does in English. The opposite of *agathos* is "bad" in the sense of "useless," or "unfitting," rather than "morally depraved" or "evil." *Agathos* can denote a "good man" *(agathos anthropos)*, but typically in the sense of "a man who does his job well," or who "displays the excellences befitting of a man." Thus, the good man is one who lives a most fitting, well-ordered, or coherent life.

In light of this notion of "good," we can begin to glimpse the sense in which the good is the source of all human action. Aristotle does not mean to suggest that all people aim at what we typically call the "morally good." This suggestion would seem implausible in light of the many instances of people who pursue unjust or evil ends. To understand what Aristotle means by the priority of the good, we must follow the more modest sense of "good" as "useful."

Every human action, Aristotle writes, aims at "some good" *(agathou tinou)*; it is action "for the sake of" *(charin)* a certain end *(telos)*.[6] Among ends there is a hierarchy. We see this clearly in cases where several pursuits are subordinate to a single end—as bridle-making is subordinate to horsemanship, which, in turn, is subordinate to generalship (i.e., being a good general in war). Now, to make sense of any of the ends, including the higher ones, which appear to be ends in themselves, we must presuppose, Aristotle suggests, a single highest end—the good as such, or as a whole. For only in light of the good as a whole do any particular ends make sense, or attain their "goodness." Without the good as a whole, writes Aristotle, all action would be "pointless" *(mataia)*.[7] ("Pointless," and not "wicked" or "evil" is the key word.) Insofar as our action has a point, insofar as it makes any sense, we

6. Ibid., 1094a.
7. Ibid.

must presuppose a single, highest good. In this sense, the good as a whole is the "supreme good" *(to ariston);* it gives being to all of the good things.

Of particular note is how Aristotle's account of action prepares Heidegger's. As for Heidegger, all action, for Aristotle, is "for the sake of" a certain end. And this end, whatever it may be, has its place within a certain hierarchy of ends, ultimately, within a certain articulated whole of ends, the good as such—the (highest) Good. In Aristotle's conception of the Good, we catch a glimpse of Heidegger's *world.*

To underscore the practical, or "situated," character of the Good, Aristotle challenges the doctrine of *ideas* according to which the Good is an abstract unity that exists apart *(choriston)* from the actual things called "good."[8] (Notably, he attributes this doctrine to the Pythagoreans, among others, but *not* to Plato. By omitting Plato from his line of criticism, Aristotle maintains the possibility that his own notion of the Good is actually *akin* to his predecessor's.) The Good, concludes Aristotle, is not an abstract form, but a "way of life" *(ergon zoein tina).*[9] It is a "practical good" *(practon agathon).*[10]

By "practical" Aristotle means that the Good is both expressed in practice and intelligible only from the perspective of practice. In other words, our knowledge of the Good is inseparable from our lived awareness of the good, and our lived awareness is inseparable from the Good itself. To grasp the Good thus requires more than theory or mere book learning. It requires life experience *(emperia).*[11] Although the term *emperia,* from which the English "empirical" derives, might suggest the sort of experience that we gain by surveying the word "out there" and then processing the data in our minds, this is not what Aristotle means. To avoid this unfortunate association, shaped by modern subjectivism, I have translated *emperia* as "life experience," not simply as "experience" (as it is typically rendered). The former, I believe, better captures Aristotle's meaning. *Emperia* is not the experience of things in a world separate from our concerns. It is a basic mode of experience by which we understand both the world and ourselves. It is the sort

---

8. Ibid., 1096b 30.
9. Ibid., 1098a 10.
10. Ibid., 1097a 20.
11. Ibid., 1142a 15–20.

of "experience" that we acquire by growing up in a certain community, developing virtuous habits, deliberating about how to act, and making moral judgments. All of these activities contribute to our understanding of the Good and enable our ability to reflect upon it.

The sense in which our understanding of the Good, according to Aristotle, can be conceived as "situated" is perhaps best captured by his claim that grasping the good requires *phronesis,* typically translated as "prudence," or "practical wisdom." The defining feature of *phronesis* is the ability to "deliberate well about what is good and advantageous for one's self—not about a part of life, such as what is good for health or strength, but about living well as a whole."[12] This deliberative ability, Aristotle continues, is irreducible to rules or principles. In this respect, *phronesis* differs from scientific knowledge *(episteme),* the model of which (for Aristotle) is mathematics. *Phronesis,* unlike *episteme,* involves grasping the particular goods at stake in a given circumstance and knowing how to balance them well.[13] It involves knowing how to act "at the right time, on the right occasion, toward the right people, for the right purpose, and in the right manner."[14] In this sense, *phronesis* is situated. It is not the knowledge of this or that object but of the situation in which one is engaged.

The situated character of *phronesis* comes to the fore in Aristotle's contrast of *phronesis* and craft knowledge *(techne).*[15] This contrast is perhaps even more crucial for understanding *phronesis* than the well-known contrast of *phronesis* and *episteme.* The importance of the former has to do with the apparent kinship of *phronesis* and *techne.* Both, after all, aim at what we loosely call "practice" in the sense of doing something, or acting, rather than merely contemplating. In Aristotle's terms, both *phronesis* and *techne* deal with "the class of things that admit of being otherwise," that, unlike the natural things, are subject to our choice and agency.[16] In this sense, both differ from *episteme,* which concerns things that "exists or come into being of necessity."[17]

---

12. Ibid., 1140a 25.
13. Ibid., 1141b.
14. Ibid., 1106b 20.
15. Ibid., 1105, 1140a-b.
16. Ibid., 1140a.
17. Ibid.

However, *phronesis* and *techne* diverge in this crucial respect: although *techne* deals with fabrication, and thus involves a certain tangible skill, it is nevertheless a sort of abstract knowledge. *Techne* requires knowledge of the product's form *(eidos)* in abstraction from its use. The workman can grasp the *eidos* before his conscious gaze, and then, as a separate matter, embody that image in the available material. (The workman need not understand how to use what he produces.) *Phronesis,* by contrast, is inescapably situated. It involves more than a formal kind of knowledge. It involves the agent's engaged understanding of a particular circumstance—an understanding embodied in the agent's action *(praxis)* rather than represented in his or her mind.

Aristotle's distinction between *phronesis* and *techne* is worth highlighting, especially as it is often overlooked by modern readers who interpret *phronesis* as a kind of detached theoretical knowledge *applied* to practice. Adam Smith, for example, makes this mistake. According to his interpretation of Aristotle, we can have moral knowledge independent of our actions and habits, and then, as a separate matter, apply that knowledge to practice. Smith thus collapses the distinction between *phronesis* and *techne,* missing the situated character of moral judgment.[18]

Of contemporary philosophers who do recognize the distinction between *techne* and *phronesis,* Arendt and Gadamer are of special note. Both draw upon this distinction to articulate a situated conception of understanding and action. Arendt develops Aristotle's contrast of *techne* and *phronesis* in her own distinction between "work" and "action." Expressing Aristotle's philosophy in terms influenced by Heidegger, Arendt maintains that action is always situated within a "web of enacted stories."[19] Only insofar as work is drawn into this web does it acquire meaning. Detached from the world of action, she argues, our ability to manipulate and fabricate things would be pointless. In that case, our plastic capacity would cease to be an expression of our agency; it would become a sort of blind know-how.

Gadamer uses the distinction between *techne* and *phronesis* to develop his situated conception of hermeneutics. Accordingly, he interprets Aristotle as

18. The tendency to misinterpret *phronesis* in this way points, I believe, to how "practical" knowledge has come to mean "applied theory."

19. Hannah Arendt, *The Human Condition* (Chicago: University of Chicago Press, 1958), §25, 181.

teaching that "man always encounters the good" in "the particular practical situation in which he finds himself."[20] Through the practice of balancing the competing goods at stake in particular situations, we gain a deeper understanding of the Good itself.

In Aristotle's terms, we come to discern the Good through exercising the particular *virtues of character,* all of which require and cultivate *phronesis.* Aristotle's account of the virtues (bravery, moderation, greatness of soul, justice, generosity, and so on) illuminates the situated conception of judgment in concrete terms. In particular, his account brings out the sense in which moral deliberation and judgment involves *prejudice.* To exercise the virtues, or to judge well, one must possess a virtuous disposition of *character (hexis).* In other words, *hexis* is the condition of *phronesis.*[21] Furthermore, the very nature of *phronesis,* as Aristotle defines it, must be understood in terms of character. For the ability to size up a given circumstance involves grasping the relative significance of the particular roles and activities that the circumstance calls into play. *Phronesis,* we might say, is a "value-laden" virtue of the intellect. To have good character and to have *phronesis* ultimately amounts to the same thing.

Aristotle's notion of *hexis* captures the sense of prejudice I mean to defend. One's disposition of character can be understood as a "prejudice" in the sense of a particular life perspective—a viewpoint from which certain actions appear desirable that otherwise might seem unworthy. But the particularity of character is not, according to Aristotle, a limitation to moral judgment—as if our judgment would be improved if only it could be freed from its conditions. As a mode of understanding, and not a mechanical or sentimental disposition, character admits of being better or worse. A virtuous character provides a broad range of view, enabling one to see the situation clearly and to judge well.

The sense in which character can be understood as a sort of prejudice emerges in Aristotle's claim that the standard of good character cannot be fully captured in a statement *(logos)* alone. If what made for good character could be so captured, it would be teachable to anyone anywhere; it would cease, in that case, to be a prejudice. The standard of virtuous character is

20. Gadamer, *Truth and Method,* 311.
21. Aristotle, *Nicomachean Ethics,* 1144a 25–35.

inseparable from its application, inseparable from whether it enables one to discern the goods at stake in any given situation and to balance them adeptly. The ability to recognize this standard presupposes that one already meets it. In other words, the competent judge of good character must himself be virtuous; he must partake of the right perspective, the right "prejudice."

These considerations introduce the way in which Aristotle's notion of *hexis* can be understood in terms of prejudice. Furthermore, his notion of *hexis* undermines the assumption that judgment influenced by prejudice is enslaved to circumstance. Although our character is forged by our upbringing *(paidea)*, it is not given from the moment of birth or acquired passively. Aristotle maintains that our character is up to *us;* we shape it through the activity of deliberating and judging. By judging well and doing virtuous deeds consistently, we come to develop a virtuous character. This is the sense in which virtuous character depends on *habit (ethos).*

Whereas Bacon, Descartes, Smith, and Kant understand habit as a sort of mechanical behavior, Aristotle teaches otherwise. Habit is not the mechanical repetition of the same thing or blind obedience to convention. For each virtuous action that we "repeat" must respond to a situation that is similar to, but never the same as, any other. Each "repeated" action requires considering new trade-offs, balancing competing goods, sorting out the essential from the less pressing. In this sense, habit involves our agency. Through deliberating and judging well, we cultivate the character we drawn upon. Our character thereby becomes a more informed perspective. This is why Aristotle insists that happiness, or the good life *(eudaimonia)*, requires the exercise *(energeia)* of virtue and not simply the capacity *(dunamis)* for virtue.[22] Not only is the exercise of virtue more fulfilling than the simple possession of it, but in order to possess it in the fullest sense, we must exercise it. For each act of moral deliberation and judgment develops our character, thereby improving our capacity for judgment. Habit is thus essential for attaining virtue, and by no coincidence, as Aristotle points out, the Greek word for ethical virtue, *arete ethike,* derives from *ethos,* or habit.

22. Ibid., 1095b 30–1096a 5.

Aristotle's Situated Conception of the Good and of Philosophy

Before turning to the details of Aristotle's situated conception of moral judgment, let us step back to review his conception of the Good and of philosophy. The philosophical study of the Good, for Aristotle, is "situated" in the sense of being bound to the practice of ethics. The Good first comes to light not in principles or precepts, but in our way of life. We come to understand the Good not primarily by theoretical study but by exercising the virtues.

However, Aristotle's notion of the Good does not suggest that he rejects or denigrates *contemplation* of the Good. We must remember that Aristotle is a philosopher whose writing is supposed to provide an account of the Good. Furthermore, Aristotle maintains that philosophy, or theory *(theoria)*, is the highest activity of the soul. Nevertheless, theory is, for Aristotle, bound to practice. He insists that the student of ethics must be educated in "fine habits" in order to grasp accounts of the Good.[23] Although knowledge of the Good may come to completion, or at least to its fullest development, in theory, this achievement remains bound to practice.

To say that theory is bound to practice is also to say that practice embodies a kind of theory—not a "theory" in the sense of a set of abstract principles that could be detached from actual life, but "theory" in the sense of a certain understanding that can be articulated and developed by philosophy.

The Good, for Aristotle, is the highest concern of theory. Not only is it the end of human action but also (as for Plato) the basis of the cosmos. For this reason, ethics and philosophy go together. A closer look at Aristotle's Good reveals a greater cosmic significance than first meets the eye. Although the Good is embodied in practice, or sustained by human action, it is by no means created by human beings. Aristotle makes clear that the Good is, rather, the condition, or *cause (aitios)* of human action, not its product.[24] Only insofar as we possess a practical awareness of the Good, an awareness embodied primarily in our disposition of character, can we deliberate, judge, and act.

23. Ibid., 1095b 5.
24. Aristotle, *Nicomachean Ethics*, 1102a.

The priority of the Good to particular human acts is captured by Aristotle's definition of the Good as *eudaimonia*—a key term typically translated as "happiness" or the "good life." Neither, however, quite reaches its meaning. Although "happiness" is often close enough to the term's typical use, it misses the sense of "blessedness," which Aristotle means to highlight. In fact, the word *eudaimonia*, broken into its parts, *eu-daimonia*, means "having a good deamon," or being shepherded throughout life by a guardian god. *Eudaimonia* suggests that the Good, the ultimate end of human action, points beyond what is merely human. It has a certain divine quality, which Aristotle calls "honorable and godlike."[25]

Aristotle attributes the Good's divinity to its being the cause *(aitios)*, or beginning *(arche)*, of human action (which, for Aristotle, is equivalent to human *life)*: "It is clear to us, from what has been said, that *eudaimonia* is honorable and perfect. It seems to be so on account of its being a beginning *(arche)*; for all human beings do all things for the sake of the Good. The beginning and the cause of all good things, we say, is something honorable and godlike."[26] Aristotle makes clear that by "cause" *(aitios)*, he means the ultimate source of human action rather than the efficient cause. For the efficient cause, he writes, is *choice (prohairesis).*[27] The Good is the unchosen condition of choice. Insofar as human beings become what they are through choice, through the particular deliberations and decisions they make, the Good, as the condition of choice, is also the condition of human life. In this sense, the Good transcends what is merely human.

The divinity of the Good suggests a certain kinship between what we today distinguish as ethics, theology, and metaphysics. At any rate, Aristotle does not distinguish among them. For him (as for Plato) there is only philosophy, which he defines as the quest for *wisdom (sophia)*. Aristotle defines wisdom as complete knowledge of the most exalted, or honorable, things *(ton timiotaton)*. Such knowledge is complete in that it "apprehends not only the things that follow from beginnings, but also has a true grasp of the beginnings themselves."[28] This definition of wisdom recalls Plato's claim that dialectic, unlike geometry, grasps not only a string of valid conclusions that

25. Ibid.
26. Ibid.
27. Ibid., 1139a 30.
28. Ibid., 1141a 15.

follow from some premise, or "beginning" (e.g., the geometric definition of a triangle) but grasps the beginning itself (the mode of being of the geometric triangle).

Aristotle strikingly echoes Plato by calling wisdom "intellect *(nous)* combined with science *(episteme)*" *(he sophia nous kai episteme)*.[29] By "intellect," or *nous*, Aristotle means a comprehensive awareness of first causes, or beginnings. By "science," or *episteme*, he means knowledge that grasps things that are unchanging, for example, statements that follow necessarily from given premises. *Sophia* combines *episteme* and *nous* in this respect: Like *episteme*, *sophia* concerns things that are unchanging. But unlike *episteme*, which relies upon unquestioned beginnings, or assumptions, and grasps only what follows, *sophia* draws upon *nous*, which grasps the beginnings themselves. In this sense, *sophia* is knowledge of the most honorable things; it is knowledge of the unchanging first causes.

Now, the Good, according to Aristotle's account, is just such a "first cause"—at least with respect to human action. As the first cause, or source, of human action, the Good, Aristotle writes, is among the "most honorable things."[30] Perhaps it is the single most honorable thing. At any rate, the Good is "beyond" the human things, and insofar as it is "among the most honorable things," it is among the primary aims of philosophy.

The difficult question, of course, is the sense in which the Good is unchanging, and, moreover, the sense in which the Good relates to the cosmos, to being as such. Aristotle's *Ethics* gives an implicit answer to the first and only hints at the second. The sense in which the Good is unchanging finds expression in Aristotle's account of *natural right*, which I discuss later in this chapter. His basic teaching is that although human life presents a multiplicity of ever-changing conventions and practices, it always aims at the same Good. In other words, the Good, in a sense, maintains its identity throughout its many expressions.

The sense in which the Good, for Aristotle, relates to the cosmos is ambiguous. If the Good, is, indeed, identical with the cosmos, then knowledge of the Good would be the single end of philosophy. And if so, then philoso-

29. Ibid., 1141b 1–5.
30. Ibid.

phy as such would be essentially situated. In Aristotle's terms, our practical or lived understanding of the Good would be the condition of our knowing the cosmos. Only on the basis of our understanding of the Good could we define the nature of the heavenly bodies and address the question of their revolution.

Although the *Ethics* does not directly address the relation of the Good to the cosmos, it provides some significant hints. For one, Aristotle describes both the Good and the cosmos in the same terms—as "more divine than man."[31] Although this description by no means establishes their identity, it at least suggests their kinship.

The most crucial evidence for Aristotle's identifying the Good and the cosmos and, thereby, for his situated conception of philosophy is the subtle, yet fundamental, link that he draws between *sophia* and *phronesis*. The link is obscured, to some extent, by the difference Aristotle highlights between the two. *Phronesis*, he insists, deals with the human things *(ta anthropeia)*, which, unlike the natural things, admit of variation. The characteristic trait of the *phronimos* is deliberative excellence *(euboulia)*, which always aims at a particular action, something that can be realized or neglected by human agency. For "no one deliberates about things incapable of being otherwise."[32] Insofar as *phronesis* deals with human affairs, things that can differ and thus are not "everywhere and always," *phronesis* is an "inferior" *(cheiron)* kind of knowledge to wisdom *(sophia)*.[33]

Aristotle qualifies this inferiority, however, by linking *phronesis* to *sophia* in an important respect: both faculties, Aristotle maintains, draw upon *nous*—a comprehensive awareness of beginnings *(archai)*, or first causes. This linkage to *nous* would suggest that both *phronesis* and *sophia* have a certain exalted character as compared to *episteme* and *techne* which can achieve their aims without considering the first cause from which they spring.

The precise character of Aristotle's conception of *"nous"* is difficult to discern, but this much he makes clear: *nous* is not a capacity for abstract intuition or thought. It is connected, rather, to life experience *(emperia)*. In a telling passage, Aristotle writes: "The beginnings of the study of nature

31. Ibid.
32. Ibid., 1141b 10–15.
33. Ibid., 1143b 30–35.

come not from abstract principles but from life experience *(emperia)*."[34] Thus Aristotle ties *nous* to *emperia*, and considers it to be the basis of the study of *nature (phusis)*. For this reason, he adds, children can be mathematicians but not philosophers. The study of mathematics concerns the relations among terms (numbers) in abstraction from what the terms represent. Children with sufficient acuity can learn such abstract relations. Philosophy, by contrast, requires a grasp of things themselves. It therefore requires lived experience, which children lack.[35]

In a passage shortly thereafter, he considers *nous* to be the basis not only of *sophia*, but of *phronesis:* "*Phronesis* lies across from *nous;* for as *nous* grasps the first definitions, which cannot simply be reached by reasoning, *phronesis* [must draw upon *nous*] to grasp what is ultimate *(eschaton)* [in the particular circumstance]."[36] Aristotle elaborates *nous* as a special sort of "perception" *(aisthesis)*—"not the perception of the senses, but closer to the sort of intuition whereby we perceive that the ultimate [or most basic plane] figure in mathematics is a triangle; for here there is a stop [or limit of analysis]."[37] But *nous* is still "of a different kind" than mathematical intuition. For *nous* grasps what the concrete circumstance, as a whole, demands. In other words, *nous* grasps the Good as it appears in whatever concrete instance. So although *phronesis* deals with human action, with what can be otherwise, it draws upon a divine sort of awareness of what is "everywhere and always." In doing so, *phronesis* not only achieves its particular aim (the action to be done), but also, however implicitly, clarifies the Good, the condition of all action.

Based on Aristotle's account of how *phronesis* and *sophia* involve *nous*, his teaching might be summarized as follows: our comprehensive awareness of the Good is the source of both moral judgment and the study of nature (all that has come into being). That is to say, the question of how to act and the question of what nature is can be answered only from within the realm of human action—from within the comprehensive perspective

34. Ibid., 1142a 15–20.
35. Ibid., 1142a 15–25.
36. Ibid., 1142a 25–30.
37. Ibid.

of the Good. Philosophical understanding, is, as such, a kind of "situated" understanding.

But lest we become mired in the depths of these obscurities, we should recognize a much clearer way in which philosophy, according to Aristotle, is situated rather than detached. This has to do with the relation of philosophy to opinion, or to "what is generally said" about the matter. Philosophical beginnings, or starting points *(archai)*, writes Aristotle, attain their credence, or justification, only in relation to opinion *(doxa)*. And the "beginning," Aristotle reiterates, "is more than half of the whole; for the beginning sheds much light on what is to be investigated."[38]

Accordingly, he writes, in the case of our starting from the notion that the Good is *eudaimonia,* "we must examine this beginning not only as a conclusion following from certain assumptions, *but also in light of what is said about the matter"* (emphasis added). For "all opinions will cohere with a true beginning, whereas they will soon diverge from a false one."[39] Opinions, then, are not merely extraneous considerations to be validated or rejected in light of a context-free, objective analysis of the phenomenon. It is not as though we first learn what the Good really is, and then, as a separate matter, determine which opinions about it are true and which are false. Opinion, suggests Aristotle, is *itself* an indispensable standard of philosophical knowledge.

How can opinion be such a standard? If we think in terms of the subject-object relation, Aristotle's claim seems obviously mistaken. For according to this way of thinking, the "truth" of an opinion (about the Good, or any topic) means its correspondence to the object, or to the "fact of the matter." Accordingly, an opinion is either "objective," that is, it corresponds to the fact, or it is "subjective," that is, it diverges from the fact and reflects our subjective error. Determining whether an opinion is "objective," or "subjective," requires knowing the object (through some sure method). The object itself is the only standard of knowledge. Aristotle does not think within this

38. Ibid., 1098b 5–10.
39. Ibid., 1098b 5–15.

framework. For him, opinion is *itself* a legitimate standard of knowledge—the standard by which our claims can and must be measured. His faith in opinion reflects the notion that "facts," or in his terms, the phenomena themselves, are not detached from what we say about them. Thus, his confidence that all opinions about the Good contain at least some insight comes *not* from his belief that such opinions, in some way, correspond to an independent, or abstract entity called "the Good." For, by his own admission, the consideration of opinions is necessary for establishing the nature of the Good in the first place. His confidence in opinion comes, rather, from his understanding that the Good, and indeed, any phenomenon, is constituted by *logos*. The Good is embodied in opinion. This statement by no means implies that any opinion reflects the complete truth, or that all opinions are equally insightful. Most are narrow and unsophisticated. Nevertheless, they all contain at least glimmers of insight.

Along these lines, Aristotle can sensibly maintain of the views about the Good, "Some are held by the many and by men of old; others are held by a few distinguished men. None of these views could be wholly mistaken. At least in part, or even for the most part, they are correct."[40] What appears to be a mere concession to authority actually contains philosophical insight. As divinations of the truth, opinions must constantly be considered in any account of the Good. For this reason, Aristotle tirelessly tests, substantiates, and revises his conception of *eudaimonia* in light of prevailing views on the matter. At one point, for example, with respect to the common opinion that the goods of the soul are higher than the goods of the body, Aristotle writes: "This opinion, being old and agreed upon by philosophers, bolsters what we have said [about happiness]."[41]

It should be clear that by thus relying on opinion, Aristotle does not capitulate to mere convention or blindly accept the word of reputable men. All relevant opinions, he maintains, must be considered in a philosophical analysis. If the opinions cohere with the starting point, they bolster its credence. If the opinions appear to clash with it, they must be rendered consistent—either by revising the starting point or by showing that the opinions, properly understood, actually substantiate it. Aristotle's appeal to

40. Ibid., 1098b 25–30.
41. Ibid., 1098b 10–20.

opinion is entirely critical. He never takes opinion—or his own starting point—simply at face value. In Gadamer's terms, we might say that Aristotle presents a hermeneutic conception of philosophy.

Character as the Condition of Ethical Knowledge

Having outlined the sense in which Aristotle presents a situated conception of ethical philosophy and perhaps of philosophy in general, let us turn specifically to his conception of moral judgment. Aristotle points to the situated character of moral judgment from the beginning of the *Ethics* by insisting that even his own teaching (i.e., the contents of the *Ethics* itself) is an insufficient guide to action. The competent student of "the fine and the just," writes Aristotle, must *already* be "cultivated in fine habits"; he or she must already possess a virtuous character.[42] Theory requires practice. Only the cultivated person has the starting point *(arche)* from which to learn.

The Greek *arche*, or "beginning," is a key term for Aristotle. Rackham translates it as "first principle," but something like "basic starting point" better captures Aristotle's meaning.[43] "Principle" is somewhat misleading, as it suggests some precept or rule that one has in mind. The *arche* of ethics, Aristotle makes clear, is not an object of knowledge, but a practical understanding of how to act well—an understanding expressed in one's actions and cultivated by experience. Thus, the person cultivated in fine habits "already has the starting point."[44]

Aristotle reiterates the practical character of ethics in his claim that children are unqualified to study it.[45] The reason is not that children lack some cognitive ability or mental sharpness that adults possess. For as Aristotle points out, children can become proficient students of mathematics. Nor is it simply that children tend to be led by their passions and lack the discipline to apply the ethical precepts they learn in class. Although Aristotle mentions this consideration, he highlights a more basic reason why children cannot learn ethics: they lack the *experience* necessary to have attained the right disposition of character. They lack the basic condition of knowing how

42. Ibid., 1095b 5–7.
43. Cf. Aristotle, *Nicomachean Ethics*, 13.
44. Aristotle, *Nicomachean Ethics*, 1095b 9.
45. Ibid., 1095a.

to act: "They are inexperienced *(apeiros)* in the activities of life, and it is from these and about these" that ethical philosophy reasons.[46] In other words, children lack the right *life perspective* from which ethical teaching makes sense. This perspective is the *arche,* the starting point, which is "of great importance for the subsequent course of the inquiry" and admittedly "more than half of the whole."[47] Without roots in actual life, warns Aristotle, the teaching of the *Ethics* will fall flat. It will become mere preaching without resonance—just as a phrase repeated many times over becomes a mere sound. Although children can repeat philosophical principles, writes Aristotle, they do so without any real conviction that what they say is true.[48]

But although a grasp of ethical philosophy requires a practical understanding of how to live well, philosophy is by no means superfluous. Aristotle indeed has moral wisdom to impart—wisdom that pertains to practice, that is supposed to improve our character. Otherwise his endeavor would be pointless—a mere repetition of what we, his students, already know. To the person brought up in fine habits, philosophy can impart a *clearer* vision of what he or she already understands. This is precisely Aristotle's aim. He seeks to give an account *(logos)* of virtue as an illuminating guideline for good judgment. At the same time, however, he aims to highlight the *insufficiency* of all such guidelines. Both teachings are equally important—not only as theoretical insights, but for the spirit in which we live.

Aristotle's first lesson addresses the second point: ethical teaching can provide only a "broad outline of the truth."[49] This statement, which Aristotle repeats several times at the beginning of the *Ethics,* is not meant to acknowledge his own shortcoming as a teacher. The claim is intended, rather, to state a truth about ethical knowledge—that because it involves practical wisdom, it evades being taught as a system of rules. His goal is to bring to consciousness the essentially practical nature of ethical knowledge and to ward off false interpretations that see ethics as purely theoretical, teachable in the same sense as number or geometry.

The imprecision of ethical philosophy is thus determined by the subject matter *(hule)* itself, not by a lack of rigor on our part. Aristotle's point is that

46. Ibid., 1095a 3–4.
47. Ibid., 1098b 5.
48. Ibid., 1142b 15.
49. Ibid., 1094b 20–25.

virtue and the Good life are inaccessible to cognition or abstract thought alone. We learn about them through practice. Moreover, our practice has a certain dynamic character, driven, in part, by theory. Any account of how to act inevitably informs our practice—quite apart from whether we explicitly affirm or reject the account. Simply in virtue of providing alternative terms of description, the account will come to recast what it describes. The ethical phenomena are never wholly unchanged by how we speak of them. Any description, any web of concepts that we attempt to throw around our practices will never contain them. For the web will inevitably dissolve into the practices themselves. An educated person knows this, and, in general, knows that one must "seek that amount of exactness in each kind [of study] which the nature of the thing admits." For example, "it seems just as unreasonable to accept probable conclusions from a mathematician as to demand [formal] demonstrations from an orator."[50] (We can imagine what Aristotle's response would have been to Descartes's claim that all knowledge is "certain and evident cognition." From Aristotle's point of view, Descartes's claim represents an overblown desire for scientific precision that fails to distinguish between the truth grasped by science [episteme] and the truth grasped by practical wisdom [phronesis].)

Thus, Aristotle claims that his own ethical teaching can serve only as a guideline for action, not as a how-to manual. This claim itself is meant as a first lesson. It is meant to draw our attention to the practical nature of ethical judgment. (Although anyone's actual judgments and actions would have expressed this insight, his account of the nature of his judgments might have failed to do so. For example, he might have claimed to be acting on principles alone when, in reality, his judgment involved practical wisdom. For such a person, Aristotle's teaching would be clarifying.)

In the following, Aristotle intends to provide his students with a fuller understanding of what practical judgment entails and a clearer account of their actions—of what it means to act bravely, generously, justly, and so on, and of what it means to live a good life as a whole. This fuller understanding is intended to cultivate the dispositions with which his students begin. The relationship of character and philosophy thus mirrors the circular movement of character and action. Just as character shapes and is shaped by action

50. Ibid.

(i.e., acting virtuously), character shapes and is shaped by philosophical understanding. (In Aristotle's final analysis, philosophical understanding is really just a special type of action, indeed the highest action of the soul.) So from the beginning of the *Ethics,* Aristotle makes clear that grasping the right thing to do presupposes a virtuous character—a practical understanding of how to live well. He does not hesitate to apply this claim to his own account of ethics. Ethical instruction can improve character but is no substitute for it.

Character as the Union of Nature *(phusis)* and Habit *(ethos)*

If we develop a virtuous character through habit *(ethos),* then it would seem that our virtue does not come from nature *(phusis)*—at least if "nature" means what is fixed and given in the species. For according to this conception, "nothing that is by nature a certain way can be altered by habit."[51] No matter how many times one throws a stone upward, for example, it will not become habituated to rise instead of fall. Its nature is to be drawn toward the earth.[52]

But although virtue does not come from nature in this sense, virtue is not "against nature" *(para phusin)* either.[53] For nature, according to Aristotle, does not simply mean what is fixed and given in the species or what arises in the absence of human action. The nature of a thing, he teaches, is defined by its *end (telos),* or the essential character toward which it tends. In the case of human beings, Aristotle suggests, the "end" must be understood in terms of *"ergon,"* or characteristic *activity.*[54] This activity is that of the *soul,* or more specifically, of the virtues that define the soul, the virtues of character and of thought. But the virtues can be realized only through habit, and for this reason, habit and nature are intertwined. Aristotle thus maintains that human beings are endowed by nature with the capacity for virtue, but this capacity "is brought to maturity by habit."[55]

The link between habit and nature is the basis for Aristotle's distinction between "natural virtue" *(phusike arete)* and "true virtue" *(kuria arete).*[56]

51. Ibid., 1103a 20.
52. Ibid.
53. Ibid., 1103a 20–25.
54. Ibid., 1097b 25.
55. Ibid., 1103a 25.
56. Ibid., 1144b.

The first refers to our capacity, or potential, for virtue that we possess from the moment of birth *(euthus ex genetes)*, but with no guarantee of realizing it. The second refers to virtue in the full sense, as perfected by habit and *phronesis*. At first, the distinction gives the impression that Aristotle proposes two kinds of virtue, a crude "natural" version and a purified "true" one. But he soon makes clear that "natural virtue" really is not virtue at all. "Natural virtue," Aristotle writes, is like a strong-bodied blind man who stumbles about heavily because of his lack of sight. There is nothing virtuous in such a man's clumsy movements. But if he were somehow to acquire sight, his powerful frame could allow him to move with strength and coordination, to move "virtuously."[57] Thus "true" virtue is altogether different from "natural" virtue. In other words, we are not born with a sullied version of virtue that we subsequently clean off through habit and *phronesis*—as when we wipe dirt off vegetables just plucked from the earth. Habit and *phronesis* are not simply cleaning agents that reveal in full clarity what was present from birth. Only through habit and *phronesis* does virtue, and hence, the entire soul, acquire its *shape*. Human beings are, by nature, what they become through their own action.

But if so, has "nature" not fallen out of the picture entirely? If human "nature" is shaped by human action, and if human action is guided by choice *(prohairesis)*, unconditioned by the merely given, then in what sense does the term "nature" describe human beings at all? It would seem that the "nature" of a human being is to have no nature, which, if true, would make the very term "nature" superfluous. And yet, Aristotle firmly maintains that human beings do have a nature. What he means by "nature" clearly is not captured by the contrast of "given from birth" to "acquired by upbringing."

To understand Aristotle's meaning, we must consider "nature" as the counterpart not to upbringing, habit, or action, but to *convention (nomos)*. Aristotle develops this distinction in his treatment of natural *(phusikon)* versus conventional *(nomikon)* justice.[58] To say that human beings have a nature is to say that the soul has an essential character whose shape is not forged by arbitrary decision. The concept of "nature" reflects the fact that human beings are not self-creative. Although the soul acquires its shape through

---

57. Ibid., 1144b 10.
58. Ibid., 1134a 20.

habit, *phronesis,* choice, and action, it still has a discernible character that, in a sense, remains the same. In this sense, the soul can be said to have a "nature." The basis of the soul's nature is its lived awareness of the Good, the unchosen source of the decisions that define its identity. Insofar as the Good retains its identity through change, so too does human life.

It should be clear, at least, that Aristotle's special sense of "nature" is altogether different from the notion that arose during the Enlightenment, the notion of a basic dimension of our being—whether an instinct, sentiment, or behavior—that obtains independent of our reason and choice. If anyone is to be charged with asserting a simple-minded sort of "biologism" or "naturalism" it is David Hume, not Aristotle.

Aristotle's view denies the opposition of human nature and habit that lies at the heart of Smith's and Hume's moral thought. Both, as we have seen, argue that moral judgment is based ultimately on natural sympathy, understood in contrast to habit and custom. They defend habit only to the extent that good habit counteracts bad habit, allowing us to consistently act according nature, that is, to sympathetically identify with humanity at large. But this natural tendency, they insist, is given independent of habit. Good habit alters bad habit but in no way alters nature. Good habit is really a mere servant to nature, defending her dignity against the unnatural social tendencies that assault her. Good habit fights bad, and in the end, nature stands pure.

Aristotle, by contrast, denies such a thing as "human nature," understood as a sentiment shared throughout the species, independent of human habits, customs, and practices. How we feel and what we want, he teaches, is always shaped by our aims and how we articulate them, ultimately, by our understanding of the good life. As we develop such an understanding through habit and education, our sentiments evolve as well. Aristotle captures this connection of reason and desire in the phrase *orektikos nous,* or "desiring understanding." To emphasize the union of the two terms, he also reverses the phrase, changing it to *orexis dianoetike,* or "understanding desire."[59] According to Aristotle's account, the notion of "pure" desire, or "natural" sentiment detached from habit and custom, is as much a phantom as "pure" reason.

What is natural for human beings is always tied to habit and custom. Thus Aristotle famously asserts that "man is *by nature* a political animal"

59. Ibid., 1139b 5.

(emphasis added).[60] Contrary to appearance, this statement does not mean that political associations *(polei)* arise spontaneously out of basic human needs—for shelter, security, and the like. For according to Aristotle, such needs could be fulfilled by nonpolitical arrangements, arrangements akin to the guarantees of peace and commerce among different cities. Human beings are by nature political in that they realize their nature only as members of a *polis*. For only by living together, by growing up in a certain community, by learning to deliberate and judge, do human beings develop the virtues definitive of soul.

Aristotle's way of thinking thus challenges the familiar contemporary contrasts between "nature" and "nurture," between "essence" and "human choice," between what is "given" and what is "socially constructed." Aristotle reveals that all such contrasts are misguided. They miss the sense in which nature involves our agency. The supposed opposition between human agency and nature could arise only when people came to understand themselves as decisively separate from the world in which they lived, when people came to see "nature" as an "objective" field of forces, governed by laws independent of human "subjectivity." On the basis of this world picture, it indeed makes sense to speak of "nature" versus "artifice" and to raise the question of whether and to what extent our behavior (or any feature of our being) is simply "given" or up to us. At any rate, this notion of "nature," the notion of a force that directs human life from "the outside," is a modern bias read back into Aristotle. It is the bias of our tendency to split the world into subjects and objects.

Because human nature, according to Aristotle, is realized by human action, our character is not a result of some natural disposition over which we lack all control. So to understand Aristotle's conception of character as a sort of prejudice productive of good judgment, we must distinguish it from Hume's and Smith's familiar notion of natural sentiment.

Character as the Condition of Its Acquisition and the Basis of Moral Judgment

Although our disposition of character is achieved and not merely given, it is neither a product of our making nor something we can acquire from "square

---

60. Aristotle, *Politics*, trans. H. Rackham (Cambridge: Harvard University Press, 1932), 1253a 2.

one." To acquire character, we must already, in a certain sense, possess it. For every virtuous deed we accomplish, each step we take toward acquiring a virtuous character, itself presupposes such a character. In other words, to grasp the standard of virtuous action, we must, in a sense, be virtuous already. Because character conditions its acquisition, character is a kind of prejudice. To get it, we must have it.

The sense of this paradox emerges in Aristotle's comparison of virtue to craft knowledge *(techne)*. In a general sense, we acquire virtue and craft knowledge in the same way—through practice, broadly conceived as "doing" rather than simply thinking. For example, "men become builders by building houses, harpers by playing the harp. In the same way, we become just by doing just things, moderate by doing moderate things, brave by doing brave things."[61] A person cannot become just simply by learning principles of justice any more than an apprentice can become a house builder simply by learning rules of house building. In both cases, the student must put his hands to the actual deeds. Only through trial and error can he acquire the right "touch," the excellence required of his role.

But in one significant respect, the mode of acquiring virtue and craftsmanship diverge. The divergence concerns the kind of standard that determines an act of virtue and the kind that determines an act of production:

> The crafts are not really the same as the virtues. The things produced
> by craftsmanship hold their goodness [or usefulness] in themselves, so
> that it is enough if they are produced having a certain character of their
> own; but acts done according to the virtues are not done virtuously—
> for example, justly or moderately—if they themselves are of a certain
> character, but only if the actor does them with a certain disposition.[62]

Herein lies a crucial distinction. When Aristotle says that works of craft "hold their goodness in themselves," he means that the standard of a good shoe, a couch, or a chair, can be read off the finished product itself. One can look at the product and thereby determine whether it embodies the form *(eidos)* appropriate to its function. One need not know the craftsman who

---

61. Aristotle, *Nicomachean Ethics*, 1103b 1–5.
62. Ibid., 1104b 25–30.

made the product, the circumstances under which he made it, or whether he took pleasure in his creation. None of this background knowledge has any bearing on whether the product is, in fact, good.

In the case of a virtuous deed, however, one cannot simply read off its merit by looking to some "finished product" (i.e., the deed done) detached from the conditions under which it was enacted. For the meaning of the deed, what it *is,* whether or not it is virtuous, is constituted by the underlying *attitude* of the actor. If a deed is to count as virtuous, writes Aristotle, the actor must "choose it knowingly, for its own sake, and from a firm and unwavering disposition [of character]."[63] If the actor fails in any of these regards, the deed itself is not entirely praiseworthy. For example, if someone gives lavishly to a friend, yet hates relinquishing the money, the act itself, however beneficial to the friend, is not truly generous. For the benefactor, in this case, prizes money more than a fine deed. By contrast, a cobbler who makes a fitting pair of shoes but despises shoemaking nevertheless produces shoes worthy of merit. His attitude does not detract from the character of the product. Similarly, as Aristotle points out, an apprentice who has not acquired a disposition toward excellence (he still makes more errors than not), may nevertheless hit the mark on occasion; and in these cases, the quality of the product is no worse for the craftsmen's inconsistency. In the case of moral virtue, however, one cannot hit the mark by chance. For the "mark" itself includes the right disposition. Aristotle summarizes the special standard of a virtuous action as follows: to be virtuous, the action must be done as the virtuous *person* would do it.[64] The action presupposes a virtuous disposition of character.

Thus emerges the circle between virtuous character and virtuous action. We acquire a virtuous character only by means of virtuous actions. But any such action presupposes that we already have a virtuous character. Thus, we cannot acquire a virtuous character from "square one." We cannot leap from a state of complete moral ignorance to a state of virtue.

In the case of a *techne,* by contrast, the "virtuous" disposition, that is, the disposition toward excellence, is not presupposed by any particular act of production. The products "hold their goodness in themselves." For this

63. Ibid., 1104b 30.
64. Ibid., 1105 5.

reason, a *techne* can truly be acquired from the ground up: by looking to the *eidos* of the product and by learning how to manipulate the materials through trial and error, we can learn a *techne* that we previously lacked. But we cannot learn a virtue in this way. In order to perform even a single virtuous deed, we must be virtuous already.

To fully understand the sense in which moral judgment, according to Aristotle, involves a virtuous disposition of character, we must examine more closely his account of the standard *(horos)* of a virtuous deed. Continuing the analogy to *techne*, Aristotle insists that both a virtuous deed and a successful act of production are done "according to right reason" *(kata ton orthon logon)*, according to a standard that the actor can, in principle, articulate.[65] A virtuous deed cannot be based on thoughtless instinct or even a "good hunch" *(eustochia)*.[66]

But what, exactly, is the nature of the standard? In the case of a craft product, the answer is relatively straightforward: the standard of "right reason" is the *eidos* suited to the product's use. The craftsman's task is to grasp the *eidos* and embody it in the right material. In the case of a virtuous deed, the standard is clearly more complicated: "according to right reason" cannot simply mean according to a distinct *eidos,* or according to a principle that one has in mind. For what makes the action virtuous is whether the actor carries it out in the right spirit—whether he does it at "the right time, on the right occasion, toward the right people, for the right purpose, and in the right manner." He must act, writes Aristotle, "always with an eye to what is fitting in the circumstance" *(ta pros to kairon skopein)*.[67] In other words, what makes the action virtuous is whether it meets what the *situation* demands.

To understand the end—the deed to be done—the actor must understand the situation. But understanding, in this case, means something quite different from beholding a fixed form, as the craftsman does when he envisions the *eidos* of his product. For the agent himself is involved in the situation he seeks to understand. As Gadamer comments: "Moral knowledge, as

65. Ibid., 1103b 30.
66. Ibid., 1142b 1.
67. Ibid., 1104 5.

Aristotle describes it, is clearly not objective knowledge—i.e., the knower is not standing over against a situation that he merely observes; he is directly confronted with what he sees."[68] The nonobjective character of moral knowledge does not, of course, mean that such knowledge is subjective. The point is that the subject-object framework fails to capture the relationship of the actor and his or her circumstance. As Aristotle's formulation suggests, the circumstance, or "situation," is *personal*. Understanding the situation means, at the same time, understanding one's self. It means grasping how to live well, understanding the relative significance of particular roles and activities, balancing competing commitments adeptly. Clearly the craftsman's understanding of successful production is not situated in this way. To make a good pair of shoes, the cobbler need not grasp on what occasion to make shoes, for whom, or for what purpose (beyond foot covering). (Nor does he even need to know how to use shoes, i.e., what shoes to wear when.) All he needs to know is the *eidos*. With that in view, he can make a pair of shoes that will be good or bad in itself depending on whether or not it meets the standard.

Aristotle's contrast of the practice of moral judgment to the practice of craftsmanship is clearly summarized by Gadamer:

> The image that a man has of what he ought to be—i.e., his ideas of right and wrong, or decency, courage, dignity, loyalty, and so forth (all concepts that have their equivalent in Aristotle's catalogue of virtues)—are certainly in some sense images that he uses to guide his conduct. But there is still a basic difference between this and the guiding image the craftsman uses: the plan of the object he is going to make. What is right, for example, cannot be fully determined independently of the situation that requires a right action from me, whereas the eidos of what a craftsman wants to make is fully determined by the use for which it is intended.[69]

The way in which actions, considered from an ethical standpoint, are never good "in themselves" but depend for their merit on the situation is exemplified by a good joke. For a joke to be funny, it must be delivered at the right moment. Even the most hilarious joke loses its charm when blurted out

---

68. Gadamer, *Truth and Method*, 312.
69. Ibid., 315.

during a solemn moment of silence. In this case, it is no longer a joke at all, but rather an inappropriate remark. The situation determines the character of the action. Aristotle claims that all virtuous deeds are so constituted.

Although we can certainly articulate the details of the right situation for a joke, or for any action, such an account will fail to fully represent the situation for someone not "there" with us. Even the most incisive accounts *(logoi)* lose their edge in abstraction from the situations they describe. Hence the difficulty of capturing the spirit of an event (perhaps a party among friends, a political campaign, a project at work) for someone who was absent. The difficulty arises not primarily because the absent person lacks information. If information were all that he or she needed, we could simply provide it. What makes the task so difficult is the *nature* of the "information" at stake—its irreducibly practical character. What the absent person lacks is a sense for the participants we describe, for their character as expressed in the cadence of their step, the tone of their voice, the timing of their actions. The words that call attention to all of these nuances for those who are there with us remain empty phrases to the person who missed the party. Thus our grasp of a situation is always itself situated. In Aristotle's terms, it involves *phronesis.*

As this example suggests, one person's account of a situation may, of course, shed light upon it and contribute to the (situated) understanding of others. When one person points out the nuances of a situation to another (who is also there), the other may gain a new way of viewing the event, perhaps a deeper appreciation for it. This sort of pointing out is what Aristotle does in his analyses of what actions (in what situations) count as brave, temperate, just, and so on. The ability to give an insightful account of the situation, what Aristotle calls "deliberative excellence" *(euboulia),* is, in fact, the characteristic quality of the *phronimos,* the person who excels in practical wisdom. Nevertheless, the accounts of such a person, or of Aristotle himself, are not self-sufficient models for how to act. They depend on the very situations they describe. To someone "outside" the actual situation, to someone without a basic practical grasp of the commitments at stake, the account would be uninformative.

Aristotle offers two ways of seeing why. First, any account intended to capture the conditions for a certain action will always admit of exceptions.

Aristotle addresses the problem of exceptions in his discussion of "legal justice" *(nomimos dikaios)* and its imperfection. The law must attempt to specify the conditions of an illegal action. But even good laws necessarily involve some error, for the law "is always a general statement, and a general statement is insufficient to cover certain cases." This insufficiency "does not make the law any worse [as a law]; for the error is not in the law or the law giver, but in the nature of the thing: the subject matter is human action, which is essentially irregular."[70] To be truly just, the law must, in certain cases, be corrected by the judgment of the rulers, by what Aristotle calls "equity" or "appropriateness" *(epiekes)*. Equity requires that the rulers supplement the law with ordinances that respond to the concrete situation. For a situation is, by its nature, indefinite, and what is indefinite, Aristotle writes, "can only be measured by an indefinite standard—like the leaden rule used by Lesbian builders." Just as that rule "is not rigid but can move around the shape of the stone, so a special decree is made to fit the particular affair at hand."[71] Aristotle's teaching on law applies, in principle, to any sort of statement about how to act, including his own accounts of the virtues. Just as the law always involves exceptions, so does any statement about the right thing to do.

Consider, for example, Aristotle's treatment of courage *(andreia)*. The mark of a courageous person, writes Aristotle, is to risk a noble *(kalon)* death for the sake of its nobility.[72] To be fearless in the face of imminent disaster is not brave. Nor is risking death in order to escape poverty or pain. For in such cases, one aims not at nobility, but at the escape from some evil.[73] Furthermore, courageous people must risk a noble death in the right manner. They must recognize the full weight of the impending danger, be aware of the potential losses involved, and push forward nonetheless. People who are excessively optimistic are not really brave. Their fearlessness comes not from conviction, but from a failure to grasp the risk of the situation.[74] The same holds true for those overcome by rage *(thumos)*. Although they often fight tenaciously, they too lack an appropriate sense of what they could lose.[75]

---

70. Aristotle, *Nicomachean Ethics*, 1137b 15.
71. Ibid., 1137b 25–30.
72. Ibid., 1115b 10.
73. Ibid., 1116 10–15.
74. Ibid., 1117a 10–15.
75. Ibid., 1117a 5.

But even this nuanced definition of bravery admits of exceptions. Aristotle suggests that a brave man "can throw away his shield, and can wheel around and run away."[76] This might be the case, for example, even if the cause is noble but victory is hopeless. It might also be the case if the person came to realize that he had too much to lose. Although this attitude would appear to be cowardly, especially in light of the Greek warrior ethic, Aristotle suggests that it may actually be consistent with bravery. For if, indeed, the person does have much to lose, for example, if he possesses many other virtues to such a degree that "life is worth most" to him, "and he stands to lose the greatest goods," then fighting might be reckless rather than brave.[77] Such a person would manifest his bravery only for a great cause. In ordinary circumstances, he might appear cowardly even though, in reality, he is the bravest of all. The "great-souled" man *(ho megalopsuchos)*, writes Aristotle, "is not someone who risks small dangers, nor is he someone who loves danger in general, for he honors very few things." He is "someone who will risk only great dangers, and, in such cases, will be ready to sacrifice his life; for he realizes that life is not worth living in all cases."[78]

These exceptions to the rule for what counts as courage illustrate the incompleteness of any account of the circumstances that call forth certain actions. Although stating exceptions, as Aristotle does, can contribute clarity to the account, at a certain point, a list of exceptions becomes gratuitous. For there will always be exceptions to exceptions, many of which cannot be foreseen.

A second way in which Aristotle expresses the situated character of moral judgment is that such judgment involves grasping "particulars" *(ta kath' hekasta)*. *Phronesis,* Aristotle writes, involves apprehending the "ultimate and particular things" *(ta eschata kai ta kath' hekasta)*. To grasp such particulars, we cannot simply look at them from a distance. We must be engaged with them in the context of our lives. This sort of apprehension is not that of science *(episteme)*, nor is it something attained by reason *(logos)*. It is a certain type of perception *(aisthesis)*, but not that of the senses. Because it appre-

76. Ibid., 1137a 10.
77. Ibid., 1117b 10.
78. Ibid., 1124b 5–10.

hends what is basic to any deliberation, it is closer to "the sort of intuition whereby we perceive that the [basic plane figure] in mathematics is a triangle; for here too there will be a stop [or limit of analysis]." But the intuition of *phronesis* is still of a different kind.[79] Aristotle describes this kind of intuition as *nous,* which he also calls the eye of the soul. What *nous* means is mysterious. Aristotle makes clear that it requires experience *(emperia).* Only the experienced person, writes Aristotle, has *nous.* He has a certain eye for particulars that a novice lacks. But only in virtue of *nous* do we "catch sight of particulars," or acquire experience, in the first place. *Nous,* as Aristotle understands it, must be a way of expressing our lived experience as a whole, our disposition of character, our fundamental awareness of the Good. *Nous,* in this sense, is the condition of our ability to give an account of particulars.[80]

To see how ethical insight requires *nous,* we might consider the familiar virtue of generosity. In Aristotle's terms, it involves giving to the right people, and the right amount, and at the right time, and for the right end.[81] The generous person must grasp all of these particulars. But how? Let us consider the "right people." The generous person does not give indiscriminately but to some more than to others. For example, he would presumably give more, or at least different things and in a different way, to friends as compared to strangers. Thus he must know who his friends are. As certain as he may be, this certainty cannot be established simply by reflection on the meaning of a friend in general. For an essential part of what makes someone a friend is not that he or she exemplifies some generic ideal of friendship, but that through shared experiences and activities, the person has become a significant part of one's life. The mark of close friends is a certain way of relating to each other, a "knowing" expressed in their actions, a mode of understanding that develops over time through living together.

The difficulty of describing what makes a particular person a friend brings to relief the practical nature of friendship. No matter how many character traits we might use in our description (for example, "loyal," "generous," "funny," and so on), we still end up describing a generic person. What makes this person and not someone else a friend slips through our fingers. A listener who had never met the person would have no way of distinguishing her

79. Ibid., 1142a 20–30.
80. Ibid., 1143b 10–20.
81. Ibid., 1120b 1–5.

from many other people who share the same qualities. To begin to capture what makes that person a friend, one is forced to become a storyteller—to speak of actual events and situations that typify the friendship and uncover the friend's unique place in one's life as a whole.

The story, unlike a set of principles or predicates, does not attempt to represent the quintessential qualities of a friend, as if the story could substitute for actually being there with the person. The point of a story is to transport the listeners to one's own actual life and, by doing so, to convey with greater depth the character of one's friend. But the life to which the listeners are transported is one's own as glimpsed through *theirs*. What makes the story effective, in other words, is the extent to which it refers the listeners to experiences (and a whole perspective) akin to one's own. The listeners' understanding of the particular (friend, or other relationship) thus remains a kind of situated understanding. It remains engaged with the particulars of their actual life. For this reason, the standard of virtue cannot be captured in an account.

The Dynamism of Virtue: How Our Way to the Good Shapes the End

To say that moral judgment is situated, or that it comes from the perspective of one's character, is to say that moral judgment is inescapably *personal*. It always follows from one's *own life*. Aristotle captures this personal aspect of moral judgment in his definition of the *phronimos* as someone best able to determine the good *for himself*.[82] In a similar vein, Aristotle writes that the ethical mean *(mesotes)*, the standard of right action, is not fixed and universal like a numerical mean, but is relative to one's own (particular circumstance).[83] It could therefore be said that Aristotle defends a certain ethic of *self-interest*. In contrast to Smith and Kant, who define morality as a kind of self-denial, as the detachment from one's particular concerns, Aristotle connects morality to self-fulfillment. He implies that moral obligation can be justified only in terms of one's own good, one's own *eudaimonia*. But Aristotle has an expansive notion of one's own. Unlike Kant, who under-

82. Ibid., 1140a 25–30.
83. Ibid., 1106a 25–1106b 10.

stands one's own as "subjective and personal," or Hume, who sees it as "private and particular," Aristotle understands one's own as public, as part of a way of life shared with others, a common good. The *phronimos* is not concerned with "himself" in contrast to "everyone else." In considering the good for himself, writes Aristotle, the *phronimos* is necessarily directed toward his domestic affairs, toward politics, and ultimately, toward the whole way of life in which these activities fit—toward the good life as such.[84]

The disposition of character, or perspective, from which we judge is not a cave of private thoughts, feelings, or conscience, but a way of life open to interpretation. And those who are there with us are all potential interpreters. That our disposition of character is an intelligible perspective, open to interpretation, means that its contours are never fixed. Furthermore, the particular practices and roles that shape our character are constantly evolving; as they evolve, so too does our character. This evolution is never, of course, a neutral process of development; for our roles and activities always express an interpretation of their worth. Any change of disposition implies a better or worse perspective—a deeper or shallower understanding of the good life. At every moment, we are acquiring such an understanding as we take up involvements and neglect others. Even maintaining a certain role, despite all appearance, is never the mere continuing of the same thing. For to continue a certain activity means to maintain it in the face of other possibilities. The activity thereby persists in a new form, as something to which we hold on despite rival opportunities. Even in cases where we speak of someone becoming "fixed" in his or her demeanor or perspective, this fixity too, for better or for worse, is really a development acquired through lived experience, always becoming more or less fixed as it is confirmed or challenged.

But although we are constantly in the process of acquiring our character, often imperceptibly, certain moments tend to shape it more significantly than others. One such moment is having to make an important moral judgment—having to size up the situation, to balance competing claims, and to decide how to act. By deliberating and judging well, we not only hit the mark in the particular case, but also develop our character; we clarify the very source that reveals the "mark" in any instance.

84. Ibid., 1142a 5–15.

By repeating virtuous actions, we develop a virtuous character. In this sense, we acquire character through *habit*. To "acquire," in this case, does not mean to gain something that we previously lacked. For any judgment is always already guided by one's character, by one's situated grasp of what the circumstance demands. In this sense, moral judgment involves prejudice.

Nevertheless, by making judgments, and by judging well consistently, we come to redefine our character, improving our basic prejudice. So in a certain sense, situated judgment has a transcendent dimension (akin to what Heidegger calls "projection"): it brings us beyond who we currently are. This transcendence, however, does not take us to some abstract realm removed from our concrete lives. To "transcend" ourselves means to clarify what we always, implicitly, are; it means to recognize certain features of our identity— certain activities, purposes, and roles—as more truly ours than we had previously realized.

Let us return, for example, to the soldier who desires to act courageously. In the midst of battle, he must consider whether to push forward or to throw down his arms and retreat. In determining how to act in that moment, in considering whether the nobility of the cause and the potential honor warrants the risk of dying, he would be forced to reflect on the things of significance in his life as a whole—on his other virtues, on his loyalty to family, friends, and country. In reflecting upon these things in light of the situation at hand, he may discover that certain loyalties actually carry greater weight than he had previously recognized. In any case, and however he decides to act, that particular moment of judgment will forever redefine the terms of certain relationships. For a country that one loves is not the same as a country for which one risked everything. And a close friend is not the same as a friend for whom one relinquished honor and returned home. The new terms in which the soldier understands these relationships changes their very character: some now evoke different feelings, demand greater loyalty, and acquire deeper significance.

Aristotle's version of the transcendent or "projective" character of understanding reveals the shallowness of Adam Smith's account of our loyalty to family, friends, and country. Smith calls such loyalties "constrained sympathies," as they arise, he claims, from our having to perpetually accommodate the same people, or from our having to constantly witness their joy and sorrow firsthand.[85] Smith's account neglects the way in which our loyalties are forged by the terms in which we interpret them and by the situations that give rise to such terms. The situations may be far removed from the physical presence of the people upon whom we reflect and come to cherish more deeply.

With the aid of Aristotle and Heidegger, we may summarize Smith's mistake as follows: Smith interprets devotion to one's own as "constrained sympathy" on the basis of a superficial analysis of "being-with-one-another." Specifically, he interprets such being (implicitly) as "the occurring together of several subjects" or as the perpetual "presence-at-hand" of those in our circle. By seeing the same people time and again, we become "habituated to sympathize with them."[86] Smith thereby derives the stronger loyalty we feel toward family members than toward cousins, toward cousins than toward "the greater part of other people."[87] The measure of loyalty is how frequently one sees a smile or tears on the face of another. Constant exposure to each other forges attachment. Captive to the subject-object worldview, Smith is blind to real source of our loyalties. He overlooks the way in which our devotion to family, friends, and country arises primarily through being together in a shared way of life. In many moments, and typically when our being together is most profound, when the spirit of our friend or relative defines our situation, such intimacy does not involve face-to-face presence. Rarely, even, does it involve having each other before the gaze of our conscious reflection.

Returning to Aristotle's ethics: what one gains through deliberation in the moment of judgment is not simply knowledge of the brave thing to do then and there, but a clearer grasp of the significance of particular relationships and ends; insofar as each part touches one's life as a whole, one gains a clearer understanding of the good as such—the very standard by which a brave action is measured.

The preceding considerations reveal the significance of habit for moral judgment. The repetition of virtuous action is not simply the means by which we

85. Adam Smith, *The Theory of Moral Sentiments,* ed. Ryan Patrick Hanley (New York: Penguin, 2009), 258–259.

86. Ibid.

87. Ibid.

become accustomed to doing the right thing, as if we knew it already and needed only to train ourselves to repeat it consistently. Habit is, rather, the condition of moral *knowledge*. Only through doing virtuous deeds do we cultivate the practical understanding that reveals the right thing to do.

Aristotle points us to the understanding involved in habit and helps correct the modern tendency to view habit in terms of mechanical behavior. According to the modern view, shaped largely by Enlightenment philosophers such as Hume and Smith, habit is, at best, a mere means for disposing people toward the right thing—where "the right thing" is conceived as knowable apart from habit. According to this familiar account, habit can be, at best, a valuable supplement to moral knowledge. For knowledge alone may not sufficiently motivate us to act virtuously. As Smith and Kant point out, even if we know the right thing to do, our opposing desires may pull us toward vice. By acquiring good habit, we counteract such desires and come to act virtuously all or at least most of the time. Smith, as we have seen, considers habit and custom to be, at best, mere means to becoming virtuous. The standard of virtue itself comes from the impartial spectator—a source supposedly detached from our habit.

In the grip of this way of thinking, Smith projects it onto Aristotle. According to Smith's reading of Aristotle, habit is separate from knowing the right thing to do: one can have a perfectly virtuous "motive and disposition of the heart," and thereby perform a single virtuous deed, quite apart from habit or a "steady or permanent character." In a striking misinterpretation, Smith claims that according to Aristotle, an action "which proceeds from an occasional fit of generosity is undoubtably a generous action," even if "the man who performs it is not necessarily a generous person."[88]

To read this view of habit back into Aristotle confuses the nature of ethical habit *(ethos)* with the type of "habit" associated with craft knowledge *(techne)*. In the case of a craft, the workman really does grasp the end in advance of attaining it. That end, moreover, the *eidos* of the product, remains the same throughout each successive act of production. In this case, "habit" is a mere means to an end. What the craftsman learns through "habit" is what kind of materials to use and how to successfully mold them; but in figuring out the right means, he does not illuminate the end.

88. Ibid., 323.

In the case of action *(praxis)*, by contrast, the standard, or the end at which bravery or moderation or justice aims, is not something that we fully know in advance and then, as a separate matter, fulfill through employing the right means. Although Aristotle writes that "we deliberate about means and not ends," he makes clear that the two are mutually dependent.[89] In Gadamer's terms:

> The relation between means and ends here is not such that one can know the right means in advance, and that is because the right end is not a mere object of knowledge either. There can be no anterior certainty concerning what the good life is directed toward as a whole. Hence, Aristotle's definitions of phronesis have a marked uncertainty about them, in that this knowledge is sometimes related more to the end, and sometimes more to the means to the end.[90]

Means and ends are inseparable: we begin with a basic understanding of the end (e.g., how to act courageously or justly), influenced by our character, which can be conceived as our life perspective, or our fundamental awareness of the Good. Through the activity of deliberating about how to fulfill the end, and simply through living our daily lives, we come to understand the end (and the Good) more clearly.[91]

The constitutive relationship of means and ends reveals the special sense in which virtue is natural, even though its meaning emerges from an

---

89. Aristotle, *Nicomachean Ethics*, 1112b 10.

90. Gadamer, *Truth and Method*, 318.

91. We see the same relationship of means and ends in Aristotle's claim about the origin of political life. The city, he writes, emerges from the needs of mere life but continues in existence for the sake of the good life (Aristotle, *Politics*, 1252b 30). Although human beings may in the first place found a city for the sake of shelter and comfort, supposing that these are the primary goods to be secured by politics, what they discover in the process turns out to be something more. For by employing the means to fulfill the end—by considering competing arrangements, arguing about which to adopt, drawing up agreements—human beings come to discover certain capacities, certain virtues of character and of thought, that point beyond the mere necessities of life. Politics, initially conceived as the means for securing necessities, turns out to be an end in itself. By engaging our capacities for virtue and for deliberating about the common good, politics gestures toward the question of the good as such—a question that can be fulfilled only by philosophy.

open-ended perspective. The natural character of virtue makes little sense without the situated character of moral judgment in view. The notion of a natural standard that nevertheless emerges from within our way of life cuts against the familiar conceptions of "nature," or "natural right," as opposed to habit, custom, and upbringing. According to Hume and Smith, for example, "nature" denotes the basic sentiments that condition moral judgment independent of our life circumstance. Although Kant understands "nature" as the realm of necessity, and thus rejects it as the source of moral judgment, he nevertheless maintains what could be called a notion of "natural right"—a universal standard of judgment, valid for all rational beings, independent of any situation or particular perspective.

Aristotle's special conception of natural right challenges the familiar opposition between nature and prejudice. Furthermore, the situated or "prejudicial" character of moral judgment is precisely the basis of its being natural as opposed to merely conventional. To see why this is so, let us consider once more the standard of moral judgment—this time, by comparison to Aristotle's definition of a merely conventional standard.

A standard is conventional "that from the beginning (*ex arches*) may be settle one way or the other indifferently"; for example, "that the ransom for a person shall be one mina" or that a "sacrifice shall consist of a goat and not two sheep."[92] A contemporary example would be that cars must drive on the right side of the road instead of on the left side (or vice versa, as the case may be). These standards may be settled indifferently because there is no higher, unchosen standard to guide the settlement. To raise the question of whether it is fitting for cars to drive on the right rather than the left, or for stop signs to be red instead of green, would make little sense.

Some people think, continues Aristotle, that the standard of virtue is determined in a similarly arbitrary manner—that some people decide upon one system of customs, others upon another. For example, "some people think that all the just things are merely conventional because whereas a law of nature is immutable and has the same validity everywhere, as fire burns both here and in Persia, the just things are seen to vary."[93] This sort of "conventionalist" view became even more prominent in modern times, largely

---

92. Aristotle, *Nicomachean Ethics*, 1134 15–25.
93. Ibid., 1134 20–30.

because of Thomas Hobbes's tremendous influence. Justice and all standards, he claimed, are the products of arbitrary human creation. This Aristotle denies. Unlike a traffic law, the standard of justice and of the rest of the virtues cannot be settled arbitrarily *ex arches*. For no matter what someone might declare as just or brave or generous—whether in a principle, a set of statements, or any sort of account—the claim is always open to the following question: By acting in this manner, do we acknowledge the full significance of all the commitments that the situation calls into play? In raising this question, we appeal to a standard of virtue irreducible to any particular opinion on the matter—a standard expressed in our commitments themselves, ultimately, in the whole way of life to which they point.

Although this standard emerges through human action, the standard is nevertheless natural. For the standard is not ordained by human beings, or created by the deeds of any particular people. Insofar as we can deliberate, judge, and act at all, we must already possess at least a faint grasp of the standard at which all action aims. By means of our deliberations, judgments, and actions, the standard of virtue comes more clearly to light. And in coming to light, the standard maintains a certain identity throughout change. In this sense, the standard really can be said to have the same force everywhere *(pantachou ten auten echon dunamin)*.[94]

The special sense in which the Good is natural answers to the basic question posed by Aristotle at the beginning of the *Ethics:* Does ethical inquiry set out from the *archai* or work toward them? The answer turns out to be both. We begin from an initial understanding of virtue—from a basic practical grasp of the relative significance of our roles and activities and a sense of how to balance them in the different situations that arise within our lives. By reflecting on this understanding, by questioning certain roles and activities in light of others, we gain a deeper understanding of their relative significance, a broader perspective as a whole, and a keener sense of what particular situations demand. In the end, we return to the beginning with greater insight. *Nous,* or the eye of the soul cultivated by experience, must therefore be "both a beginning and an end" *(kai arche kai telos nous)*. It is "both the starting point and the subject matter for demonstration."[95]

94. Ibid., 1134 15–20.
95. Ibid., 1143b 5–15.

With the situated character of virtue in view, we can also understand Aristotle's claim that the good life is blessed and therefore worthy of honor rather than praise. The word *eudaimonia* itself, typically translated as "the good life" or "happiness," really means "having a good deamon"—being shepherded throughout life by a guardian god. We might consider the good life blessed for the obvious reason that it depends, to some extent, on chance. No matter how virtuous a person may be, he still needs a god on his side. Without one, he may eventually meet the doom of an Orestes or Oedipus.

But the good life is blessed for a deeper reason, having to do with the very source of virtue. What counts as brave, generous, just, or magnanimous, Aristotle teaches, is not of our own making. In one sense, we do become virtuous by our agency: by the judgments we make, the deeds we execute, and the activities we carry out. But in another sense, virtue is not within our own power. For to judge well in the first place, we must already have a basic understanding of virtue expressed in the way we live. Ultimately, our acquisition of virtue depends on a pre-given standard—upon our lived awareness of the Good. Prejudice, in this comprehensive sense, is essential to moral understanding.

6

Prejudice and Rhetoric

If prejudice is indeed an indispensable feature of judgment, then what are the implications for politics? In this final chapter, I consider how the situated conception of judgment might lead us to reconsider some familiar views about the nature of political argument and how it should proceed. In particular, the situated conception forces us to rethink the familiar assumption that political rhetoric is a lowly kind of discourse—one that engages people's passions, interests, loyalties, and not their reason. This assumption figures prominently in contemporary discourse. It underlies the way we often dismiss a politician's speech as "mere rhetoric," as high-flown eloquence without substance, as a kind of deception, or as an attempt to mask a weak argument in rousing language.

One way of articulating the suspicion of rhetoric is that it appeals to people's *prejudices*. The best orators rarely persuade by stating abstract principles addressed to no one in particular. They typically persuade by speaking to different people differently—depending on who they are, where they live, and what they care about. The most persuasive speakers are often brilliant raconteurs, masters at using stories, images, and metaphors geared specifically to the audience at hand. In short, great orators are skilled at persuading people from within their particular life perspectives. In this sense, they are skilled at appealing to people's prejudices.

For precisely this reason, rhetoric tends to arouse suspicion. Some maintain that policies and principles should be justified in abstraction from the perspective of a given audience—in terms ideally accessible to anyone anywhere. Perhaps the most well-known statement of this view comes from John Rawls. According to his notion of "political liberalism," arguments about "constitutional essentials" (i.e., rights and the basic structure of society) depend for their validity on principles that can be justified "nonrhetorically," so to speak—without reference to the perspective of this or that group. In Rawls's terms, "public reason" means that "we do not view persons as socially situated or otherwise rooted . . . as having this or that comprehensive doctrine [this or that religious, philosophical, or moral worldview]."[1] According to this conception, we should justify our positions in terms of principles that do not depend on any particular moral or religious convictions. Although Rawls later revised his position to allow for arguments drawn from "comprehensive doctrines," he added a proviso that in "due course," people must give "properly public reasons to support their principles and policies."[2] But Rawls's notion of "properly public reasons" admits rhetoric only as an adornment to a legitimate political argument justified independently.

A helpful way of clarifying the suspicion of rhetoric, in both political theory and practice, is by considering what Bryan Garsten calls the "twin dangers" of persuasive speech—pandering and manipulation. He argues that rhetoric need not devolve into these perversions. At its best, rhetoric neither follows the crowd nor moves people like puppets on a string. Nevertheless, we tend to conflate rhetoric with such evils. We tend to assume that speech tailored to the passions and concerns of a given audience is, by its very nature, an uncritical kind of discourse, one that fails to engage people's reason. According to Thomas Nagel, for example, reason must be "a way of distancing one's self from common opinion and received practices."[3] This detached conception of reason leads to the disparagement of rhetoric as a

---

1. John Rawls, "The Idea of Public Reason Revisited," in *Political Liberalism* (New York: Columbia University Press, 2005), 481.

2. Ibid., 453.

3. Thomas Nagel, *The Last Word* (New York: Oxford University Press, 1997), 3.

kind of smooth talking that leads people astray, getting them to accept what their better judgment would denounce.

Perhaps not surprisingly, the disparagement of rhetoric as a brand of pandering or manipulation aligns with what I have called the two strands of the case against prejudice—the idea that prejudice is at odds with truth, or sound judgment, on the one hand, and with freedom, or agency, on the other. To say that rhetoric is pandering is to denounce it as uncritical, as simply telling people what they want to hear, encouraging them to follow their narrow self-interest, and leading them to judge without reflection. In this instance, the concern is with poor judgment or a failure to consider the common good. To say that rhetoric is manipulative is to denounce it as inimical to freedom, as a kind of speech that coerces those who hear it. The suspicion is that by appealing to passions, hopes, fears, pleasures, and pains, rhetoric leads people to slavishly accept the speaker's position.

The tendency to reject rhetoric as a kind of uncritical or manipulative discourse reveals the link between the wariness of rhetoric and the case against prejudice. In fact, if we reexamine those who develop the case against prejudice, many of them also disparage rhetoric. Recall, for example, how Bacon denounces ancient Greek philosophy as "rhetorical and prone to disputation," therefore, "inimical to the search for truth."[4] According to his view, truth is wholly independent of the terms that make it compelling for a given audience. Recall too how Adam Smith denounces the poets of his day for trying to sway public opinion in favor of their literary styles. He disparages these rhetorical tactics as "the mean arts of intrigue and solicitation," as attempts "to obtain praise, and to avoid blame, by very unfair means."[5] His belief that these means are "unfair" comes from his prejudice-free ideal of judgment. The best literary critics, he assumes, are blank-slate minds, people unaffected by public opinion or by the author's defense of his own style. Rhetoric, Smith implies, is a force that corrupts aesthetic judgment, that taints the minds of those who hear it, illicitly predisposing them to favor a certain kind of art.

4. Francis Bacon, *The New Organon*, ed. Lisa Jardine and Michael Silverthorne (Cambridge: Cambridge University Press, 2000), 58.

5. Adam Smith, *The Theory of Moral Sentiments*, ed. Ryan Patrick Hanley (London: Penguin, 2009), 150.

Perhaps the sharpest critique of rhetoric that we have so far considered comes from Kant. He summarily rejects it as the lowly business of "talking men round and prejudicing them in favor of anyone."[6] By arousing people's passions, and by appealing to their particular interests, rhetoric, Kant argues, leads people to thoughtlessly accept the speaker's position. In doing so, it not only leads the listeners to judge poorly, or unfairly, but it also "robs" them of their "freedom."[7] It "[moves] men like machines to a judgment that must lose all its weight with them upon calm reflection."[8]

Thomas Hobbes's Critique of Rhetoric and Its Link to the Detached Conception of Judgment

The basic critique of rhetoric that we find in all of these thinkers—the idea that rhetoric plays upon prejudice and is thus opposed to reason—finds its most powerful expression in Thomas Hobbes. Although Hobbes does not discuss prejudice as explicitly as the thinkers we have so far examined, he articulates a well-known version of the detached, or prejudice-free, ideal of judgment. At the center of this ideal lies his critique of rhetoric. To understand our contemporary suspicion of rhetoric and to see its connection to the case against prejudice, we should consider Hobbes's notion of how rhetoric inhibits detached judgment.

Hobbes's version of the detached ideal emerges in his conception of reason, which he defines as "nothing but Reckoning (that is, Adding and Subtracting) of the Consequences of generall names agreed upon."[9] For Hobbes, reason requires putting aside our own experiences and perspectives and beginning from fixed premises accepted by all in advance. Hobbes's favorite examples of such reasoning are mathematics and logic:

For as Arithmeticians teach to adde and subtract in numbers; so the Geometricians teach the same in lines, figures (solid and superficiall,)

6. Kant, *The Critique of Judgment*, trans. James Creed Meredith (Oxford: Oxford University Press, [1790] 1952), §53, 192.

7. Ibid.

8. Ibid., §53, 193.

9. Thomas Hobbes, *Leviathan*, ed. Richard Tuck (Cambridge: Cambridge University Press, 1996), 32.

angles, proportions, times, degrees of swiftnesse, force, power, and the like; The Logicians teach the same in Consequences of words; adding together two Names, to make an Affirmation; and two Affirmations, to make a Syllogisme; and many Syllogismes to make a Demonstration; and from the summe, or Conclusion of a Syllogisme, they subtract one Proposition, to find the other . . . In summe, in what matter soever there is a place for addition and subtraction, there is also a place for Reason; and where they have no place, there Reason has nothing at all to do.[10]

Reason, as Hobbes understands it, refers merely to the formal or abstract operations of thought that proceed from given premises—from "generall names agreed upon." Reason has nothing to do with determining the premises or "general names" themselves. The premises, Hobbes insists, come not from reason, but from *agreement,* from what Aristotle calls *convention.* According to Hobbes, reason has nothing to say about basic assumptions; it can attain no higher knowledge. *Geometry,* he writes, "is the only Science that has pleased God hitherto to bestow on mankind." For in geometry, "men begin at settled significations of their words . . . and place them in the beginning of their reckoning."[11]

The notion that reason is merely formal and can attain no higher knowledge is today a commonplace. At least in the Anglo-American tradition, the restriction of reason to formal argument, or to method, is widely accepted. This predominance attests to the tremendous influence of Hobbes's way of thinking. Although contemporary philosophers might cavil with Hobbes's claim that basic premises come from mere convention, they still tend to accept that rational discourse depends on clear premises shared in advance. But for Hobbes himself, the restriction of reason to "reckoning" was something of which he sought to convince people. Given the reigning influence of Aristotle, who did teach the possibility of higher knowledge, Hobbes could not assume the limits of reason uncritically.

But why was Hobbes bent on restricting reason in this way? First, he found it a philosophically compelling position. In light of his chaotic vision

10. Ibid.
11. Ibid., 28.

of the universe, as matter in motion, he did not believe in any sort of higher reality. In particular, he rejected the idea of a "highest good," or *summum bonum*. But Hobbes also had a practical stake in defending this philosophical position. As Garsten points out, Hobbes's philosophy was, in large part, a reaction against the Protestant revolutionaries of his day who invoked divine revelation as a justification for civil disobedience and rebellion. The Puritan preachers tended to dogmatically assert their opinions, claiming to have received them directly from God. They were unwilling to question or revise what they claimed to be a call from their inner conscience. Such recalcitrance led to conflict, and eventually, to the wars of religion. As a witness to and victim of this turmoil, Hobbes had a clear political interest in denying the possibility of so called higher knowledge.

The experience of religious dogmatism and war seems to have led Hobbes to the view that reasoning from within people's perspectives is a contradiction in terms. People's particular loyalties and religious views, he claims, are merely private feelings and beliefs. As such, they provide no basis for reasoned argument about justice or the good life. "Good" and "bad," "just" and "unjust," "holy" and "profane," are, according to Hobbes, utterly subjective labels that different people attach to different objects, objects which, in themselves, are meaningless: "One man calleth Wisdome, what another call feare; and one cruelty, what another justice; one prodigality, what another call magnanimity."[12]

We might say that the experience of religious dogmatism coupled with the conception of subjectivity that was emerging in his day led Hobbes to overlook what Aristotle recognized as the reason, or sense, embodied in common opinion and everyday life. At any rate, Hobbes severed the link between reason and *logos* upon which Aristotle had insisted.[13] According to Aristotle, reason inheres in the simple yet enigmatic fact that human beings

12. Ibid., 31.

13. The significance of this split should not be underestimated. It implies, as Hobbes teaches us, the nonexistence of the good, or that the "good" is merely subjective. As evidence of how the split between reason and speech has influenced contemporary thought, I refer to the following passage from Rawls: "All ways of reasoning—whether individual, associational, or political— must acknowledge certain common elements: the concept of judgment, principles of inference, rules of evidence, and much else; otherwise they would not be ways of reasoning but perhaps rhetoric or means of persuasion. *We are concerned with reason, not simply with discourse*" (Rawls, *Political Liberalism*, 220; emphasis added). It is no coincidence, I believe, that Rawls also defends the priority of the "right" over the "good." For to separate reason from discourse, as Hobbes shows, is also to deny the possibility of a highest good—at least as would be intelligible to human beings.

are able to give an account of what they do. Reason and speech are thus inseparable. On the basis of this unity, Aristotle maintains the possibility of ascending to higher wisdom, to knowledge of the Good.

In separating reason from speech, Hobbes denies the possibility that reason can lead to higher wisdom. Reason, by his account, is nothing but calculation, and speech is nothing but a system of subjective labels. In line with this understanding, Hobbes stresses the need for agreeing to "general names." For without such initial agreement, he argues, reason cannot proceed. The "first cause of Absurd conclusions," he writes, is "the want of Method; in that [people] begin not their Ratiocination from Definitions; that is, from the settled significations of their words: as if they could cast account without knowing the value of numerall words, one, two, and three."[14]

Thus emerges the source of Hobbes' strange affinity for geometry. What otherwise appears to be a rather unremarkable sort of knowledge is, for Hobbes, the model of the kind of thinking that begins from settled, uncontroversial premises and moves to uncontroversial conclusions. Geometry, in short, is the model of detached reason, the model of a method whose validity obtains regardless of any particular perspective.

But geometry was not Hobbes's ultimate ideal of reason. He set his sights higher. Geometry was for him merely a model of the sort of certainty that he hoped his political theory could impart to social life. What Hobbes proposed as an instrument of such certainty was the state as "Leviathan." As Garsten highlights, Hobbes intended the Leviathan state to replace people's own judgment as the sole arbiter of decent conduct.[15] By setting all social standards once and for all, by informing everyone "what he should call his own and what another's, what he should call just and unjust, honourable and dishonourable, good and bad," the Leviathan, Hobbes hoped, would allow people to confidently apply instrumental reasoning to social relations, and, thereby, to coexist with minimal controversy and conflict.[16] Hobbes

---

Although Rawls does not explicitly deny such a possibility, one is compelled to wonder whether a deep skepticism about the existence of the good motivates his thought.

14. Hobbes, *Leviathan*, 34.

15. Bryan Garsten, *Saving Persuasion: A Defense of Rhetoric and Judgment* (Cambridge, MA: Harvard University Press, 2007), chap. 1.

16. Thomas Hobbes, *On the Citizen*, ed. Richard Tuck and Michael Silverthorne (Cambridge: Cambridge University Press, 1998), 79.

hoped that the Leviathan could bring the certainty and stability of geometry to human affairs.

We might restate Hobbes's ideal as the attempt to overcome perspective, or prejudice, by replacing it with a fixed, external standard of judgment. This standard is, of course, itself a kind of prejudice. But its authority quells the conflict among competing prejudices. According to Hobbes, people's particular life perspectives are wholly *subjective.* They provide no footing for reasoned argument. In this regard, his thought falls in line with that of Bacon, Descartes, Smith, and Kant. Hobbes, however, adds his own pessimistic twist: The viewpoint shaped by one's desires, loyalties, and religious views is not only a "cave," as Bacon calls it, but the source of irreconcilable conflict. Perspective, or prejudice, Hobbes teaches, is the source of both ignorance and war.

Hobbes's critique of rhetoric is an outgrowth of his attempt to banish prejudice as a feature of political argument. He denounces rhetoric as a force that rouses people's passions, that distorts the true proportion of the things they care about, and that hinders their ability to reason in a calm, calculating, detached manner. The "task of eloquence," Hobbes writes, "is to make the Good and the bad, the useful and the useless, the Honourable and the dishonourable appear greater or less than they really are, and to make the unjust appear Just as may seem to suit the speaker's purpose . . . the result is that votes are cast not on the basis of correct reasoning but on emotional impulse."[17]

A familiar feature of rhetoric to which Hobbes takes particular exception is the use of metaphor. He goes so far as to identify the "sixth cause" of absurd thought as "the use of Metaphors, Tropes, and other Rhetoricall figures, in stead of words proper." In "reckoning, and seeking of truth," he writes, "such speeches are not to be admitted."[18]

A poet would no doubt resist the notion that metaphor and truth are so radically opposed. To a poet's sensibility, the purpose of metaphor is to convey truth, to breathe life into abstract concepts, to make them concrete rather than empty. But from Hobbes's point of view, the concrete quality of metaphor is precisely what puts it at odds with reason. The whole point of

17. Ibid., 123.
18. Hobbes, *Leviathan,* 35.

reason, according to Hobbes, is to abstract from the concrete and particular, to begin from "general names agreed upon." The concrete, or particular, he claims, is something that distorts rather than clarifies the general. Insofar as the point of metaphor is to connect general concepts to people's particular experiences, metaphor, as Hobbes sees it, merely adds inconsistency to definitions. It thus undermines the consensus necessary for reason's operation. Metaphor, Hobbes writes, leaves one "entangled in words, as a bird in lime-twiggs, the more he struggles, the more belimed."[19] As this evocative line suggests, Hobbes does approve of at least one kind of metaphor—that which aims to reveal the folly of metaphor itself. In a larger sense, the only rhetoric of which Hobbes approves, and, indeed employs to powerful effect, is, in Garsten's terms, "the rhetoric against rhetoric" itself.[20] Through the image of the Leviathan, Hobbes sought "to end the practice of rhetoric as it had traditionally been understood."[21] He sought to convince his contemporaries to cede their own judgment to the supreme word of the sovereign.

Against the background of Hobbes's political theory, we can better understand the contemporary suspicion of rhetoric. Although few today share Hobbes's fear that rhetoric will lead to war, many accept his basic idea that rhetoric is opposed to reason and thus is an illegitimate mode of political discourse. As Garsten compellingly argues, the familiar defense of "liberal public reason," as an alternative to rhetoric, actually emerges from Hobbes's defense of the Leviathan. For despite the apparent difference between contemporary liberalism and Hobbesian absolute rule, both seek a standard of right that is detached from citizens' particular life circumstances, above all, from their moral and religious views. Both rest on the assumption that our life circumstances are caves that blind us and lead to conflict rather than perspectives that inform our reason.

But with the situated conception of judgment in view, we can see how the suspicion of rhetoric is misguided. It is misguided at least insofar as it rests on the wholesale rejection of prejudice, or on the opposition of prejudice and reason. To be sure, what is often denounced as mere rhetoric is, indeed, pandering, or worse, speech that shamelessly propagates lies, that manipulates people by distorting or withholding the relevant facts about an

19. Ibid., 28.
20. Garsten, *Saving Persuasion*, 25.
21. Ibid., 28.

issue. But speech that persuades by appealing to people's particular experiences, to their roles, loyalties, and desires, is not by necessity opposed to reason. Rhetoric can be a way of reasoning from within people's life perspectives, a way of engaging their situated understanding.

Prejudice and Rhetoric Reconsidered

Perhaps not surprisingly, many proponents of situated understanding are also, in one form or another, defenders of rhetoric. Aristotle is a case in point. Contrary to the suggestion of Socrates that rhetoric is mere flattery, a sort of unsophisticated knack for pleasing people and winning their support, Aristotle argues that rhetoric requires a more nuanced kind of knowledge. *Persuading* one's listeners, he argues, involves knowing them at a deeper level than their superficial preferences. An orator cannot be like a chef who simply cooks to the taste of his customers. He must understand the regime in which his audience lives and have a sense for the political climate of the day. He must be able to interpret the prevailing passions and to invoke the myths, proverbs, and metaphors that bear upon the situation at hand. Only by drawing upon this wealth of knowledge can an orator effectively persuade his listeners. Although such knowledge is irreducible to rules or principles, it admits, Aristotle shows, of a kind of rational analysis— precisely the sort that he offers in his *Rhetoric*. He thereby challenges the claim of Socrates that rhetoric "has no account to give of the things [i.e., the means of persuasion] it applies."[22]

Aristotle recognizes that persuasive speech appeals to people's experiences, concerns, and loyalties—even, in a sense, to their self-interest. But this, he argues, is not necessarily bad. Although Aristotle points out that people can be poor judges in their own case, he also sees in self-interest (or "one's own," *ta heautou*) the basis for deliberation. People who have a stake in a given debate, Aristotle observes, tend actually to judge more considerately than those who look on as neutral spectators. For example, in the assembly when addressing issues of common concern, people deliberate with greater care than when sitting in the law courts as judges of other people's

22. Plato, *Gorgias*, 465a. *Lysis, Symposium, Gorgias*, Loeb Edition, ed. Jeffrey Henderson, Harvard University Press, 1935.

business.[23] Aristotle's conception of situated judgment thus leads him to a nuanced defense of rhetoric.

We find a similar defense of rhetoric in Gadamer, who connects rhetoric to hermeneutics. Both, he writes, occupy the same realm: "the realm of arguments that are convincing (which is not the same as logically compelling)." It is the realm, he continues,

> of practice and humanity in general, and its province is not where the power of "iron clad conclusions" must be accepted without discussion . . . but rather where controversial issues are decided by reasonable consideration. . . . If rhetoric appeals to the feelings, as has long been clear, that in no way means it falls outside the realm of the reasonable. . . . Only a narrow view of rhetoric sees it as a mere technique or even a mere instrument for social manipulation. It is in truth an essential aspect of all reasonable behavior.[24]

In the rest of this chapter, I aim to develop the sense in which rhetoric is a mode of situated reasoning. As I have suggested, this conception of rhetoric follows in the tradition of Aristotle and Gadamer. It finds its most powerful contemporary expression in Bryan Garsten's *Saving Persuasion*. Garsten argues that "rhetorical appeals to people's partial and passionate points of view can often be a good means of drawing out their capacity for judgment and so drawing them into deliberation."[25]

My approach to showing how rhetoric is a kind of situated reasoning is to examine several political speeches from American history that cannot be dismissed as mere flattery or deception. These speeches seek to initiate significant political *reform*. But they do so not by appealing to some abstract standard of justice. Instead, they work by invoking tradition and appealing to the life perspective of the listeners. Because the speeches I examine all offer compelling arguments in defense of liberty and because they support positions that, in Rawls's terms, are "reasonable," they appear to derive their

23. Aristotle, *On Rhetoric*, trans. George A. Kennedy (New York: Oxford University Press, 1991), 1354b. I am indebted to Garsten for highlighting this theme in Aristotle (cf. Garsten, *Saving Persuasion*, 119, 124).

24. Gadamer, *Truth and Method*, 571.

25. Garsten, *Saving Persuasion*, 13.

moral force from abstract principles alone. As I try to show, however, the speeches actually derive their persuasive and *moral* force by appeal to situated understandings that make the principles intelligible.

By considering rhetoric, I hope to conclude the account of situated understanding in two respects. First, I hope to draw out its implications for the nature of political argument. As Garsten observes, persuasive speech is "the currency of the democratic realm." Although democracy means "rule by the people," in practice it means rule by the most compelling orators. It may be true, concedes Garsten, "that in Washington 'money talks,' but campaign strategists and lobbyists often value money for its ability to buy speaking time and a large audience. In general, if people want to wield political power in a democracy, they must look for opportunities to talk to their fellow citizens, to impress them, and to persuade them."[26] To influence politics, money still needs the support of smooth talking. So whether we like it or not, rhetoric, in some form or another, rules the day. But it makes a great difference whether we understand rhetoric as a regrettable fact of democracy, or as practice, which, in certain forms at least, is worth cultivating. By viewing rhetoric in light of the situated conception of understanding, we can understand it as a kind of reasoned argument that lies at the heart of democracy.

Second, by examining political rhetoric, I aim not only to apply but also to clarify the phenomenon of situated understanding. Through an analysis of several speeches, I hope to elicit the way in which reason proceeds from within the world rather than from abstract principles alone. Moreover, by considering the rhetoric of reform, I hope to highlight how *agency* is connected to situated understanding, how argument and judgment influenced by prejudice is not merely consistent with agency but an integral expression of it.

Rhetoric of Reform

During the 1960 presidential election campaign, Lyndon B. Johnson of Texas, the vice-presidential running mate of John F. Kennedy, spoke throughout the South in support of civil rights. Instead of appealing to abstract principles of fairness and equality, Johnson invoked common experiences to

26. Ibid., 2.

which his southern audience could relate. As Henry Fairlie recounts, Johnson would often evoke feelings of moral outrage against the daily indignities of segregation:

> How would you feel, he demanded of [his listeners] if your child was sick, and you could not take him to the hospital in this town, but had to go twenty miles away? How would you feel, if you were shopping and your child was thirsty, and you could not give him a cold soda at the counter in the drugstore? Again and again, he won the sullen audiences.[27]

By this account, Johnson does not explicitly appeal to principles at all. He does not argue, for example, that segregation is wrong because it violates equal basic rights and liberties or because it fails to respect citizens as free and equal persons. He appeals not to his listeners' abstract reason, but to their feelings. The kind of emotion he arouses, moreover, is not some context-free "natural sympathy," of the sort that Adam Smith claims to be basic. Instead, Johnson arouses a *particular* sense of sympathy, tied to the concern of parents for their thirsty child on a hot day or their sick child in need of a doctor. Furthermore, Johnson asks them, "How would *you* feel?" By emphasizing the second person, Johnson connects his message to the lives of the particular crowd in front of him. To evoke the moral outrage he intends, Johnson presents two everyday examples of how black children and their parents cannot share in the common life that white southerners take for granted.

In presenting these examples, Johnson speaks to his southern audience as situated. He refers to the hospital in this town, to the activity of shopping at the local drugstore. Most strikingly, the cure for thirst he invokes is not water, but a "cold soda" (presumably the kind served in a glass bottle that was popular in the 1960s South). Johnson's speech addresses things that are readily familiar to his southern listeners and that have meaning for them. His speech is geared to a specific audience that can relate to buying a cold soda at the local drug store. To an audience of businessmen in the Northeast, this

27. Henry Fairlie ("The Decline of Oratory," *New Republic,* May 28, 1984, 17) in Garsten, *Saving Persuasion,* 193.

typical southern activity would probably lack the same resonance. Johnson (like other politicians including Bill Clinton) was even known to speak in a thicker southern accent in the South in order to establish a rapport with his audience. He referred to himself as "a man whose roots go deeply into Southern soil."[28]

The resonant phrases in Johnson's speech gesture toward the principle "segregation is wrong" without formulating it in such terms. Johnson provides the potent images and examples and lets his listeners see the principle for themselves. Their understanding of the principle is tied to the way of life in which the principle acquires meaning for them.

A person examining Johnson's words from an abstract, analytic standpoint might contend that I have failed to scrutinize the speech systematically enough. The reason why Johnson's words carry moral weight, one might argue, is because they appeal to an implicit basic principle: we should judge our attitudes and actions by putting ourselves in the shoes of others. Although Johnson does not explicitly state this principle, it lies just below the surface. The principle unifies and explains the particular examples of your feeling a sense of unfairness that someone else is denied the opportunities that you have. By this account, Johnson presents two particular cases to his listeners, each of which evokes a sense of unfairness. These cases of unfairness, in turn, imply the abstract moral principle to "put yourself in another's shoes." Segregation is wrong according to this principle.

But to recast Johnson's argument in terms of an abstract principle is to miss the significance of the examples that make the principle concrete. We should consider that the full meaning of the principle "Put yourself in another's shoes," its moral force or lack thereof, is tied to how Johnson *expresses* it. Johnson's examples reveal the "other" as similar enough to the listener, so that for the listener "to put himself in the other's shoes" is an appropriate test in the first place.

The meaning of the principle, in other words, is inseparable from its application. To fully understand the principle "put yourself in another's shoes," one must be able to apply it in the right situation, toward the right people. In Aristotle's terms, knowing the principle means "recognizing the

28. Lyndon Baines Johnson, "We Shall Overcome," address to a Joint Session of Congress on Voting Legislation, Washington, DC, 15 March 1965.

particulars" *(ta kath' hekasta)*—recognizing to whom the principle applies—in this case, to equal human beings. For it would not necessarily make sense to put one's self in another's shoes if the other was fundamentally different from one's self.

Johnson's genius, what really makes his words compelling, is his ability to find the right examples to show white southerners that they actually share much in common with black southerners. Johnson suggests that under segregation, black southerners suffer the same injustices that would frustrate white southerners. In this way, he establishes common ground between the two groups. Once Johnson's speech forges this common ground, the white listeners can recognize the imperative to put themselves in the shoes of blacks. But this abstract imperative crucially depends for its proper application, and thus for its very *sense,* on the particular examples that show something like "they suffer in the same ways you would suffer."

To someone analyzing the speech from an abstract perspective, Johnson's particular examples seem to be mere cases that evoke intuitions of unfairness, which, in turn, can be captured in a general principle. But the abstract perspective fails to account for the way in which Johnson finds the right examples and presents them in the right way to evoke the intuitions of unfairness in the first place. This rhetorical skill is not a mere knack for finding the means to persuade people of a principle that they should accept independently. Stripped of all its relevance to the listener's own interests and concerns, the principle would be an empty moralism. To insist that people simply accept it as "reasonable" would be pointless finger wagging. Otherwise put, the standard of "reasonableness" says why anyone should accept a principle but not why *these* people *here* should. But, as Aristotle teaches us, the abstract "anyone" is always a sort of fiction. Insofar as people are always, in a sense, *these* people *here,* Johnson's rhetoric is more than an adornment to the real argument. Johnson's rhetoric is part of the principle's justification—at least for the audience to whom he speaks.

It should be clear, then, that Johnson's knack for speaking to the interests and concerns of his listeners involves a critical *interpretive* faculty—the ability to see things from within their perspective, to understand the activities that articulate their way of life, to identify some good within those activities, and to highlight how the good, properly understood, reveals other activities to be confused or mistaken. Johnson's genius is his eye for small things, such as a bottle of cold soda, that point beyond themselves and that refer to roles and activities of significance for his audience. Johnson brings to expression the significance of such things and uses it to evoke a sense of unfairness.

Nor could it be said that Johnson manipulates his listeners. To be sure, he tries to move them to his side. But he does so precisely by appealing to their *own* lives—by challenging certain aspects of their perspective in light of others. In thus persuading his listeners, Johnson exercises a kind of authority, or rule over them. But the term "over" is somewhat misleading. Johnson does not rule his audience from above, as a marionette handles his puppets, or from outside, as wind bends the branches of a tree. To bring his listeners around, Johnson relies on their self-interpretive agency. He urges them to consider the particular things they care about, the things that define their daily lives, and to judge accordingly. This sort of rhetorical appeal exemplifies how judgment shaped by perspective, or prejudice, is nevertheless critical. We see how prejudice provides the basis for its own revision.

Lyndon Johnson's rhetoric is a clear example of speech that appeals to concrete experiences and activities rather than to abstract principles. But what about rhetoric that invokes abstract principles without explicit reference to particulars? What are we to make of such cases? Do they show that speech can, indeed, transcend its situation? Let us consider a well-known speech: Abraham Lincoln's Gettysburg Address. Upon examination, what appears to consist of abstract language alone actually depends on the particular setting and narrative in which the speech is situated.

The purpose of Lincoln's address was to commemorate the Union soldiers who died at the Battle of Gettysburg and also to persuade the Union troops to keep fighting. The entire speech is only 272 words long, and the language is notably abstract. The speech begins: "Four score and seven years ago our fathers brought forth on this continent a new nation, conceived in Liberty, and dedicated to the proposition that all men are created equal."[29] Although Lincoln mentions the date of the founding, he leaves

29. Abraham Lincoln, "Gettysburg Address," Gettysburg, Pennsylvania, 19 November 1863. http://www.americanrhetoric.com.

out other specifics. Even his more particular references are notably general. For example, he refers to "our fathers," instead of to Washington, Madison, and Hamilton. He refers to "this continent" instead of to North America or the United States. Most significantly, he refers to an abstract proposition that "all men are created equal."

As historian Garry Wills observes, Lincoln's address contains no proper names—"not even the name of the battle, or of the cemetery he is dedicating with his speech." When Lincoln refers to "this ground," the ground "is only a testing place where the 'proposition' is to be vindicated by 'these dead.' "[30] But in spite of its abstract wording, and perhaps even because of it, Lincoln's speech is an instance of compelling rhetoric. And, moreover, it was persuasive. The address reinvigorated the spirit of the Union and the founding principles of the Declaration of Independence. It motivated the soldiers to keep fighting.

Does the apparently abstract eloquence of the Gettysburg Address undermine the dependence of general principles on particular references and narratives? Not at all. The speech only seems to rely on abstract statements alone. Its commemorative and persuasive effect really comes from the conspicuous *absence* of particulars—ones well known to the audience that day and for generations to come. To grasp the full meaning of the Gettysburg Address, we must pay as much attention to what Lincoln *omits* as to what he explicitly states. Paradoxically, what gives the address its transcendent character is precisely the concrete circumstance that Lincoln could have invoked yet did not. In this sense, the speech is firmly situated rather than detached.

The Gettysburg Address illustrates Gadamer's point that "to say what one means . . . to make one's self understood—means to hold what is said together with an infinity of what is not said in one unified meaning and to ensure that it is understood in this way."[31] Under the circumstances, Lincoln could have said many things, indeed, an "infinity" of things that he decided, consciously or unconsciously, to pass over.

What, in particular, were Lincoln's resonant omissions? Most conspicuously, he did not enumerate the details of the battle and its bloody aftermath. As Wills recounts, the Battle of Gettysburg had left the Pennsylvania

30. Garry Wills, *Lincoln at Gettysburg: The Words That Remade America* (New York: Simon & Schuster, 1992), 54.

31. Gadamer, *Truth and Method*, 464.

battlefield blanketed with rotting bodies. There were so many dead men that General Meade of the Union army had no time to collect them, and in many cases, the locals had to move aside bodies in order to plant their crops.[32] According to one Gettysburg banker, "arms and legs and sometimes heads protrude and my attention has been directed to several places where the hogs were actually rooting out the bodies and devouring them."[33] The Battle of Gettysburg was not even a decisive Union victory despite the high price the Union had paid. Lee's Confederate army had escaped, and both sides had sustained heavy casualties.

Lincoln's audience was all too familiar with the gruesome and demoralizing particulars of the battle, which had been brought into sharp relief by Edward Everett's speech, which preceded Lincoln's. Everett was actually the main speaker. He gave a two-hour speech that set the battle "in a larger logic of campaigns that had an immediacy for those on the scene." He "excoriated the rebels for their atrocities," as he recounted the three bloody days of fighting.[34] Only against this all-too-worldly background, brought to powerful expression in Everett's words, does the Gettysburg Address emerge as distinctively transcendent.

Lincoln's words, which omit the details of the battle, of victory and defeat, conspicuously hover above the particulars, and, in this sense, depend on them. As Wills comments, "The general or generalizing articles—*a* great civil war, *a* great battlefield, *a* portion, *any* nation—make this military engagement part of a larger process. . . . The draining of particulars from the scene raises it to the ideality of a type."[35] The key phrase is the "draining of particulars." The lofty, *idealistic* quality of Lincoln's speech comes from the particulars over which the speech hovers: the tragedy of "the macerated bodies, the many bloody and ignoble aspects of this inconclusive encounter, are transfigured in Lincoln's rhetoric. . . . His speech hovers far above the carnage. . . . The nightmare realities have been etherealized in the crucible of his language."[36]

---

32. Wills, *Lincoln at Gettysburg*, 20.
33. Ibid., 21.
34. Ibid., 33.
35. Ibid., 54.
36. Ibid., 37.

By pointing to the significance of Lincoln's omitting the "nightmare realities," Wills, on one level, acknowledges the dependence of the Gettysburg Address on its concrete circumstance. But his conclusion that the "nightmare realities have been *etherealized*" is somewhat misleading. If by "etherealized" he means *evaporated* into the principle, or "larger process" (i.e., that "all men are created equal," or that "American history is marching toward freedom"), this would overlook the sense in which the principle, or the process, still depends on the particulars. Only insofar as the particulars are *preserved* as essential elements of the struggle for equality does the principle of equality or the march toward its fulfillment attain its depth, its transcendent character. Without the particulars lurking conspicuously in the background, the principle would lose much of its meaning. It would be a hollow statement, not a principle worth fighting for.

The particulars and the principle, we might say, sojourn together in Lincoln's speech. By relating the particulars, in their silent presence, to the proposition that "all men are created equal," Lincoln recaptures them within a certain ideal framework. He thus preserves their horror while evoking their nobility. In Wills's terms, Lincoln "transfigures" the tragedy. The term "transfigures" is more apt than "etherealizes" or "idealizes." For Lincoln does not sugarcoat the particulars, as if the grave losses were fully justified in light of abstract equality. Precisely by omitting the particulars, and thus letting them speak for themselves, he avoids terms that would entirely dissolve their horror into a higher cause. He avoids treating the sacrifices as mere means, however laudable, for a cause that retains its force regardless of the fight in its favor. Instead of dissolving the "nightmare realities," Lincoln builds on them to breathe life into the proposition that "all men are created equal." In other words, the higher cause of liberty *itself* is transformed by the circumstance in which Lincoln invokes it.

Lincoln's speech highlights the sense in which meaning depends on *silence* as much as on utterance. The significance of silence, in turn, points to the situated character of speech. For only within a situation, in relation to what someone might typically say in a certain circumstance, does speech attain its distinctive character. According to Hobbes's notion of language, which conceives of words as subjective labels for objects, silence is meaningless. For the absence of sound or gesture cannot designate anything. It merely betokens agreement or the lack of a need to speak. Only a situated conception of language can make sense of the weight of silence, of how the most powerful words often speak to us without voice.

Perhaps the most compelling instance of rhetoric that reasons clearly from within the world is Frederick Douglass's Fourth of July speech against slavery. On Independence Day, 1852, Douglass was invited to address the citizens of Rochester, New York. Instead of singing a hymn to liberty, Douglass delivered a scorching attack on the hypocrisy of celebrating Independence Day. He begins his speech by asking: "Why am I called upon to speak today? What have I or those I represent to do with your national independence?"[37] With this question, Douglass alerts his northern, largely sympathetic audience, to the life circumstance of the millions of Africans still enslaved. A striking feature of Douglass's speech is the way it works from within the life perspective of his listeners, including from within the perspective of slaveholders themselves.

To make his case against slavery and for the equality of black Americans, Douglass rejects abstract, formal arguments:

> Must I argue the wrongness of slavery? Is that a question of republicans? Is it to be settled by the rules of logic and argumentation, as a matter beset with great difficulty, involving a doubtful application of the principle of justice, hard to understand? How should I look today in the presence of Americans, dividing and subdividing a discourse, to show that men have a natural right to freedom, speaking of it relatively and positively, negatively and affirmatively? To do so would be to make myself look ridiculous, and to offer an insult to your understanding. . . . I will use the severest language I can command, and yet not one word shall escape me that any man . . . shall not confess to be right and just.[38]

Douglass resolves to speak justly without applying principles of justice. In dispensing with "rules of logic and argumentation," he ridicules the kind of

37. Frederick Douglass, "What to the Slave Is the 4th of July?" Rochester, New York, 4 July 1852. http://www.americanrhetoric.com.
38. Ibid.

speech so prized by Hobbes. What Hobbes considers the paradigm of reason, Douglass considers stupid in the current circumstance. To invoke "natural right" or principles of justice against slavery would be an insult to the understanding of his audience. It would be an insult because it would presume to teach his listeners what they don't *already know,* what they do not already grasp from within the perspective of their own laws and practices:

> Must I undertake to prove that the slave is a man? That point is conceded already. Nobody doubts it. The slave-holders themselves acknowledge it . . . when they punish disobedience on the part of the slave. There are seventy-two crimes in the State of Virginia, which, if committed by a black man (no matter how ignorant he be), subject him to the punishment of death; while only two of these same crimes will subject a white man to like punishment. What is this but the acknowledgment that the slave is a moral, intellectual, and responsible being? The manhood of the slave is conceded. It is admitted in the fact that Southern statute books are covered with enactments, forbidding, under severe fines and penalties, the teaching of the slave to read and write. When you can point to any such laws in reference to the beasts of the field, then I may consent to argue the manhood of the slave.[39]

The reason for the wrongness of slavery, suggests Douglass, is not to be found in some ideal realm detached from the world. The fact that slaves are equal human beings is embodied in American life itself, most obviously in the laws that hold slaves responsible for disobedience, that disproportionally punish them for crimes, and that forbid their being taught to read and write. Douglass does not simply mean to highlight the unfairness of such practices. His deeper point is that the practices actually acknowledge the humanity of slaves, however negatively.

Douglass thus reveals that on the slaveholders' *own* terms, as expressed by their own laws, blacks are equal human beings. To be sure, the slaveholders fail to acknowledge the humanity of blacks in full. For to do so would be to already reject slavery. Nevertheless, the slaveholders possess a keen awareness of the humanity of blacks, at least in part. Douglass elicits this

39. Ibid.

partial knowledge, and holding it before the eyes of his audience, he challenges them to revise their attitudes. By calling attention to what the slaveholders see hazily, Douglass hopes to make them recognize the equality of blacks more clearly. By doing so, he hopes to turn them against slavery. Like Lyndon Johnson, Douglass appeals to the self-interpretive capacity of the listeners. He implores them to revise their practice in light of their own lives.

Douglass continues this approach in the conclusion of his speech, but in a more inspiring tone this time. Instead of pointing to nefarious laws that implicitly attest to the humanity of black Americans, Douglass points to a range of distinctively human activities in which black and white Americans both participate:

> Is it not astonishing that while we are ploughing, planting, and reaping, using all kinds of mechanical tools, erecting houses, constructing bridges . . . that while we are . . . acting as clerks, merchants, and secretaries, having among us doctors, lawyers, ministers, poets, authors, editors, orators, and teachers; that we are engaged in all the enterprises common to other men—digging gold in California, capturing the whale in the Pacific, feeding sheep and cattle on the hillside, living, moving, acting, thinking, planning, living in families as husbands, wives, and children, and above all, confessing and worshipping the Christian God, and looking hopefully for life and immortality beyond the grave—we are called upon to prove we are men?[40]

The equality of black Americans is not to be found in heaven, or in the stars, or in some ideal realm. It is expressed in American life itself—in the activities and occupations that blacks and whites share.

By appealing to life activities instead of only to principles, Douglass might seem to evoke feeling instead of reason. But to assume so would be to miss the real force of his speech. It misses how the feelings he evokes arise, in the first place, in light of his words. By pointing to certain activities and by placing them alongside each other, Douglass does not just recall a way of life or trigger an already-formed set of sentiments. His words *clarify* the activities they describe, allowing the activities to evoke the feelings that they do.

40. Ibid.

To fully appreciate the creative and critical character of his words, we should consider that "feeding sheep and cattle on the hillside" is not a self-evident description of farming. If one were to ask a farmer for an account of his activity, he might offer a range of answers, perhaps "tending the flock" or "making a living." The different terms of description, which might appear to be different ways of describing the same thing, actually express very different activities. To understand farming as "making a living" is to see it as something necessary, something to be mastered (if only for the sake of preservation), and something to be done away with if we could. If farming is indeed "making a living," a merely necessary activity that aims at self-preservation, it would have no place in Douglass's speech in defense of freedom. It would not attest to the distinctively human qualities that Douglass seeks to elicit.

In contrast to "making a living," "feeding sheep and cattle on the hillside" defines the activity not merely as something necessary or something to be mastered, but as something to admire. It evokes the Jeffersonian vision of the independent farmer, walking among peaceful animals on the firm ground of rolling pastures. It evokes this vision all the more clearly in contrast to the whaler wrestling with nature on violent seas. Douglass's descriptions do not merely represent instances of farming or whaling whose character is already manifest. The descriptions clarify the activities themselves, allowing them to evoke the admiration of the audience. If these activities point to distinctively human qualities, then black Americans, Douglass argues, are equal human beings. For they too participate in such activities. In this way, Douglass allows his listeners to see why slavery is wrong. He does not take them to an abstract standpoint that casts judgment on human affairs from above; he brings his listeners before themselves. He allows them to see that the wrongness of slavery is already implicit in their way of life properly understood.

The Unity of Philosophy and Life

By examining rhetoric in light of the situated conception of understanding, we can better appreciate the character of political argument. We can see that argument from within people's life perspectives is not necessarily pandering or manipulation. Properly conceived, rhetoric is a compelling instance of the situated understanding that defines our relation to the world.

This understanding, as I have tried to show, is at once passive and active, neither blind slavery to circumstance nor detached mastery of it. Different philosophers have expressed this insight in different terms. Heidegger and Gadamer speak of thrown-projection, of our horizon, or world, and the interpretive acts that reshape it. Aristotle speaks of the good and its relation to human practice. Although virtue, he teaches, is expressed in our action, it rests ultimately on our implicit awareness of the good—an awareness that we clarify through the judgments we make and the actions we carry out.

Rhetoric is an example of situated understanding at work. In its most striking instances, rhetoric is both accepting and critical of the way things are. In this way, it reveals the passive and active sides of situated understanding. Precisely by invoking custom, tradition, and pre-given loyalties, rhetoric can be the vehicle of reform.

The accepting and critical aspects of rhetoric point to what is ultimately at stake in the situated conception of understanding. At stake, we might say, is the relation of critical thought to steadfast commitment, of philosophy to our concrete lives. By philosophy I mean the "love of wisdom," the age-old desire to *know*—not just to know this or that—how to write a computer program, or to cure a disease, or to succeed at business—but to comprehend anything and everything worth knowing—to raise the Socratic question "What is?" with respect to justice, piety, beauty, friendship, the good life, and, ultimately, to hazard a sufficient answer. In short, philosophy is the desire to know not only some aspect of life, but to "see the ground and background of all things."[41]

By life, I mean our basic experience of the world—life as we live it every day. Above all, life means *commitment,* especially to one's family, friends, and country. Life, in short, means love of *one's own*—not in the sense of one's own self-interest, but of one's own household, occupation, city, reli-

---

41. Friedrich Nietzsche, "The Wanderer," in *Thus Spoke Zarathustra,* pt. 3, in *The Portable Nietzsche,* trans. Walter Kaufmann (London: Chatto & Windus, 1971), 265.

gion. The defining feature of this sort of love, or commitment, is the way it comes naturally to us, the way it precedes our explicit choice to commit. Even when, in certain moments, we consciously affirm some aspect of our life, it seems that life most fully commands our allegiance, that life is most fully *itself*, only when it absorbs us, only when when we are engaged in the activity of living.

So conceived, philosophy and life might seem opposed, indeed radically so. For if philosophy means the *reflection on life*, in all its essential aspects, philosophy might seem, by its very nature, to separate us from life. It might seem to detach us from our commitments by the very act of questioning them. For to question something, whether a relationship, role, or practice, is always, in a sense, to step back from it, to bring its claim within the range of our consideration and thus to break its natural hold on us. In other words, to ask the basic philosophical question—the question "What is?"—means to aim at justice, friendship, or goodness *as such*. The question is primarily unconcerned with *this* particular practice, *this* particular friend, or *this* particular goal. Philosophy would seem, therefore, to be "indifferent to the fate of individuals"[42]—indifferent, indeed, to life itself. For life, however expansively conceived, always means my *own*.

Philosophy might seem, even, to inflict a sort of *violence* upon life. For not only does philosophy seem to detach us from our commitments; it seems also to subject them to the sovereignty of reason. By the very act of questioning the things we care about most, we seem to weaken their intrinsic claim to our allegiance. We seem to sacrifice them for the sake of the truth and thus to commit a sort of disloyalty.

The apparent link between philosophy and disloyalty reminds us of the drama of Socrates. Socrates never explicitly renounced Zeus, or any of the Olympian gods. Nor did he found a new religious cult or recommend civil disobedience. And yet, Athens sentenced him to death for corrupting the youth and introducing new gods. The Athenians, at least certain ones, saw in the very activity of his *questioning* a certain disloyalty to the city, an impiety toward its divine basis. For this reason, they sought to halt his search for wisdom.

---

42. Allan Bloom, "Interpretive Essay," in *Plato's Republic*, trans. Allan Bloom, 2nd ed. (New York: Basic Books, 1991), 405.

The Athenian reaction to Socrates belies the familiar suspicion that critical thought undermines serious commitment, that philosophy undermines life. In modern times, the suspicion comes to dramatic expression in Nietzsche's claim that the truth is *deadly*. By this he means that the theoretical analysis of life, if taken seriously, destroys the researcher's loyalty to his own. "Deadly" thus applies to truth *as such* (at least, as Nietzsche claims, to "truth" as it has so far been understood.)

If this suspicion is well founded, if, indeed, philosophy *as such* attenuates our particular loyalties, then, I believe, we must have some sympathy for Nietzsche's defense of life, some sympathy, indeed, for those who condemned Socrates. At least we should not denounce them in full. We must ask, with Nietzsche: "Could Socrates have been the corrupter of youth after all? And did he deserve his hemlock?"[43] For why should the call of life, of instinctive commitment, not fight back against the desire to know, against the deadly grasping for sufficient reason? Any serious thinker, must, at some point, venture an answer to this question—to "the problem of the value of truth." Suppose we want truth, asks Nietzsche, *"why not rather* untruth? and uncertainty? even ignorance?"[44] In asking this question, Nietzsche aims to arouse the Athenian demos lurking in all of us. Even the most fervent lovers of truth, he suggests, harbor a certain love of life—of their *own*—that cannot be entirely extinguished: "For all the value that the true, the truthful, the selfless may deserve, it would still be possible that a higher and more fundamental value for *life* might have to be ascribed to deception, selfishness, and lust" (emphasis added).[45]

By invoking these shocking terms, Nietzsche does not mean to valorize petty lies, narrow self-interest, or crude sexual desires. "Deception, selfishness, and lust" are, rather, counter-concepts to "unconditional truth." "Deception" means "appearance"; "selfishness," "one's own"; and "lust," "eros." In short, these terms are meant to capture *life*—full-blooded life as we live it—life as distinct from *reflection* upon life—as distinct from *knowledge* or the quest for knowledge. Nietzsche forces us to consider the potential conflict between philosophy and life. A thinker who fails to see this potential conflict, he suggests, must fail to take philosophy seriously. For to take it

43. Friedrich Nietzsche, preface to *Beyond Good and Evil*, in *Basic Writings of Nietzsche*, 193.
44. Nietzsche, "Aphorism 1," *Beyond Good and Evil*, 199.
45. Nietzsche, "Aphorism 2," *Beyond Good and Evil*, 200.

seriously is to follow the argument *wherever it may lead*. And might it not lead away from family, friends, and country, away from everything one holds dear? The very activity of questioning seems already to point in this direction.

A familiar solution is to assert the higher pleasures or greater freedom associated with wisdom. You only experience it once you get there—so they say. But one gets the sense, as Nietzsche so vividly highlights, that the lovers of wisdom are really those who despise life because they live diseased and decaying ones: "These wise men of all ages—they should first be scrutinized closely. Were they all perhaps shaky on their legs? late? tottery? decadents? Could it be that wisdom appears on earth as a raven, inspired by a little whiff of carrion?"[46] Nietzsche suggests that someone truly full of life, someone in the moment of living, would laugh at the supposedly higher pleasures of wisdom. To a person truly committed to his family, friends, or city, the philosopher's assertion in favor of wisdom would have no purchase. The conflict is between two irreconcilable perspectives—each with a claim on its side.

Another potential solution is to recognize the weight of both claims—to view human beings as essentially torn between critical thought and serious commitment. We find a clear expression of this apparent solution in Allan Bloom's interpretation of Plato. Invoking Plato's terms, Bloom interprets the conflict between philosophy and life as between "the good and one's own." Although Bloom has a certain sympathy for the philosopher and his quest for the good, he also gives due credit to the claim of one's own:

> Men, in fact, do love their own things, and because they are their own things, especially their countries, their families, and themselves. This is the first and perhaps the natural way, before men ever learned of the good. When they do learn of it, they sophistically identify the good with their own in order to remain at peace. If they really wanted to pursue the good simply, they would have to give up their cities, their homes, those whom by habit they call friends, and even perhaps themselves. This is what Socrates actually does. He lives in Athens, but is not

46. Friedrich Nietzsche, "The Problem of Socrates," *Twilight of the Idols*, §1, in *The Portable Nietzsche*, 473.

really of it, he is married and has children but pays little attention to them. Socrates' life illustrates the sharpness of these conflicts and makes him appear monstrous to the decent people who love their own. . . . The problem that Socrates poses for all of his interlocutors is that he urges them to break with their own in favor of the good. Hardly any are willing to go the whole way, and this willingness to go the whole way defines the potential philosophers, such as Plato himself.[47]

Bloom thus acknowledges the claim of both the good and one's own, of philosophy and steadfast commitment. Humanity, he maintains, is torn between these two irreconcilable desires: the desire for wisdom, which means transcending one's city, friends, even one's self, and the desire for a home. The most comprehensive insight, Bloom suggests, is to recognize the tension of these claims, to acknowledge the "essential split in man" rather than to cover it up. To recognize the split means to be neither Socrates, who loves only the good, nor someone who sophistically identifies the good with his own. But how to live in light of this tragic insight remains unclear.

At this point, we may recall the significance of situated understanding: philosophy and life, the good and one's own, are not necessarily opposed. On the contrary, they unfold together. To assume an essential opposition between these terms is to mistakenly conceive of philosophy as *detached*, to assume that the truth at which philosophy aims is some standard or form or idea external to the world—external to our cities, homes, and friends. For if the truth indeed lies outside of life as we live it every day, then the problem of divided loyalties inevitably arises. Do we elect to remain in the cave or to seek the sunlit world above? As Bloom puts it, we are presented with the "harsh choice" between the good and our own, between a "monstrous" indifference to life and a fanatic devotion to it. The only way out would seem to be an honest recognition of the essential conflict.

When Nietzsche wrote that the truth is deadly, he was referring not to truth *as such,* but truth conceived as *unconditional,* truth as detached from the perspective of life. His charge was not against philosophy *per se,* but against the theoretical analysis of life that looks upon it from the remote-

47. Allan Bloom, "The Ladder of Love," in *Plato's Symposium,* trans. Seth Benardete (Chicago: University of Chicago Press, 1993), 137.

ness of a birds-eye view.[48] In particular, he was concerned with the kind of historical science that Gadamer also criticizes—the historicism that teaches us to leap out of our own perspective and into the worldview of a people "back then"—to think in terms of "its ideas and thoughts" and thus to advance toward historical "objectivity." Nietzsche saw in this way of thinking a deadly tendency. He saw that it would lead the researcher to inevitably look upon his *own* life as a detached spectator, to view his own thoughts and commitments as merely contingent and transitory, and hence, of no ultimate value. In short, Nietzsche foresaw that historicism would lead to the devaluation and denial of life—to nihilism.

But contrary to appearance, Nietzsche did not defend irrational commitment over theory, or "pleasing illusion" over truth. He sought instead to replace the detached conception of theory with a situated, or life-bound, one. The detached conception, he argues, not only degrades life; it also fails to understand it. Only from the perspective of life, he insists, from the perspective of *one's own* commitments and concerns, does the true meaning of life *as such,* including the life of others, reveal itself. Nietzsche sought to develop a sort of theory rooted firmly in the world, a theory that would view the world "from inside," that would attempt to grasp its deeper truths, but that, at the same time, would strengthen life rather than destroy it.[49] What might such a theory look like? In what sense can reflecting upon life cohere with whole-heartedly living it?

What at first appear as two conflicting stances toward life come together in the situated conception of understanding. As I have tried to bring out, the answer to the Socratic question "What is . . . ?" or to the familiar puzzle "How should I act?" is not lurking behind opinion and appearance, or hovering over and beyond our lives in some ideal realm. The answer is expressed in the world itself, inscribed in our projects, commitments, and loyalties as we live them every day. But the answer is never intelligible "down to the smallest letter," or present for us to see without effort. We discern it, always provisionally, only through a certain kind of practical deliberation or philosophy—a kind overlooked by the impartial spectator but familiar to all of us. This sort of reasoning questions life from within. It proceeds from our

48. Nietzsche, "Aphorism 41," *Beyond Good and Evil,* 242.
49. Nietzsche, "Aphorism 36," *Beyond Good and Evil,* 238.

lived awareness of the whole and at the same time works toward it. By questioning particular practices, aims, and loyalties in light of others, we come to clarify the comprehensive awareness from which we began. And by doing so, we simultaneously clarify the particulars. We come to see them in their true proportions, undistorted by the superficial concerns that initially occupied the forefront of our attention. In this way, critical reflection actually strengthens our particular commitments. It guarantees that although certain relationships fade away, others come to the fore; although some no longer claim our loyalty, others now command our stronger allegiance.

Thus conceived, philosophy is not "indifferent to the fate of individuals" but a source of their integrity. By pointing us to the universal, philosophy returns us to the particular with deeper insight and appreciation. This basic tie between the universal and the particular, or between the whole and its parts, finds concrete expression in the situated conception of understanding. In short, we learn what it means to reason from within the world, what it means to be led by the light of our horizon and, at the same time, to be the source of its flame.

BIBLIOGRAPHY

ACKNOWLEDGMENTS

INDEX

Bibliography

Abramson, Jeffrey. *We, the Jury.* New York: Basic Books, 1994.

Arendt, Hannah. *The Human Condition.* Chicago: University of Chicago Press, 1958.

Aristotle. *Nicomachean Ethics.* Translated by H. Rackham, edited by Jeffrey Henderson. Cambridge, MA: Harvard University Press, 1926.

———. *On Rhetoric.* Translated by George A. Kennedy. New York: Oxford University Press, 1991.

———. *Politics.* Translated by H. Rackham. Cambridge: Harvard University Press, 1932.

Bacon, Sir Francis. *The New Organon.* Edited by Lisa Jardine and Michael Silverthorne. Cambridge: Cambridge University Press, 2000. First published 1620.

Benardete, Seth. "On Plato's Symposium." In *Plato's Symposium,* trans. Seth Benardete. Chicago: University of Chicago Press, 1993.

Bloom, Allan. "Interpretive Essay." In *Plato's Republic,* trans. Alan Bloom. 2nd ed. New York: Basic Books, 1991.

———. "The Ladder of Love." In *Plato's Symposium,* trans. Seth Benardete. Chicago: University of Chicago Press, 1993.

Burke, Edmund. *Reflections on the Revolution in France.* Edited by Frank M. Turner. New Haven, CT: Yale University Press, 2003. First published 1790.

Demos, Raphael. Introduction to *The Dialogues of Plato.* Translated by B. Jowett. New York: Random House, 1937.

Descartes, René. *Discourse on the Method.* 1637. In Descartes, *Selected Philosophical Writing,* trans. John Cottingham, Robert Stoothoff, and Dugald Murdoch. Cambridge: Cambridge University Press, 1998, 20–56.

———. *Meditation on First Philosophy.* 1641. In Descartes, *Selected Philosophical Writings,* 73–122.

———. *Objections and Replies to the Meditations.* 1641. In Descartes, *Selected Philosophical Writings,* 123–159.

———. *Principles of Philosophy.* 1644. In Descartes, *Selected Philosophical Writings,* 160–212.

———. *Rules for the Direction of Our Native Intelligence.* 1628. In Descartes, *Selected Philosophical Writings,* 1–19.

———. *Selected Philosophical Writings.* Translated by John Cottingham, Robert Stoothoff, and Dugald Murdoch. Cambridge: Cambridge University Press, 1998.

Douglass, Frederick. "What to the Slave Is the 4th of July?" Rochester, New York, 4 July 1852. http://www.americanrhetoric.com.

Dreyfus, Hubert L. *Being-in-the-World: A Commentary on Heidegger's* Being and Time, *Division I.* Cambridge, MA: MIT Press, 1991.

Dworkin, Ronald. *Law's Empire.* Cambridge, MA: The Belknap Press, 1986.

Gadamer, Hans-Georg. "Hermeneutics and Historicism." In *Truth and Method,* trans. Joel Weinsheimer and Donald G. Marshall. Rev. ed. New York: Continuum, 1989.

———. *Truth and Method.* Translated by Joel Weinsheimer and Donald G. Marshall. Revised edition New York: Continuum, 1989. First published 1960.

Garsten, Bryan. *Saving Persuasion: A Defense of Rhetoric and Judgment.* Cambridge, MA: Harvard University Press, 2007.

Guignon, Charles B. "Authenticity, Moral Values, and Psychotherapy." In *The Cambridge Companion to Heidegger,* ed. Charles B. Guignon. Cambridge: Cambridge University Press, 2006.

Hegel, G. W. F. *The Phenomenology of Spirit.* Translated by A. V. Miller. Oxford: Clarendon Press, 1977.

———. *Philosophy of Right.* Translated by T. M. Knox. Oxford: Oxford University Press, 1952.

Heidegger, Martin. *Basic Writings.* Edited by David Farrell Krell. New York: Harper & Row, 1977.

———. *Being and Time.* Translated by John Macquarrie and Edward Robinson. Malden, MA: Blackwell, 1962. First published 1927.

———. "Building Dwelling Thinking." In *Poetry, Language, Thought,* 143–159.

———. *The Concept of Time.* Translated by Ingo Farin with Alex Skinner. New York: Continuum, 2011. First published 1924.

———. "Letter on Humanism." In *Basic Writings,* 213–266.

———. "The Origin of the Work of Art." In *Poetry, Language, Thought,* 15–86.

———. *Poetry, Language, Thought.* Translated by Albert Hostadter. New York: Harper & Row, 1971.

————. "The Thing." In *Poetry, Language, Thought*, 163–180.

————. "The Thinker as Poet." In *Poetry, Language, Thought*, 1–14.

————. "What Is Metaphysics?" In *Basic Writings*, 89–110.

Hobbes, Thomas. *Leviathan*. Edited by Richard Tuck. Cambridge: Cambridge University Press, 1996.

————. *On the Citizen*. Edited by Richard Tuck and Michael Silverthorne. Cambridge: Cambridge University Press, 1998.

Hoffman, Piotr. "Death, Time, Historicity: Division II of *Being and Time*." In *The Cambridge Companion to Heidegger*, ed. Charles B. Guignon. Cambridge: Cambridge University Press, 2006.

Hume, David. *An Enquiry Concerning the Principles of Morals*. Edited by J. B. Schneewind. Indianapolis, IN: Hackett, 1983. First published 1751.

————. *A Treatise of Human Nature*. Edited by L. A. Selby-Bigge. 2nd ed. Oxford: Oxford University Press, 1978. First published 1740.

Johnson, Lyndon Baines. "We Shall Overcome." Address to a Joint Session of Congress on Voting Legislation, Washington, DC, 15 March 1965. http://www.american rhetoric.com.

Kant, Immanuel. "An Answer to the Question: What Is Enlightenment?" In *Practical Philosophy*, trans. and ed. Mary J. Gregor. Cambridge: Cambridge University Press, 1996. First published 1784.

————. *The Critique of Judgment*. Translated by James Creed Meredith. Oxford: Oxford University Press, 1952. First published 1790.

————. *The Critique of Pure Reason*. Translated and edited by Paul Guyer and Allen W. Wood. Cambridge: Cambridge University Press, 1998.

————. *Groundwork of the Metaphysics of Morals*. Translated and edited by Mary Gregor. Cambridge: Cambridge University Press, 1997.

Lincoln, Abraham. "Gettysburg Address," Gettysburg, PA, 19 November 1863. http://www.americanrhetoric.com.

Marx, Karl. *Economic and Philosophical Manuscripts of 1844*. In *The Marx-Engels Reader*, ed. Robert C. Tucker. 2nd ed. New York: W. W. Norton, 1978.

Michalski, Krzysztof. *The Flame of Eternity*. Translated by Benjamin Paloff. Princeton, NJ: Princeton University Press, 2012.

Mulhall, Stephen. *Inheritance and Originality: Wittgenstein, Heidegger, Kierkegaard*. New York: Oxford University Press, 2001.

Nagel, Thomas. *The Last Word*. New York: Oxford University Press, 1997.

Nietzsche, Friedrich. *Basic Writings of Nietzsche*. Translated and edited by Walter Kaufmann. New York: Modern Library, 2000.

————. *Beyond Good and Evil*. 1886. In *Basic Writings of Nietzsche*, 179–435.

————. *The Birth of Tragedy*. 1871. "Attempt at Self-Criticism" (added by Nietzsche as a preface, 1886). In *Basic Writings of Nietzsche*, 1–144.

———. *The Portable Nietzsche.* Translated by Walter Kaufmann. London: Chatto & Windus, 1971.

———. *Thus Spoke Zarathustra.* 1883–1885. In *The Portable Nietzsche,* 103–440.

———. *Twilight of the Idols.* 1889. In *The Portable Nietzsche,* 463–564.

Nussbaum, Martha. *The Fragility of Goodness.* New York: Cambridge University Press, 1986.

Polt, Richard. *Heidegger: An Introduction.* London: Routledge, 1999.

Plato. *Apology.* Edited by Jeffrey Henderson. Cambridge: Harvard University Press, 1914.

———. *Gorgias.* Edited by Jeffrey Henderson. Cambridge: Harvard University Press, 1925.

———. *Phaedo.* Edited by Jeffrey Henderson. Cambridge: Harvard University Press 1914.

———. *The Republic of Plato.* Translated by Allan Bloom. 2nd. ed. New York: Basic Books, 1991.

———. *Republic.* Translated by Paul Shorey. Cambridge: Harvard University Press, 1935.

Rawls, John. "The Idea of Public Reason Revisited." In *Political Liberalism,* 435–490.

———. *Political Liberalism.* Expanded Edition. New York: Columbia University Press, 2005.

Ross, Sir David. *Plato's Theory of Ideas.* Oxford: Oxford University Press, 1951.

Rousseau, Jean-Jacques. *The Social Contract and Discourses.* Translated by Donald A. Cress. Indianapolis: Hackett, 1983.

Smith, Adam. *The Theory of Moral Sentiments.* Edited by Ryan Patrick Hanley. New York: Penguin, 2009.

Strauss, Leo. *The City and Man.* Chicago: University of Chicago Press, 1964.

———. *Natural Right and History.* Chicago: University of Chicago Press, 1953.

Taylor, Charles. *Hegel.* Cambridge: Cambridge University Press, 1975.

———. *Philosophical Arguments.* Cambridge, MA: Harvard University Press, 1995.

Wills, Garry. *Lincoln at Gettysburg: The Words That Remade America.* New York: Simon & Schuster, 1992.

Acknowledgments

As I look back on this book, I am returned to the places from which it grew and to the people who gave it life.

I am grateful to my early teachers at Harvard University who sparked my interest in philosophy: Jeffrey Abramson, Richard Fallon, David Grewal, and Sandy Levenson. Thanks to the generosity of the Clarendon Scholarship Fund, I was able to spend four years of graduate study at Jesus College, Oxford, reading my way from Plato and Aristotle to Heidegger and Gadamer. Much of what I studied during those years was not the standard fare of Oxford philosophy. So I am especially grateful to teachers who offered sympathetic guidance and support, despite my somewhat unorthodox interests: Michael Freeden, who influenced my thinking on rhetoric; Stephen Mulhall, whose lectures introduced me to Heidegger; Richard Tuck and Lois McNay, who made my dissertation defense a stimulating seminar; and above all, my D.Phil. supervisor, Jeremy Waldron. With enthusiasm and good cheer, he encouraged me to draw out the full implications of the case for prejudice and to interpret classical texts in my own voice.

I also owe thanks to my friends Edward Brookes, Julius Krein, Noelle Lopez, John Perry, Abdallah Salam, and Julian Sempill, all of whom either read drafts or helped shape my thoughts and strengthen my belief in the project.

I am especially grateful to informal mentors and advisers who were generous with their time, advice, and encouragement: Tony Kronman, Harvey Mansfield, and Charles Taylor. Paschalis Kitromilides gave me the opportunity to study Greek philosophy in Athens during the summer of 2010. Russ Muirhead provided wise counsel, incisive commentary, and buoyant support from start to finish. Bryan Garsten offered a major source of intellectual inspiration. His work on rhetoric and situated judgment is a powerful influence on this book. Krzysztof Michalski, who hosted me during the summer of 2012 at his Institute for the Human Sciences in Vienna, guided my reading of Heidegger and Gadamer and led me to consider the crucial link of situated understanding to time. Though he died just before this book was completed, his influence on it is one of the many ways I will remember him.

I also want to thank my editor at Harvard University Press, Michael Aronson, for the care and thoughtfulness with which he brought this book to publication, and Edward Wade for his expert management of the book's production.

If all understanding is situated, then philosophy is inseparable from family. My brother, Aaron, often alerts me to my prejudices and forces me to think twice about them. Above all, I owe thanks to my father, Michael Sandel, and my mother, Kiku Adatto, my first and foremost teachers. From the time I began this project, we've spent many days and nights, at home and abroad, discussing prejudice, situated understanding, and other philosophical themes. This book took shape with their insight, support, and love.

Index